ROUTLEDGE LIBRARY EDITIONS: MANAGEMENT

Volume 33

THE FUTURE 500

THE FUTURE 500
Creating Tomorrow's Organizations Today

CRAIG R. HICKMAN
AND MICHAEL A. SILVA

Routledge
Taylor & Francis Group

LONDON AND NEW YORK

First published in 1988 by Unwin Hyman

This edition first published in 2018
by Routledge
4 Park Square, Milton Park, Abingdon, Oxon OX14 4RN

and by Routledge
605 Third Avenue, New York, NY 10017

Routledge is an imprint of the Taylor & Francis Group, an informa business

British Library Cataloguing in Publication Data
A catalogue record for this book is available from the British Library

ISBN: 978-1-138-55938-7 (Set)
ISBN: 978-1-351-05538-3 (Set) (ebk)
ISBN: 978-1-138-48005-6 (Volume 33) (hbk)
ISBN: 978-1-138-48006-3 (Volume 33) (pbk)
ISBN: 978-1-351-06390-6 (Volume 33) (ebk)

Publisher's Note
The publisher has gone to great lengths to ensure the quality of this reprint but points out that some imperfections in the original copies may be apparent.

Disclaimer
The publisher has made every effort to trace copyright holders and would welcome correspondence from those they have been unable to trace.

THE FUTURE 500

CREATING TOMORROW'S ORGANIZATIONS TODAY

by

Craig R. Hickman

and

Michael A. Silva

UNWIN
PAPERBACKS

LONDON SYDNEY WELLINGTON

First published in Great Britain by Unwin Hyman, an imprint of
Unwin Hyman Limited, 1988
First published in Unwin ® Paperbacks in 1989
Published in the United States by New American Library

UNWIN HYMAN LIMITED
15/17 Broadwick Street, London W1V 1FP

Allen & Unwin Australia Pty Ltd
8 Napier Street, North Sydney, NSW 2060, Australia.

Allen & Unwin New Zealand Ltd with the Port Nicholson Press,
Compusales Building, 75 Ghuznee Street, Wellington, New Zealand

ISBN 0 04 440437 9

A CIP catalogue record for this book is available from the British Library.

Printed in Great Britain by Cox & Wyman Ltd

ACKNOWLEDGEMENTS

Many people have contributed to the development and writing of this book. Michael Snell continued to perform feats of genius as he assisted us through every phase of this project, from helping shape our original ideas into book form to the editing of several manuscript drafts. We express our deepest appreciation and admiration for his unique talents and capabilities. He has taught us a great deal about the art of book writing. Also, we deeply appreciate the support and guidance of Arnold Dolin and Jill Grossman, our editors at New American Library. Their persistence and patience have helped us forge a better book than we ever imagined.

Several people provided valuable and insightful research. Rob Page, currently a Ph.D. candidate at the University of California, Irvine, took painstaking care with the details of business history and provided an invaluable sounding board for our ideas. Marcello Hunter supplied important background materials and resources in the early phases of our research and Steve Bennett and Nancy MacDonald worked later to amass detailed research on the companies we chose to highlight. We wish both of them well in all their future endeavours. Les Forslund, a business associate, provided important information on the struggles of contemporary corporations, while Mike Davidson, special advisor to Arthur Young & Company, gave us interesting perspectives on the evolution of executive concerns in this century. We owe special thanks to Mary Kowalczyk and Word Masters for their skillful retyping of all the drafts that led to the final manuscript.

In addition, a number of people directly and indirectly influenced our work: Larry Senn, John Childress, Stan Varner, Kirk Benson, Floyd Mori, Larry Wilson, Sherm Hibbert, Shiro Terakawa, Takashi Sakai, Charles Dahlquist, Max Lundberg, Dan Garrison, Terry McGann, Alan Wilkins, Paul Thompson, Bill Leigh, Max Knudsen, Dixie Clark, John Baird, Jim Christensen, Lee Conant, Nan Conant, William Bush, Phil Lear, Don Mangum, John Dyment, Peter Wimbrow. Paul Moncur, Tom DeLong, Paul McKinnon, Reid Robison, Neil Anderson Tim Baird, and Tom Fries.

Finally, and most importantly, we thank our wives and families, without whose support and encouragement this effort would have been meaningless. The happiness we enjoy with them makes all our professional and personal achievements worthwhile.

CONTENTS

Part I A New Way of Thinking about Management

Part II Eight Dimensions of the Corporate Future

FOREWORD

THE NEW BUSINESS CONCEPT

The View from America

Hickman and Silva have written a thoughtful and practical book about business that is today perhaps even more relevant in Europe than in America. For, unlike the much heralded Peters and Waterman who went "back to basics", these two American management consultants claim that managers should learn how to manage complexity. Why should this be so?

For thousands of years, historically, as well as at the start-up phase of its development, business was and is regarded primarily as an independent enterprise. For the past fifty to a hundred years, as well as at the consolidated phase of its development, business was and is regarded primarily as a public corporation.

For the next fifty years, though, according to Hickman and Silva, and through what I have termed the "architectural"[1] phase of business's evolution, a new interorganizational form will be emerging. It is this transformation, from a moderately complicated public corporation to a much more complex "corporate ecosystem" in which *The Future 500* are engaged.

If that is Hickman and Silva's thesis, based on their observations of American management theory and practice, what is the comparative situation in Europe in general, and in Britain in particular?

The European Perspective

From a business point of view, an ecological perspective does in fact have deep roots in European soil. In the 1920s, the Austrian philosopher, agronomist and economist, Rudolph Steiner, was advocating an approach to business and economics based on ecological principles of association. Some seventy years ago, Steiner anticipated an inevitable move towards both greater business autonomy, via privatization, and interdependence, via different forms of joint venture.

> Economic life is striving to structure itself according to its own nature, independent of political institutionalisation and mentality. It can only do this through associations, comprised of consumers, distributors and producers, which are established according to purely economic criteria. Actual conditions would determine the scope of these associations. Practical necessity would indicate how interassociational relations should develop.[2]

viii

Hickman and Silva have updated Steiner's economic thinking, now expressing it in contemporary business terms:

> When we talk about the networking organization, we're referring to a new type of umbrella organization that nurtures and protects other forms. You might think of network organizations as mentors, with the skills and resources to provide guidance, nourishment and protection to other forms.
>
> The network organization sits atop the management pyramid, creating an internal and external environment that synchronizes the success factors, promotes corporate renewal, manages paradoxes, and perpetuates itself through the growth and development of other entities.
>
> It unites the warring forces of dependence and independence, facilitating true interdependence among units.

THE COMMERCIAL CONTEXT

Dimensions of Business's Future

The Future 500, in fact, is less of an academic treatise and more of a practical proposition. It is based on prevailing business conditions in America. To what extent do these apply in Europe?

Hickman and Silva refer to eight major "dimensions" which will affect and characterize the operations of *The Future 500*. These are:

- the *globalization of enterprise*, in a world of increasing homogenization, on the one hand, and specialization, on the other
- the advent of *government–business alliances* to replace the hostile and suspicious relationships of the past
- ever-increasing *collaboration amongst enterprises*, to balance against competition, without destroying the free enterprise system
- *innovative investor–company relations* to counteract the accompanying trend towards short-term financial manipulations
- *ethical and social leadership*, working towards a heightened level of business values and practices
- the proliferation of *new organizational forms*, in the context of a dynamic environment
- corporate success hingeing on *integrated subcultures*
- *individual fulfilment*, above all, providing for the fulfilment of the needs of all the stakeholders in *The Future 500*

Let me now deal with each of these within a British and European context.

The Globalization of Enterprise

When ICI, Britain's best-known manufacturing company, announced to its shareholders in 1985 that a greater proportion of its asset base was now

ix

out of the United Kingdom than within, there was a shocked reaction. Two years later, this situation is generally welcomed rather than spurned. Large-scale business, in Europe as in America, has to operate on a global scale.

In the 1980s companies like ICI in Britain, Siemens in West Germany, Thomson in France, Olivetti in Italy, Phillips in Holland, and Ericsons in Sweden, have been leading the global way. At the same time, the inter-nationalization of London's stock market, with the advent of the Big Bang, and the massive, recent wave of British investments in the United States of America, have accelerated this global trend.

Perhaps even more important, though, from a global perspective, has been the impact of Japan on the European as well as on the American management consciousness. For we in the West have been obliged to recognize, and accommodate, an Eastern way of running businesses that is totally unlike our own, yet which, if anything, is more successful. Globalization has thus become as much an attitude of managerial mind as a territorial expansion of our business operations.

Diversity within unity, as Hickman and Silva have indicated, becomes a way of management within our globally based corporate ecosystem.

Government–Business Alliances

Hostility between government and business has traditionally been less of an issue in Europe than in America. In France and West Germany, in particular, collaboration between public and private sectors has come with relative ease.

Undoubtedly, the need for greater interdependence between business and government in Europe has arisen in recent years, for two major reasons. For one thing, the growing gap between the "haves" and the "have nots" – on a local, national and international scale – has called for increased public–private intervention.

Locally, inner city regeneration has called for the pooling of business and government resources in initiatives such as the "enterprise agency scheme" in Great Britain. Some 300 agencies have been established round the country to promote small businesses in the context of local economic development. Each scheme, moreover, involves a partnership between local and nationally based companies and both local and national government.

On the international scene, the growing interdependence between lender and debtor nations has called for new and coordinated approaches to international economic development. Private sector banks and public sector aid agencies, not to mention voluntary organizations, are obliged to work closer and closer together.

Collaboration

Collaboration between European companies, and between Europe and America, Japan and China has increased enormously in the last five years.

Within Europe itself a recent feature in *Newsweek* suggested that it is the businessmen rather than the politicians who are leading the way towards real

European integration. The scale and complexity of both the new technologies and the market-place are inducing such business leaders as Olivetti's de Bennedetti, in Italy, to engage in European-wide coalitions.

As the European economic correspondent, Guy de Jonquières commented, in 1986, in the context of the collaborative Eureka project: "Partnerships are proliferating across Europe in an effort to harness innovations for the fierce global technology race."[3]

Innovative Investor–Company Relations

The celebrated Channel tunnel project, linking Britain and France beneath the sea, is being undertaken, on the UK side, by a consortium of companies representing the Eurotunnel Group. That in itself is another example of interorganizational collaboration. At the same time, the funding of the huge project is being undertaken jointly by no less than 176 different banks.

Such innovative investor–company relations, of an intensive and long-term nature, are now becoming commonplace in Europe. They are also represented in the financing of an ever-increasing number of management buy-outs. Such arrangements serve to counteract the short-term financial manipulations that are as common in London as in New York, and which played their important part in the stock market crash of October 1987.

Ethical and Social Leadership and New Organizational Forms

A heightened level of business's social awareness within Europe has probably manifested itself most in Sweden, at least over the past twenty years. Volvo's "quality of working life" experiments represent a good case in point.

This call for a greater awareness, in recent times, has stemmed from the increase in unemployment and the job regeneration schemes that have emerged as a result. In that context Rank Xerox International has played a notable part, not only in redeploying its people but also in experimenting with new forms of work and organization.[4]

Rank Xerox, like "F" International, another British company working with computers and office systems, has experimented with homeworking, telecommuting, and the interweaving of part-time employment, self-employment and conventional job roles. These new work patterns[5] are gradually spreading across Europe.

Individual Fulfilment and Integrated Subcultures

One of the champions of the new work patterns, in recent years, has been Charles Handy.[6] Drawing on a tradition of English individualism, and relating it to European diversity, he has drawn up his equivalent of Hickman and Silva's unity in diversity.

The chief delight of Europe is the variety it offers of climate and culture
. . . So too, anyone who has spent time with a variety of organizations will
have been struck by the differing atmospheres . . . Earlier management
theory, in its search for universal formulae, or cure all remedies, did a
great disservice in seeking to disseminate a common organizational
culture.[7]

Handy advocates, therefore, not only a variety of organizational cultures,
within or between European nations, but also a mix of subcultures within a
particular company. He labels these "power" and "role", "task" and
"person" "cultures".

In the final analysis, in Europe, there is perhaps even greater emphasis on
diversity than on unity. Therefore, the kind of "corporate ecosystem" that
Hickman and Silva have evolved is particularly appropriate. If anything the
scope for transformation is greater in the more diverse European context than
in America. We can now move on to hear what the authors themselves have
to say.

RONNIE LESSEM
Director: *The City University
Business School*

Bibliography

1   Lessem, R., *The Global Business*, Prentice Hall, 1987.
2   Steiner, R., *Toward Social Renewal*, p. 17, Anthropological Press, 1977.
3   De Jonquieres, G., *European High Technology*, June 30, 1986.
4   Judkins, P., *et al, The Rank Xerox Experiment*, Gower, 1986.
5   Clutterbuck, D., (ed.), *New Patterns of Work*, Gower, 1985.
6   Handy, C., *The Future of Work*, Blackwell, 1986.
7   Handy, C., *Understanding Organisations*, pp. 185–6, Penguin, 1976.

PREFACE

In the three years since the publication of our first book, *Creating Excellence: Managing Corporate Culture, Strategy and Change in the New Age,* we have met with thousands of talented executives and managers throughout the world. After each seminar, speech, or workshop, we have often been asked to discuss a topic or concept in more depth. Again and again, we discovered scores of business people genuinely seeking deeper understanding and extended knowledge about managing their organizations. Many expressed their dissatisfaction with the superficial, technique-oriented, and often conflicting management advice they have been receiving in recent years. Won't future success require more than a mere sharpening of traditional approaches? they ask. This and other questions related to the future of business have caused us to think long and hard about what executives can do to create tomorrow's organizations today.

We vividly recall a particular experience with a well-known Fortune 500 firm. After we had conducted a day-long workshop with executives from various divisions and operations of this company, several of the participants engaged us in a free-wheeling discussion of the future of management thought and practice. One executive complained about the fragmented nature of current management theory and practice; another criticized the superficiality of so-called new management techniques; and still another suggested that managers really need a better integration of existing approaches. One soft-spoken manager summed up the frustration of all by suggesting that what we were really searching for was a new way of *thinking* about management. This observation coincided so closely with our most recent experience and research that we shared with the group our ideas about what we had begun to call the Future 500. By the end of a rather long and involved discussion, we were gratified by the enthusiastic response to our developing ideas about how business people might better manage their organizations by moving beyond a preoccupation with specific actions and outcomes to gain a broader view of the complexity that surrounds so many contemporary business issues. Such a view, we argued, would better enable business leaders to unravel the apparent paradoxes their organizations face today—the increasing size of organizations as well as the growing need to emphasize individual performance and the advancement of technical systems and controls, together with the need for greater freedom to innovate—and to deal with the need for managers to pull unifying principles from a bewildering array of perspectives in a global marketplace.

Stimulated by this and similar experiences with private and public sector leaders in the United States, Japan, Germany, Italy, and elsewhere, we found ourselves, surprisingly, looking more closely at the history of modern management and business development. The keys to the future, we concluded, lay in the past as well as the present. Thus began the development of *The Future 500*.

As you read what follows you may wonder why a book on the future of business and management pays so much attention to the evolution of management thought over the last hundred years. But we hope you will find the unfolding saga as enlightening and informative as we did, and that you will come to share our view that what happened yesterday can provide useful insights into what may happen tomorrow. To be sure, future executives will continue to hone the skills they have acquired over the years, but we doubt that simple refinements of past lessons will enable us to create the outstanding organizations of the future.

More than anything else, this book proposes a new way of thinking about the art and science of management. We call this new way of thinking "complexity management," and its goal is to unite all the essential aspects of past and present management concepts into a comprehensive new framework that addresses the major problems of contemporary and future business.

We have written this book for anyone who wants to stretch beyond old skills and techniques. It is our hope that this book will start you thinking about management in new ways and that such thinking will help you acquire a new set of abilities that can help make your own organization more purposefully profitable and humanly fulfilling.

CRAIG R. HICKMAN
MICHAEL A. SILVA

PART I

A NEW WAY OF THINKING ABOUT MANAGEMENT

CHAPTER ONE

The Future 500

Without the past the pursued future has no meaning.

—Loren Eisley

The Best-Run Companies of the Future

None of today's active business leaders had even been born when General Electric, American Express, Johnson & Johnson, Proctor & Gamble, and Dow Jones came into existence, and few of those leaders could detail exactly how those companies evolved to secure strong positions on *Fortune* magazine's Industrial and Service 500 listings. By the same token, few could explain precisely why other companies such as International Harvester, USX (U.S. Steel), New York Central, Studebaker, and Montgomery Ward, also formed near the turn of the century, have dropped from their formerly dominant positions, or why once-healthy R.C.A., J.C. Penney, Bank of America, Western Union, and Borden have become only marginal performers.

In the first two decades of the twentieth century, all fifteen of these companies appeared destined for greatness, but only five made it, while the other ten ran into trouble. Now, in the last two decades of the century, a number of prominent companies— among them Sears; General Motors; IBM; Analog Devices; W.L. Gore and Associates; Cummins Engine; Frito-Lay; Dayton Hudson; Morton Thiokol; Control Data; Citicorp; Merrill Lynch, and AT&T—seem to be positioned now in much the same way as those earlier fifteen were at the turn of the century. Which will make it, which will stumble, and which will fail?

Fortune magazine's Industrial and Service 500 listings may not necessarily represent the country's best-run companies, but they do represent the largest organizations in corporate America. And although size alone cannot guarantee dominance, most of the Fortune 500 have managed over the last 50–100 years to weather all manner of corporate storms, from unexpected crises and internal mismanagement to adverse economic conditions, new competitive forces, and changing consumer trends. We think their histories can provide insight into what it has taken in the past—and what it may take in the future—to sustain competitive advantage.

General Motors pioneered many early management trends prior to the 1950s, then fell behind in the area of strategic thinking until, by the mid to late 1970s, GM found itself reeling from an international competitive crisis. GM has undertaken a massive transformation virtually unprecedented in a corporation its size, but will the changes come soon enough for it to retain a respectable ranking among what we call the Future 500?

Most people would agree that IBM deserves high marks today, but "Big Blue" did not achieve its worldwide leadership position overnight. While pieces of the present IBM organization existed even before 1924, when the Computing-Tabulating-Recording Corporation officially became IBM, the company did not fully establish itself until the mid 1960s, when it turned strategic thinking into a powerful competitive tool. Since then IBM has continued to lead the way in important aspects of management. Will it continue to dominate in the future? Some observers have serious questions.

At Sears, after decades of prosperity under the leadership of General Robert E. Wood, performance suffered for years until Edward Telling, a recent CEO at Sears, set a bold new course for the company. Today Sears seems imbued with new vitality, versatility and vision, but will the lessons of its past continue to propel it forward?

Later in this book we will examine these companies' histories in some detail and consider how they and many others—including General Electric; Frito-Lay; Morton Thiokol; Cummins Engine; Control Data; Merrill Lynch; Citicorp; Dayton Hudson; and AT&T—might apply a new way of thinking about management to secure their eminence on the Future 500 list.

As we planned this book and pondered how business leaders might set about ensuring strong futures for their organizations, we quickly saw that the task should begin not with an imagined future but with the very real and instructive past. The study of business history used to strike us as a dry and lifeless undertaking, but as we began to examine it with an eye to what it might tell us about the future, it suddenly came alive. Far from being dull and plodding, the stories of how major organizations such as IBM, GM, and Sears developed over the past 100 years are full of excitement and insight and tell us a lot about how their futures might unfold. Historian Richard Cobb summed it up nicely: "The frontiers between history and imagination are very little more than Chinese screens, removable at will." Our aim in this book will be to try to remove those screens. Although we will ultimately discuss the future of organizations and suggest how a new theory of management might help shape that future, we will first analyze the events that have brought us from the last great revolution in business management to the threshold of another.

Business Transformations

Most students of business history would agree that the last great transformation in American business took place between 1890 and 1910, when American enterprise, after a century of evolutionary growth, reached a major crossroads. In the mid 1800s the typical enterprise, whether a shop, factory, bank, or transportation line, operated out of one office, performed only one economic function, handled one product line, functioned in a single geographical area, and was run by one or a few owners; senior, middle and first-line managers did not exist. However, a number of historical developments between the late 1700s and the late 1800s created both the need and the opportunity to devise a new structure. These developments included the western expansion of population that spurred industrial and business innovation in the early 1800s, the building of railroads in the mid 1800s, the growth of national and large urban markets in the late 1800s, and the beginnings of the widespread use of electricity and the internal combustion engine at the turn of the century. The cumulative effect of all this set the stage for a monumental transformation from what Adam Smith called the "invisible hand" of market mechanisms to what Alfred Chandler labeled the "visible hand" of management.

Prior to the 1890–1910 transformation, the invisible hand of the marketplace had governed the conduct of business worldwide, but the very growth it promoted resulted in a level of complexity that lay beyond the scope of existing approaches. And so American business leaders, prompted by their pioneering spirit, the flexibility of the free enterprise system, and a nudge from government, forged the modern corporation, which displayed two new characteristics: multiple operating units and managerial hierarchies with salaried executives. Once the modern business enterprise emerged, a new century of managerial evolution began.

Since the early 1900s a variety of developments have continued to affect our business organizations: more sophisticated forms of organization, scientific approaches to productivity, elaborate systems for controlling operations, painstaking planning processes, complex strategic positioning concepts, renewed attention to the value of healthy corporate cultures, and a growing emphasis on innovation. Combined together, these evolutionary changes have now brought us to the brink of another revolutionary transformation that can be every bit as remarkable as the rise of management's visible hand.

Companies such as Frito-Lay, General Electric, and Proctor & Gamble appear to have already recognized and acted on the possibilities of this transformation. Others, such as Borden, USX, and F.W. Woolworth lag behind, perhaps because they fear rather than welcome the future, but most likely because they have not heeded some important lessons from the past.

Competitive Advantage and the Future

High-tech company observer Dick Foster, a McKinsey & Company management consultant, describes technological innovation and progress as an S-curve phenomenon. The development of a new product or process progresses slowly in the beginning, then accelerates rapidly as knowledge accumulates, until finally the progress slows again as additional funds and efforts produce marginal benefits. When companies reach this point, they can only achieve rapid advances by moving to a new product, process or venture, and a new S-curve.

A similar S-curve might be applied to the last major business transformation. Scrutiny of events surrounding the 1890–1910 transformation reveals the three key characteristics that precede any great transformation. First, there is a long period of cumulative change, formed by a series of distinct transitions from one era to another. During each era organizations adjust existing approaches, methods, philosophies, and orientations to fit the needs of an evolving environment, but eventually such transitions produce only marginal benefits. Second, when a period of cumulative change through a series of eras concludes its acceleration and begins to slow, the opportunity arises for a fundamental and comprehensive shift from past methods, approaches, philosophies and orientations. The old ways do not disappear overnight but rather provide fertile soil from which new ways can spring. Third, the transformation launches a new series of transitions and eras during which people adjust to the new approach in light of continually evolving conditions. Once again, changes begin to accumulate and accelerate toward yet another transformation.

What stimulates an individual, organization, or economy to make these small improvements or these great leaps forward? Our study of business history has convinced us that the answer is found in an underlying, perhaps instinctive, drive for competitive advantage or comparative gain. Business investments of time, people, and money tend to flow along the path of least resistance and expense. If a company has several alternatives for achieving competitive advantage, it will usually choose the one that creates the most advantage at the least cost. However, as firms within an industry pursue their chosen paths to gain competitive advantage, they find that the opportunities for doing this cheaply diminish as they exhaust the alternatives or duplicate each other's efforts, bringing about heightened competitiveness and fewer obvious opportunities for differentiation in the industry. In either case, an individual firm seeking further advantage must eventually make a major, risky, and expensive change. Consider the U.S. steel industry, which ground to a halt as firms such as USX failed to find new ways of gaining competitive advantage. Eventually, other firms, like Chaparral Steel, broke out of the mold to find new means of differentiation and competitive advantage. This phenomenon not only occurs within industries, it also occurs across industries, and when a majority of firms across many industries begin to develop similar management practices in their ongoing effort to gain or duplicate advantage, a business-wide transition or new management era emerges. When the competitive advantage gained from new management practices lessens, because of their increasingly universal application, a few firms, seeking new competitive advantages, begin charting the course to yet another business-wide transition or management era. Eventually, successive business-wide transitions and management eras begin producing only marginal advantages and benefits, thus setting the stage for a fundamental shift or transformation.

As we see it, American enterprise is currently in the midst of what we call a "threshold era," during which the first two characteristics of a transformation have already become apparent. It has arrived at the top of the S-curve where further progress hinges on its ability to go beyond mere refinements and adjustments to a fundamental revolution (a new S-curve) in the way it manages its organizations. Unless we embrace this revolution, we may well stumble into a period of stagnation and decline.

Our Current Threshold

Though most observers of the current business scene agree that our business organizations have approached an important crossroads, they have failed to achieve a useful overall perspective of the phenomenon. Instead, they have tended to see isolated "from-to" shifts. Some of the best-known observations appear in the following chart:

"From-To" Shifts

From	To	Primary Observers
A managerial society	An entrepreneurial society	Peter Drucker
Management	Leadership	Warren Bennis
Industrial society	Informational society	John Naisbitt

Official, formal authority	Unofficial power & influence	John Kotter
Complex, bureaucratic management systems	Simple, back-to-basics business fundamentals	Tom Peters
Numerous foreign economies	A single global economy	Kenichi Ohmae
Government regulation	Government coordination	George Lodge
Individualistic independence	Collective interdependence	Robert Bellah, Richard Madsen, William Sullivan, Ann Swidler, and Steven Tipton
Multidivisional organizations	Dynamic networks	Ray Miles
Segmentalist companies	Integrative companies	Rosabeth Kanter
Strategic planning	Strategic management	Fred Gluck
Entrepreneurial innovation	Institutional innovation	James Botkin, Dan Dimancescu, and Ray Stata
Organizational maintenance	Organizational adaptation	Quinn Mills
Designing & controlling structures & processes	Creating & managing cultures	Ed Schein
Labor power	Brain power	Robert Kelley
Implementing successful traditions	Creating new traditions	Donald Clifford and Richard Cavanagh
Juggling variables	Balancing variables	James O'Toole

Although we respect these observations and think each of them contains some part of the truth, even when all the threads are woven together, they do not present a full picture of the current state of business. We suggest adopting what we call an ecological perspective, because ecology—the study of the relationships of living organisms with each other and with their environment—involves the widest possible view, including not only present relationships but past and future ones as well.

Like ecosystems in nature, corporations include all levels of organization, from recently hired secretaries to the enveloping global economy itself, and they consist of the entire collection of living and nonliving elements, from the most coolly efficient computers to the most vibrant throbbing cultures. Organizational ecology is thus the study of the relationships within business organizations and among different organizations both domestically and internationally. We urge executives who want their companies to secure their positions among the Future 500 to begin thinking about and managing their enterprises from this kind of ecological perspective. By doing so, they can replace the "from-to" orientation with more useful "combined with" ideas, and take an important step toward the transformation we envision. That transformation, we believe, depends on augmenting Adam Smith's invisible hand of the marketplace not only with Chandler's visible hand of management, but with the "synchronizing hand" of leadership. An ecological perspective allows for such synchronicity. While over the years executives, consultants, and academics may not have expected a particular management era's overriding concerns to solve all organizational problems, they did tend to preoccupy themselves with one concern at the expense of others. But now they can and should combine all the lessons of the past.

Some organizations, like Frito-Lay and its parent company, Pepsico, have moved toward greater synchronicity. Back in 1983 Frito-Lay conducted extensive corporate culture surveys, and since then the company has been wrestling with the problem of how to institutionalize innovation. In 1984, drawing upon the best existing knowledge about organizational structure, strategy, culture, systems, and operations, Frito-Lay combined field sales and marketing activities to bring about more integration. In 1985 it began experimenting with the concept of a parallel organizational structure that would allow it to create, test, and integrate innovative products faster and more efficiently. Not wanting to grow an isolated entrepreneurial culture that could not eventually be integrated into the rest of the organization, Frito-Lay has tried to resolve an apparent paradox: size gives you power, but it also tends to stymie the entrepreneurial and innovative spirit.

In order to complete a transformation into the next age, executives must learn to live with and manage complexity by turning paradoxes to their advantage. Paradoxes abound in contemporary management, and they tend to baffle us whenever we apply "either-or" or "from-to" thinking to them. However, when the mind combines their seemingly contradictory elements they become more comprehensible.

Think about some of the paradoxes corporate leaders face

today. If a $100 million-a-year company sets its sights on reaching $1 billion at the ambitious rate of 20 percent a year, year after year, its very growth may thwart ultimate success. As Frito-Lay and Procter & Gamble have discovered, massive size can rob an organization of quick responses in the marketplace. Strategies never unfold exactly as planned. A "hot" corporate culture can make as many mistakes as a "cold" one, if leaders don't direct the heat toward the proper goals. Increased productivity, often achieved by taking care of people, also comes from increased automation, which paradoxically reduces the need for people.

Complexity Management

Executives face a dilemma during this threshold era. On the one hand, many may feel tempted to cure their organizational ills with specific skills they have procured over the years, treating a sinking competitive advantage with a dose of strategic thinking or boosting sagging employee morale with a shot of culture building. Although the last several decades have given us several cures for ailing organizations, none of them alone, or even a few of them combined, can accomplish the sort of full-blown transformation we see ahead.

To bring that transformation about, we propose a new theory of "complexity management." Just as the concept of leadership has complemented the old notion of management (leaders do more than merely manage), so skillful complexity management can complement leadership (complexity managers do more than merely lead and manage).

Chapters 2 and 3 will set the historical stage for our introduction of complexity management in Chapter 4, where we will discuss how executives can create and maintain successful companies by applying three key concepts:

- *Perspective management,* which harmonizes the diverse desires and outlooks of stakeholders in the corporate ecosystem through what we call mutually benefiting principles. The perspective manager forges commitment to a common purpose by constantly relating and integrating the purposes of individual stakeholders with those of the organization, achieving both individual and collective fulfillment. The perspective manager recognizes the value of diversity within unity.

- *Power management* unleashes the creativity, the drive, and the determination of individuals and groups for the benefit of the entire corporate ecosystem. The power manager also bridles the freedom of those stakeholders who will not or cannot commit themselves to the common purposes and the well-being of the whole.

- *Pivot management* nurtures relationships among individual stakeholders to ensure their maximum fulfillment and peak performance. The pivot manager rises above the structures, processes, systems, and procedures of the organization to focus on unique individuals. The pivot manager recognizes that the individual must gain genuine fulfillment and achieve peak performance for the organization as a whole to attain its purposes.

Our ideas about complexity management represent an attempt to devise a new way of thinking about management. With the precepts of perspective, power, and pivot management, executives can continue to sharpen past management practices within a larger, more comprehensive ecological context. While complexity management leads to specific applications, it first and foremost embraces a new outlook or mind-set, redefining the world of management and organizations to include not only people's actions and their outcomes, but also the desires and outlooks of all stakeholders within the corporate ecosystem. These three precepts of complexity management can provide the basis for the creation of tomorrow's organizations. In Chapter 4 we will review and exemplify these precepts in detail, and then in Part II we will apply them to eight critical dimensions of the future.

Dimensions of the Future

While Part I of this book outlines the history of modern organizations and suggests a new way of thinking about management for the future, Part II applies the lessons of history and our theory of complexity management to future problems. In every instance we think the problems of the past and present will persist and become ever more complex, creating an ever more pressing need for new thinking.

In an effort to help those willing to think about the futures of their organizations in new ways, we have identified eight dimensions of the future that we think will make or break the Future 500. Our selection of these eight issues has grown out of our historical research and our ideas about complexity management. From the most macro to the most micro considerations, they span the full continuum of business problems:

- The *globalization of enterprise* demands global marketing and new far-reaching business strategies in a world of increasing homogenization and specialization. In Chapter 5, we will outline General Electric's rise to international prominence, and consider what lies beyond for it and other global companies.

- *Government-business alliances* must replace the suspicious and hostile relationships of the past. In Chapter 6 we will explore what Morton Thiokol has learned over the years about working with the government and how the recent shuttle disaster might expedite the search for less adversarial government-business partnerships.

- *Collaboration* can balance head-to-head competition without destroying our prized free-enterprise system. In Chapter 7, we will detail how Control Data helped establish a high-tech consortium that may attain the benefits of win-win competitive coordination without compromising free enterprise.

- Innovative *investor-company relations* can go a long way toward reducing short-term financial manipulations. In Chapter 8, we will follow Merrill Lynch's history to illustrate the evolution of public ownership, Wall Street, and the crucial drive away from short-sighted capital markets toward long-term, patient ones.

- *Ethical and social leadership* and what we call responsible leadership should work toward a heightened level of business values and practices. In Chapter 9, the story of Cummins Engine reveals how morality can positively influence all business undertakings.

- *New organizational forms* will proliferate in the future. In Chapter 10, we will review Frito-Lay's history, and then explore how its current organization points the way toward new dynamic organizational environments.

- Corporate success hinges on *integrated subcultures.* In Chapter 11, we will see how Dayton Hudson has honored subcultures by reinforcing and integrating rather than destroying them.

- *Individual fulfillment* should become the greatest achievement of the Future 500. In Chapter 12, we will recount the history of AT&T and watch as the newly divested organization struggles to provide fulfillment to all the stakeholders in its corporate ecosystem.

At the end of each of the chapters in Part II, we will apply the precepts of complexity management to each of these eight dimensions of the future. Our aim is to show how the application of perspective, power, and pivot management can help produce the Future 500.

That list will be dominated, we believe, by organizations whose executives and managers weave together the lessons of the past with a comprehensive new outlook, a new way of thinking that can govern all their decisions and problem-solving efforts, from the most global to the most personal. The complexity managers we envision for the future will transcend their own prejudices and personal points of view by respecting the differing perspectives of others; they will restrain their inclinations to control and police their people by granting individuals the maximum freedom to act and grow; and they will tie their own self-interests to the interests of all who come into contact with their organizations. Not doing so, we fear, will result in the sort of organizational decline that has beset so many of the turn-of-the-century companies that once seemed destined for greatness.

CHAPTER TWO

Management's History: A Perspective for the Future

The whole of science is nothing more than a refinement of everyday thinking.
—ALBERT EINSTEIN

The simple belief in automatic material progress by means of scientific discovery is a tragic myth of our age.
—SIR BERNARD LOVELL

An Overview of the First Six Eras of Management

Throughout the twentieth century, executives and business theorists have studied the practice of management, and many have found some deep insights into the subject. Such insights have allowed business people to get a better grasp on the progressively more complex issues and problems that affect their organizations. Prior to the late 1880s, an accumulation of problem-solving advances helped make the railroad industry an agent of transformation. As early as 1846 Louis McLane, president of the Baltimore and Ohio Railroad, and his chief engineer, Benjamin Latrobe, recognized that the increasing demand for railroads to transport machinery and equipment to new and expanding businesses, particularly coal mining operations in Pennsylvania, required a new approach to business administration. The company's plans to cross the mountains between the eastern seaboard and the Ohio River demanded smooth administration and coordination of a tremendously complex undertaking, and a com-

mittee of the board offered its conclusions about solving the problem in the company's 1847 annual report. Among other things,
the committee recommended the close supervision of all departments, a stricter system for the collection and disbursement of
money, streamlined mechanical operations, and the economical
purchase and application of materials. By setting forth and attempting to achieve such goals, railroads like the Baltimore &
Ohio became the first modern business enterprises.

Since the advent of this visible hand of management, organizations have improved on the original model by making adjustments to it rather than fundamental alterations. For convenience
we have divided these adjustments into what we see as seven eras,
of which three deal with the science of management, three with
the art of management, and the last with an attempt to combine
all the lessons of the previous six.

As you consider the first three of these eras—as well as the
succeeding ones—bear in mind that the overriding executive concerns and organizational responses reflect general trends rather
than hard-and-fast boundaries:

The Three Eras of Rational/Scientific Management

Era	Executive Concerns	Organizational Response
1. 1910–1935	Well-functioning multiunit organizations and management hierarchy	Structure building
2. 1935–1955	Maximization of production and operations output and efficiency	Productivity enhancement
3. 1955–1970	Increased management control over all business variables	Systems design

We refer to these first three eras of modern management as
"rational/scientific" because at this point in organizational history
executives generally strove to deal rationally, quantitatively, and
scientifically with the increasingly complex tasks of management.
By drawing from the sciences of organizational structure, administrative hierarchy, quantitative analysis, operational efficiency,
and management control, American management did, in fact,
achieve competitive advantages for almost sixty years. However,
by 1970, it became harder and harder to achieve increased profit
margins from these and related approaches. Large production

capacity and economies of scale had become commonplace among both national and international competitors; the technological advantages of certain processes, systems, and products had eroded; sophisticated management structures and control systems had lost their distinctiveness; and levels of quality and service had so steadily improved in so many industries that they no longer exerted the power they once had.

When executives found that they'd squeezed as much competitive advantage as possible from rational and scientific approaches, they began searching for other sorts of advantages. While they still needed rational management to determine capital investments, they realized they needed something else when it came to human investments. Beginning with the strategic planning era in 1970, the three eras of "qualitative/humanistic" management brought us right up to the late 1980s:

The Three Eras of Qualitative/Humanistic Management

Era	Executive Concerns	Organizational Response
4. 1970–1980	Successful competitive positioning in the marketplace	Strategic planning
5. 1980–1985	Superior performance and execution to achieve excellence	Culture shaping
6. 1985–late 1980s	Adaptation to increasing and accelerating of change	Innovation management

The strategic planning era provided a natural transition between rational/scientific and qualitative/humanistic management. At first, executives and their organizations approached strategic planning in a mechanistic, rational, and scientific manner, but as the strategy era unfolded, they shifted more and more to humanistic and qualitative strategy implementation issues, which eventually led them into the culture era. Clearly, an organization not only needed a brilliant strategy, it needed the right sort of people and skills to implement it; and the right sort of people, it turned out, were often those who could innovate. Thus the culture era quite naturally evolved into the innovation era as organizational cultures strove to institutionalize innovation. Let's look at each of these six eras in detail, examining along the way how three major corporations—General Motors, IBM, and Sears—dealt with them.

Era 1: Structure (1910–1935)

Adam Smith's invisible hand of the marketplace was joined by the visible hand of management as the first era of modern management got under way in the early 1900s. The visible hand had to come to grips with three new facts of business life:

1. The volume of economic activity had increased greatly, making it possible and necessary for business enterprises to grow in size and number.

2. Larger, multiunit organizational structures could produce more sales, achieve lower costs, and deliver greater profits only through greater management coordination.

3. Management coordination depended on establishing meaningful management hierarchies.

Given the newness of multiple operating units and managerial hierarchies, executives naturally preoccupied themselves with refining, enhancing, and perfecting organizational structures.

The educational institutions of the day, recognizing the need for training in basic business skills, began offering the first modern business courses. Prior to the turn of the century, business education had consisted of courses in bookkeeping and secretarial skills offered through small, specialized private schools of commerce, but during the first years of the twentieth century, the nation's most respected colleges and universities introduced business education into their curricula.

Through the late 1920s and 1930s, the *Harvard Business Review* and other journals, including *Management Review, Journal of Business,* and *Advanced Management,* printed a great number of articles dealing with the structure of business enterprises. Also during this period the first management consulting firms emerged to help the new managers find better ways of organizing and functioning. Prior to World War I, engineering consultants such as Taylor, Emerson, and Cooke began providing much more than factory management advice, and by the time the war ended, firms like Arthur D. Little, Day & Zimmerman, and Frazer & Torbet had become the precursors of today's management consultants.

What about the executives of this era? During World War I most of them enjoyed a spurt of economic activity as wartime demands stimulated opportunities to expand their operations more rapidly than they would have during peacetime. Then, in the years following the war, these same executives grappled with the effects of a cycle of growth, recession, growth, and depression. To handle the dramatic growing pains and the accompanying economic upturns and downturns of this period, business leaders continued to emphasize structure. General Motors offers an instructive example. Needing to match the flow of raw materials and finished products more closely to fluctuations in demand, GM formed what we now call the multidivisional structure, a cross between the two primary forms of organization used by companies at the beginning of this era—the centralized functional organization and the decentralized holding company.

Under the leadership of president Pierre S. Du Pont, GM created autonomous divisions to monitor and control production and distribution by coordinating the flow of materials and products within different markets. A new set of middle managers took over operation of divisions and functional departments, and they, in turn, fell under the authority of administrative staffs. In the late 1920s General Motors president Alfred P. Sloan introduced another structural innovation, interdivisional relations committees that he hoped would reduce emerging friction among line, staff, and general executives. Committees chaired by members of the executive committee oversaw major functional activities such as product development, works management, power and maintenance, sales, and institutional advertising.

Following the lead of General Motors, many other industrial companies adopted the multidivisional organizational structure in the 1920s and 1930s. In the case of mergers and acquisitions this structure proved quite effective, because under it merged entities could enjoy more autonomy than they could under a centralized functional organization and more coordination than under a holding company. To allow for internal expansion or external growth through merger or acquisition, holding companies such as Allied Chemical, Union Carbide, General Electric, and United States Steel turned increasingly to the multidivisional form.

Tom Watson, Sr., Chairman and CEO of IBM, forged a superior sales and service organization from the start of his tenure. Watson's IBM sales and service organization would end up blanketing the country. While Watson's genius lay in the fields of sales and service, he also spent a great deal of time working on structure and organization. Under the mentoring of John Patterson at NCR, Watson had learned how to organize and structure guaranteed sales territories, sales conventions, reporting relationships, high-performance clubs, and training programs. He also learned how to destroy the competition in the second-hand cash register market by structuring a network of ostensibly independent cash register outlets next to competitors' locations and undercutting their prices. Watson and other NCR officers, including Patterson, who had assigned the young and unwary Watson the task of eliminating NCR's competition, eventually were convicted of violating the Sherman Anti-Trust Act, but the Court of Appeals found the original indictment defective, and a retrial never took place.

The early years of Sears, Roebuck also mirror this era's preoccupation with structure. In 1886 a station agent for the Minneapolis and St. Louis Railway named Richard Sears began the R.W. Sears Watch Company as a moonlighting project. The small enterprise bought watches from manufacturers, then resold them to consumers. Before long the entrepreneurial Sears hired Alvah Roebuck, a watchmaker, to help him develop the business. In 1893 the two men changed the company's name to Sears, Roebuck and Co., and by 1895 they were printing a 532-page catalog that offered much more than watches. Operating out of one central location, the enterprise grew phenomenally, but as it enlarged it could not keep pace with order fulfillment and soon found itself too often shipping the wrong item or experiencing unacceptable shipment delays of 3 to 4 months. In 1895 Julius Rosenwald, a Chicago clothing manufacturer, bought into the company, and with him came the organizational expertise Sears, Roebuck & Co. sorely needed. Under Rosenwald's direction the company built the world's largest business building at the time, a 3-million-square-foot mail-order facility located on Chicago's West Side. By 1906 activities and processes within the huge facility ran according to a "systematic organization" that could handle an unprecedented amount of order processing. In the years that followed, Sears opened three more mail-order plants around the country.

In 1924 Rosenwald brought Robert E. Wood into the company

as a vice president. After an illustrious military career, General Wood had worked for Montgomery Ward for four years after World War I, but he was fired by Ward president Theodore Merseles after a sharp disagreement over the company's direction. Merseles, an advertising and mail-order man, could not accept Wood's belief that the future lay in retailing to the country's growing urban centers. Though Sears had always targeted its mail-order products to rural America, Rosenwald agreed with Wood, who quickly implemented his own organizational ideas on a grand scale, structuring the company in such a way that it could integrate mass distribution with mass production and provide the public with the merchandise it wanted and needed.

When Wood became president of Sears in 1928, the company was running 27 retail stores; by the end of Wood's first calendar year as president, the number had risen to 192. During this time Wood created a centralized structure to administer the growing number of stores, but when that approach eventually proved inadequate for the sprawling empire, Wood decided Sears needed something radically new. In 1929, Wood hired George E. Frazer, a principal in the management consulting firm of Frazer & Torbet (where the famous James O. McKinsey was also a partner), to help design a structure that could accommodate an increasing number of stores, coordinate the complex flow of merchandise from producers to mail-order plants to stores, and weld the whole operation into a smoothly running mail-order/retailing machine. In January 1930 Frazer and a committee of five senior executives produced a report that continues to influence Sears's operations to this day. The report recommended combining geographical and functional operations within five territories comprised of thirty-three districts, with each district manager supervising a group of stores and reporting to territory officers, who managed several districts and the entire territory's mail-order plants. The old functional structure that included merchandising, operations, accounting and finance, would be replicated at the territory, district, and local levels. Though functional vice presidents at the corporate level would retain responsibility for their functions at all levels, territory officers, district managers, and store managers would direct all functions at their respective levels.

This type of dual reporting structure would evolve into the matrix form of organization so popular later in the century. Although this structure served Sears well, in 1935 Wood, still obsessed with getting Sears's organizational structure "right," concluded that individual store managers were learning so much under the new system that they should be awarded even more autonomy and independence. Consequently, he eliminated the district level of management and ordered store managers to report directly to the territory managers, who in turn reported to top management. Justifying this adjustment to the Sears organizational machine, Wood said, "If we devise too elaborate a system of checks and balances, and have too many inspectors going out as representatives of the parent organization, it will be only a matter of time before the self-reliance and initiative of our managers will be destroyed and our organization will be gradually converted into a huge bureaucracy."

By the mid 1930s many American companies besides GM, IBM, and Sears had developed sound enough organizational structures that they could now turn their attention to greater operational efficiency and increased production.

Era 2: Productivity (1935–1955)

Just as the economic fluctuations associated with World War I reinforced the preoccupation with organizational structure, the Great Depression, which began in 1929 and lasted late into the 1930s, stimulated concern with operational efficiency. Later, during World War II, production output moved into the spotlight as wartime needs for a wide variety of products lifted the country out of the Depression and brought in its wake full employment and a growing demand for consumer products.

World War II pushed businesses to their productive limits, and the general mobilization of the economy spread the increasingly scientific methods of management to even the smallest companies which, serving as subcontractors for the large industrial firms, adapted them to their own needs. At the same time the war effort encouraged businesses to develop technologically sophisticated products, forcing them to emphasize product development and to seek scientific ways to employ assets and resources more productively. Food companies began producing chemicals; electrical and radio companies began making a wide range of new products; and rubber, metal, and petroleum companies attempted to develop a number of synthetic materials.

As the economy continued to spurt after the war, concern for productivity remained high as a mass market far greater than any previously known in history sprang up, with regional markets becoming as large as the national market of the late 1800s. To satisfy the exploding demands of this mass market, many executives and organizations searching for enhanced productivity turned to technology for the answer. Factory automation, technological advancements, and new materials such as plastic helped increase output, particularly in continuous process plants and high-volume operations. Before long, mass production techniques dominated both new and old industries.

Since modern managerial procedures, processes, and structures could increase operational efficiency and production output, management became increasingly professional during this era. Modern methods of forecasting, accounting, controlling inventory, and scheduling production helped the new professionals increase their companies' productivity, supply the growing consumer demand, and improve profit margins. In nonmanufacturing industries such as banking, food retailing, hotels, and restaurants, executives increased sales and profit margins by building or buying branches in other geographical areas, a practice that not only increased the volume and efficiency of their businesses, but also served to stimulate further growth and demand, which in turn led to more preoccupation with productivity enhancement.

As executives shifted their attention from structure to productivity, they still based their philosophies on the theories espoused by Frederick Taylor in his book *Scientific Management*, and on the work of Henri Fayol and Max Weber, who extended Taylor's work. These and other popular works of the day maintained the "economic man" view of people in organizations, a view that assumed that an organization could maximize productivity by continually reducing workers' jobs to minute, specialized, even mindless tasks. In the early years of the productivity movement, executives like Henry Ford pushed Taylor's industrial doctrine to its limits. As Ford himself insisted, "The man who puts in a bolt does not put on the nut; the man who puts on the nut does not tighten it." Attitudes like Ford's reduced people in large and mid-sized industrial companies to interchangeable production-process units that executives needed merely to analyze, quantify, and manipulate in order to increase efficiency and output. Taylor's doctrine held that companies should not base production costs on actual experience but on standard time and output measures arrived at "scientifically" through comprehensive job analyses and time and motion studies.

While this mentality did lead to significant increases in production and efficiency, it also fueled the labor union movement in the United States as workers united to demand, among other things, that the management of the mass production industries fulfill their needs as people and stop treating them as interchangeable disposable units of the production line. Previously, work itself had been largely governed by the traditional master-servant relationships between foremen and workers. Foremen exercised the power to hire and fire workers, and craftsmen determined how (and at what rate) they would perform their work. However, scientific management transferred such responsibilities from the foremen and craftsmen to the managers. By shifting control of the production process in this way, and by breaking down the tasks of skilled craftsmen into simple components, management reduced its dependency on skilled craftsmen, who, not surprisingly, formed the first line of the new labor movement. Workers, especially craftsmen, viewed unions as their primary, if not only, defense against scientific management and dehumanizing work.

On the other hand, as the productivity movement progressed, enlightened thinking did emerge from some quarters. The so-called "Hawthorne Experiment" confirmed that "human reactions of people engaged in productive work have a much more important effect on their morale and efficiency than had previously been realized." Gradually managers paid more attention to morale and work conditions, but they did so only to boost productivity, and their relationships with workers often remained adversarial.

In 1935 GM president Alfred Sloan, wanting to assess production capacity in light of forecasted sales increases, commissioned both a comprehensive survey of GM's manufacturing facilities and a production-related study of the impact of a shorter work week, an anticipated reduction of operating efficiency, and interruptions in production caused by labor difficulties. These studies marked the beginning of a focus on productivity at GM that would accelerate during the war years as GM scrambled to find every means possible for increasing production capacity and maximizing efficiency. In 1940, on the brink of America's involvement in the war, GM's defense production stood at $75 million, but it rose to over $400 million in 1941, then to $1.9 billion in 1942, and finally to a high of $3.8 billion in 1944. Total company sales increased from $1.4 billion in 1939 to $4.3 billion in 1944. In the years following the war, GM made huge investments in plants and equipment to meet the growing consumer demand and increase overall productivity. In 1945 the company also created a centralized manufacturing staff. Under the continuing leadership of Sloan as chairman and Charles Wilson as president, GM's approach paid off handsomely as the company became a universally accepted model of productivity and profitability. Its market share of U.S. car sales rose from 38 percent in 1946 to 51 percent in 1955.

IBM revenues increased from $22 million to $564 million between 1935 and 1955, a period when IBM consistently rang up profits from two to five times higher than those of Burroughs, NCR, Remington Rand, and Underwood, all of whom shared similar levels of revenues. What made the difference? The incredible efficiency and productivity of IBM's organization, particularly its sales force. To this day IBM trains its new sales people twice as long as any competitor and doesn't allow them to take on a full quota until they've been with the company twelve to eighteen months. Once the salespeople hit the field, a bombardment of communications, contests, conventions, and promotions continues to keep productivity and spirits high. During the era of productivity enhancement, IBM inaugurated its commitment to customer service. To ensure that IBM could continually service its customers, the company favored rental or leasing of its machines, sorters, tabulators, time clocks, and typewriters. Watson knew that his salespeople would develop a totally different attitude toward customers if the company retained ownership of the equipment. This self-enforced guarantee that IBM would always take care of its customers not only gave customers what they wanted, it turned IBM into the most productive customer relations operation in the world.

IBM set high standards for its people and enforced strict codes of conduct and dress, but it took good care of them, too. During the Depression IBM retained its people and, in fact, continued hiring salesmen while competitors were letting them go. During World War II Watson created a fund for families of IBM men killed in action, and paid a week's salary every month to the families of employees serving in the armed forces. IBM, wanting happy, satisfied customers and fulfilled, productive employees, would go to extraordinary lengths to accomplish those goals. After the war IBM grew stronger and more powerful than ever. The pressure for increased production during the war years had caused revenues to quadruple between 1939 and 1945, and during peacetime IBM continued to increase its strong position in the business machine industry with its unbeatably productive work force. By the early 1950s IBM had perfectly positioned itself to exploit the coming computer age.

In its own industry Sears had solidly established its retailing structure by the mid 1930s, and, despite the Depression, it inaugurated an aggressive expansion and improvement campaign. Although Wood moved from president to chairman in 1939, he remained chief executive officer until 1954. During the latter half of the 1930s, Sears continued to open stores, increasing the number to over 600 by 1941. The war years brought a halt to Sears's retail expansion, but as soon as the war ended, expansion resumed. Just as he had earlier anticipated the urban retailing boom, Wood foresaw great opportunities in the postwar years. While Montgomery Ward CEO Sewell Avery, expecting a postwar slump, grew cautious after the war, Wood turned aggressive, putting every available dollar into new, expanded, and more efficient facilities. Not long afterward, Montgomery Ward saw the error of its caution and began duplicating Sears's aggressive expansion. In the eight years following World War II, Sears opened 134 new retail stores, relocated 83, and enlarged 149. In addition, it invested millions of dollars in larger parking lots, warehouses, mail-order plants, and other facilities. To increase productivity Sears categorized its stores into types: "A" stores were full-line department stores, "B-1" stores were modified department stores, "B-2" stores were scaled-down versions of department stores, "B-3" stores were department specialization stores, and "C" stores were small specialized automotive and hardware stores. Such groupings made Sears's operations more efficient and profitable than ever.

Wood's commitment to providing value to the customer by offering better-quality goods at lower prices sat at the heart of his obsession with efficiency. Contrary to the norm of the day, Sears constructed its stores outside central downtown districts, on major traffic arteries easily reached by consumers who were depending more and more on their personal automobiles for transportation; it situated Allstate Insurance desks inside stores to make it easier for customers to take care of their insurance business; and it set up telephone sales offices to make shopping convenient for customers who did not wish to travel to the store. By 1954, when Wood stepped down as chairman and CEO, Sears had become the world's largest merchandising organization, with sales of $3 billion and profits of $141 million. The company employed 200,000 people in 11 mail-order plants, 694 retail stores, and 570 catalog sales offices; it blanketed every state in the union; and it held ownership interests in 59 manufacturing companies that supplied over 25 percent of its sales. Almost seven million American families were paying on Sears current time-payment accounts (long before the introduction of charge accounts and credit cards) and one dollar out of every twenty spent by Americans on general merchandise flowed into Sears's cash registers.

As these and other companies perfected the efficiency of their operations and achieved greater productivity, they found it increasingly necessary to design systems to control their organizations.

Era 3: Systems (1955–1970)

Two major forces precipitated the move into this era: the appearance of the conglomerate on the American business scene, and the intense drive for foreign markets. The mergers and acquisitions made possible by the multidivisional organizations that appeared as early as the 1920s and 1930s eventually gave rise to the contemporary conglomerate. The conglomerate differed from its predecessor both in its fundamental structure and in the way it invested capital. While the old multidivisional organizations grew primarily through internal expansion, investing in plants and equipment related to their original lines of business, new conglomerates expanded externally, acquiring and merging with businesses often unrelated to their original lines. The resultant diversity spurred the need for tighter control over operations and set the stage for a systems movement that included a focus on investment and financial planning, control systems, and long-range capital budgeting.

Companies moving into overseas markets required a similar focus. American companies did not aggressively penetrate foreign markets until the mid 1950s and early 1960s, but with the opening of the European Common Market to them, direct American investment in Europe rose from $1.7 billion in 1950 to $24.5 billion by 1970. To manage their investments abroad, many companies established international divisions to oversee all foreign operations, thus extending the multidivisional form of organization to far-flung corners of the globe. The need for better control over sprawling domestic and international operations increased the pressure on executives to design systems that would strengthen planning capabilities and help standardize and simplify the task of management.

Some observers of business history have called the period from 1955 to 1970 a "golden economic era" during which business organizations encountered few obstacles to prosperity and growth. With improved structures in place, with productivity rising to all-time highs, and with new systems promising comprehensive integration, coordination, and control, the outlook seemed bright indeed. However, executives were also exerting and feeling greater pressure than ever before. In fact, George Odiorne, a prominent business analyst of the day who later became known as a proponent of management by objectives, described the management style of the late fifties and early sixties as "management by pressure." Management, seeking ways to beef up profits in an increasingly complex environment, sought more and more control over costs, people, and operations. The heaviest pressure came to bear on the points where costs were getting out of line. As a result, organizations began looking for more action-oriented managers who could make things happen and in whose hands management control systems could become a kind of thumbscrew they could twist for results. Of course, the introduction of elaborate information, planning, control, and accounting systems increased the general level of management sophistication, and even businesses that did not play the international or conglomerate games enlarged their top management ranks, increasing the administrative staffs needed to design and implement the new control systems.

The automation that had begun during the previous era spawned a tool that, more than any other, would make it possible for the enlarged staffs to track mountains of controlling data: the computer. Although the first computer was introduced in 1944, the computer did not begin to assume its key role in business administration until the systems movement was under way. By 1970, over 50,000 computers were processing corporate America's information, gathering and storing and reporting the facts and figures executives needed to control their organizations.

The actions of executives at General Motors, IBM, and Sears during this period provide some interesting insights into the nationwide preoccupation with systems. From 1955 to the mid 1960s General Motors enjoyed its most prosperous years, and its success derived in no small part from the management controls that made GM a model for all large organizations seeking greater control over their operations. Although the recession of 1958 caused GM sales to plunge 22 percent from the prior year, the company used its controls to moderate the impact on earnings.

GM's management systems were widely admired and many companies, including the Ford Motor Company, imitated them. After World War II, Henry Ford II, in desperate need of turning his company around, decided to institute a management system similar to GM's. He hired Ernest Breech, then president of Bendix Aviation and a former GM executive, as executive vice president, and the two men in turn assembled a group of ex-Air Force officers who had worked on managerial and financial controls and came to be known as the "Whiz Kids." Among them were Robert McNamara and Arjay Miller, both of whom later became presidents of Ford. Under their leadership between 1955 and 1970, Ford built management control systems that, in part, enabled Ford to assume its solid number-two position behind GM.

During World War II, IBM had joined forces with the U.S. government to engineer the first computer, the Automatic Sequence Controlled Calculator (ASCC), later known as Mark I. On its heels followed the ENIAC and the SSEC, but IBM failed to push these machines to the commercial market, and was caught with its guard down when the first commercial computer, UNIVAC, hit the market in 1951. The Eckert-Mauchly Computer

Company had developed the UNIVAC with the help of American Totalizator, and the two firms sold out to Remington Rand just as the new machine was ready for delivery. It appeared as though Rand, which in turn merged with Sperry Corporation in 1955 to form Sperry Rand, had beaten IBM to the punch in the computer field. In fact, *Fortune* magazine suggested that the union of Sperry's technological base with Rand's sales force might overwhelm IBM. However, *Fortune* and others failed to take into account the strength of IBM's sales and service organizations and the extremely high productivity of its people.

When Tom Watson, Sr. died in 1956, Tom Watson, Jr. took the company's helm while his younger brother became head of World Trade, the foreign arm of IBM. Under the younger Watson's leadership the company embarked on a massive management restructuring program, hoping for firmer control over operations. He brought in John Burns, a management consultant with Booz, Allen & Hamilton, to help develop the new system. Interestingly, management control systems and the new information processing machines fueled each other's growth. It is our belief that had the systems movement not arisen, the computer probably would not have made its early inroads into American business, and without the computer, the systems movement might not have been able to change the landscape of American business so drastically. With its own improved management system in place, IBM began developing and marketing first the 600 and 700 series computers, then the 1400s, 1600s, and later the 7000s.

IBM did not produce technically superior machines during this period, but it did provide the best service, which won the company dominance in the market. So much could and often did go wrong with the new machines from all manufacturers that corporate users worried about making them essential parts of their organizations. Enter IBM, whose superior sales and service personnel provided much-needed reassurance. Many executives who had purchased a UNIVAC from Sperry Rand, or another machine from Control Data, Honeywell, or Burroughs, soon regretted that they had not selected old, reliable IBM. By 1965 IBM's revenues soared to $2.5 billion, twice those of Sperry Rand, and its market share rose to 65 percent, compared to Sperry's 12 percent, Control Data's 5 percent, Honeywell's 4 percent, and Burroughs' 3.5 percent. Louis Rader, head of Sperry's UNIVAC division during this period, admitted defeat, saying, "It doesn't do much good to build a better mousetrap if the other guy selling mousetraps has five times as many salesmen." By 1970 IBM had become one of the most admired U.S. corporations and would soon replace General Motors as the model of American corporate success.

Unlike GM and IBM, Sears did not respond as effectively to the overriding concerns of the systems era. By the mid to late 1950s Sears, the model for the entire retailing industry, had already developed state-of-the-art controls over its operations to achieve greater efficiency and productivity. However, when the visionary Wood stepped down, several succeeding CEOs depended mostly on the momentum built up prior to 1955. Despite attempts to maintain and increase long-range forecasting systems, sophisticated approaches to store design, and systematic analyses of traffic patterns, all aimed at exposing shoppers to the greatest amount of related merchandise in the shortest possible time, Wood's successors contributed little to his original philosophy. Many of the company's controls that focused on customer needs, such as parking space—the formula for which calculated that there should be 3.5 to 4 square feet of parking space for every square foot of shopping space and that for every $1 million in volume there should be room in the lot for 125 cars—did not need changing during this era.

Sears's budgeting and accounting systems did become more and more sophisticated during this period. In a unique departure from traditional methods, Sears's budgeting system generated its initial figures from the field instead of from corporate headquarters. To give store managers high incentive to manage more efficiently, the company installed compensation systems based on store profit. Although these and other measures helped Sears sales grow to almost $10 billion by 1970, the company's overall performance clearly declined in the mid 1960s. To be sure, Sears continued to grow, but its rate of growth was slipping, its operating costs were rising, and its profit margins were sagging. At the same time, the competition (J.C. Penny, K Mart, and a growing number of discounters and department stores) was getting better at doing business "the Sears way." As Sears lost market share, internal management problems began escalating. While Sears management had improved control systems during this era, it had done so in a maintenance rather than a pioneering fashion. After competitors followed Sears's example by streamlining their own operations, many quickly moved ahead of the giant with more forward-looking systems. Depending for too long on the momentum established in a prior period, Sears entered a stage of declining financial performance that would inhibit its response to the concerns of the coming era.

Once the systems movement had increased management's control over the internal workings of organizations, the scientific/rational school of management gradually gave way to more qualitative and humanistic approaches.

Era 4: Strategy (1970–1980)

Throughout the first three eras discussed so far, the business schools turned out well-trained professional managers who, with a core set of quantitative and other similarly rational skills, could successfully manage organizations. The best business decisions were supposedly the most analytically justifiable ones. Therefore, production, finance, and marketing, with their overriding emphasis on quantitative analysis, dominated the business school curricula, and detailed reports, analyses, and studies ruled the day. While such an approach put useful tools in the hands of executives, it almost completely overlooked the roles of intuition and subjectivity in decision making.

For decades rational management held sway partly because, during the first half of this century, business naturally flourished, and on those occasions when it did not, the downturn could be attributed to insufficient professional management or unfavorable economic conditions. America enjoyed the world's strongest economy between the end of World War II and the late 1960s, a time when American management expertise commanded universal respect in the business world. However, by the early 1970s, it became increasingly clear that business could not live by science alone. Accelerated change, international competition for markets, scarce energy resources, and a constant need for innovation ushered in a series of eras dedicated to the art of management.

With executives riding high on their ability to control internal operations, their concern naturally shifted to the external world of markets, industries, and trends in the business environment.

This outward look brought with it an overriding concern for competitive positioning, and *strategy* became the buzzword of the day.

By the end of the 1960s executives could see that all the profit planning and long-range forecasting systems in the world would not help them position their products in an increasingly complex domestic and international environment. While some companies and consulting firms had been experimenting with strategic planning systems during the preceding era, those earlier systems primarily involved long-range forecasting, which, despite its value in other areas, did not effectively address the problems of competitive positioning and realignment. As a result, a number of trend-setting companies, such as General Electric, and a few leading consulting firms, like McKinsey & Company, began searching for new techniques that would help them address important external issues.

The results of McKinsey's and General Electric's study eventually led to the reorganization of GE's 190 departments into 43 strategic business units (SBUs) and to the development of a 9-block matrix the company could use to summarize business and investment strategies. This matrix compressed complex strategic planning data into one efficient display, enabling CEO Fred Borch to evaluate the business strategies of each SBU on an annual basis. With these tools, GE executives could measure the performance of each SBU without shuffling through reams of unrelated documents. GE's experience marked the beginning of a trend that would make strategic planning the hottest topic in boardrooms and business schools throughout the 1970s.

Other consulting firms, such as Boston Consulting Group and Arthur D. Little, joined the effort. For the first time the strategy movement brought to executives and their organizations a set of concepts, methods, and tools for analyzing economic and competitive possibilities and for implementing a competitively advantageous course of action over the long term. As the movement gathered momentum, a whole new generation of tools and techniques arose, although the fundamental principle underlying a good business strategy remained the same. Bruce Henderson, founder of the Boston Consulting Group and considered by many to be the father of modern corporate strategy, summed it up when he urged executives to "concentrate your strength against your competitor's relative weakness." Unfortunately, applying that simple principle in the midst of an increasing number of aggressive competitors, fluctuating market conditions, changing customer preferences, and accelerating economic and industry discontinuity was not so easy. As embattled executives applied all the strategy formulas and techniques in a mechanistic fashion, they quickly grew disillusioned with the rational, scientific, quantitative approach. It was this disillusionment, coupled with greater focus on qualitative aspects of decision making, like strategy implementation, human resource development, and long-term rather than short-term results, that laid the foundations for the next era. But before it began, strategic management practices had shifted from quantitative to qualitative, from formulation to implementation, and from mechanistic planning to creative thinking.

General Motors, IBM, and Sears responded in different ways to the decade-long concern with strategy. Roger Smith, later to become chairman of General Motors, had been pushing strategic planning at the mammoth car company for many years, but the company didn't respond promptly enough to avoid the onslaught of foreign competition in the mid to late 1970s. Smith's struggle to turn GM's line managers into strategic planners paid off for GM in the long run, but the company's lack of a corporate strategic planning system in the early 1970s presaged the difficulties GM and other American car manufacturers would soon face. During these years GM lost its preeminent position as the most admired corporation in the U.S., and was badly burned by its shortsightedness in not switching more quickly to smaller, more economical cars, improving workmanship, keeping pace with technical developments abroad, abandoning support of gasoline price controls, and dealing with the UAW's persistent demands for higher wages and benefits. GM did not begin to get back on track until the end of the strategy movement.

By contrast, IBM marched in the vanguard of the new movement, committing the company as early as the mid 1960s to strategic thinking and planning. At that time the fledgling computer industry was still testing its wings. Second-generation computers had matured, and the third generation was nearly ready. Tom Watson, Jr. had made an early strategic commitment to the sort of technology development that would raise IBM's technical expertise to the level of its sales and service expertise, and his vigilant attention to strategy and competitive positioning helped produce the family of computers that made IBM the technology leader, expanded the company's markets, won further advantage over competitors, and unified the company.

In the late 1960s, IBM took a gamble on its strategic positioning of its new 360 computers. The risks, including the threat of new competitive technology, possible antitrust legislation, substantial financial losses, and the potential endangerment of an incomparable customer service reputation were huge. In fact, inside IBM the decision to move ahead with the 360s became known as the "bet your company" decision. But as Watson saw it, he had little choice but to place that bet. With third-generation computers on their way, IBM could either lead the charge or risk losing its existing advantage. By the time the rest of corporate America had flocked to the strategy movement, IBM's strategic positioning had already paid off handsomely. Just two years after its introduction, the 360 line accounted for nearly half of the total value of IBM's installations in the U.S., and it buried the competition abroad. Wisely, Tom Watson, Jr. had raised the company's technical prowess without overshadowing its sales and service capability. IBM's strategy also restructured the entire industry, accelerating the growth of several subindustries that exploited the success of the 360 series, creating a new group of leasing companies that purchased and rented out 360s, spawning service bureaus that bought or leased 360s and sold data or computer time to users, and opening new markets for manufacturers whose products filled niches the 360 machines couldn't.

Sears, still lacking strong leadership, again failed to fully respond to the demands of the new era. By 1975 return of average equity had fallen to 9.8 percent, nearly half of what it had been in 1955. Investors lost confidence in the company, causing a sharp drop in its stock price. When the business press began bemoaning an "identity crisis" at Sears, it became clear that the company's once-brilliant and unifying merchandising strategy had fallen upon hard times. Internally, field and corporate managers often worked at cross-purposes, creating even more confusion throughout the firm. To outside observers, the organization appeared top heavy, with almost 900 stores, 1,700 catalog and sales offices, 13 massive distribution centers, 124 warehouses, and over 450,000 employees. Many speculated that Sears had grown too large for anyone to manage effectively.

Acknowledging the company's problems, Arthur Wood directed management to "catch up" by focusing on the concerns of the prior systems era. He reduced overhead, streamlined the organization, improved communications systems, updated inventory and expense control systems, corrected problems with incentive compensation systems, and generally stengthened managerial functions. As a result, Sears's performance markedly improved by the latter part of the 1970s. However, the catch-up game delayed Sears's evolution into the strategy era until the mid-to-late 1970s when, under the inspirational leadership of Edward Telling, who assumed the chief executive spot in 1978, the company began moving in a positive new direction. Realizing the strategic significance of the company's customer base, with 25 million active credit card users, representing approximately 55 percent of all American households, and its image of trust and security, Telling began to reshape his management's thinking about the future. He masterminded a strategy that would allow Sears to operate an even wider variety of merchandising and service businesses than it already did, extending the company's existing Allstate Insurance and Homart Development (a wholly owned shopping center development subsidiary) into other financial and real estate services. The culmination of this logical extension of its businesses came when Sears acquired Dean Witter and Coldwell Banker in 1981. Although Sears attacked strategy somewhat late in the era, its eventual response seemed to promise success.

As Sears and other American organizations mastered the science and art of strategy, they soon found that competitive positioning alone could not assure success. No matter how brilliant a company's strategy, it needed the right people to carry it out.

Era 5: Culture (1980–1985)

Around 1980 a growing number of executives realized that an organization's successful competitive positioning demanded superior performance from its people, spurring many to seek new ways of building healthy and productive corporate cultures. Two major factors made the culture movement inevitable: the recognition that planning in a vacuum could not guarantee successful execution and implementation of even the most brilliant strategies, and the discovery that Japanese companies were out-performing their U.S. counterparts. The Japanese, it turned out, relied heavily on an internal socializing process, the philosophies and values of which produced what came to be called "corporate culture." These two factors thrust American business into a virtual state of panic as executives groped for ways to put people back into the excellence equation.

Experts have offered many different definitions of corporate culture, using words such as guiding beliefs, dominant values, organizational regularities, rites and rituals, superordinate goals or philosophy, organizational feeling and climate, rules of the games, and organizational norms. However, we think Edgar Schein, a professor of MIT's Sloan School of Management, articulated the most complete and concise definition in his book *Organizational Culture and Leadership:* "A pattern of basic assumptions—invented, discovered, or developed by a given group as it learns to cope with its problems of external adaptation and internal integration—that has worked well enough to be considered valid and, therefore, to be taught to new members as the correct way to perceive, think, and feel in relation to those problems." Building on Schein's definition, we would add three common manifestations of strong corporate cultures: commitment to a common purpose, competence in delivering superior performance, and consistency in passing the common purpose and competence to others.

One by-product of the culture movement has been a maturation of the field of human relations. As we pointed out in our analysis of the productivity era, human relations practices arose when studies and experience confirmed that well-treated employees can accomplish more than ill-treated ones, an idea that eroded the old notion of employees as interchangeable units of production whom management could apply to specialized, scientifically controlled tasks. However, when management initially adopted human relations, it did so in a fairly manipulative fashion, especially during the systems movement. Then, the concern with controlling the allocation of resources through more sophisticated systems led to quantitative performance appraisals and compensation systems that could supposedly better evaluate and control the "human resource." The strategy movement sought the maximization of human resources, climaxing in a situation where organizations built wonderful structures, systems, and strategies but paid scant attention to personnel who needed not only security, belonging, and recognition, but also a satisfying quality of work and self-actualization. At the start of the culture movement executives began to discover that if they could match their people's personal goals and ambitions to the corporate mission they could achieve incredible levels of organizational productivity and high levels of personal satisfaction and fulfillment.

The stories of GM, IBM, and Sears during this period manifest that concern for superior performance and the resulting attention to people and corporate cultures. Under Roger Smith's leadership GM began promoting a stronger corporate culture in the early 1980s. Smith's master plan called for integrating strategic planning into the daily lives of GM people, and he was fond of saying, "The team isn't going to score if the QB is the only one who knows the game plan." Understanding that strategic planning would not become part of the lives of GM's people unless the corporate culture could easily grasp it, GM set forth the following precepts:

S— Stick-to-it-iveness (Commitment to self-discipline, competitive advantage, and excellence in the basics)
T— Thinking Through (What we are, will be, and should become)
R— Risk, Responsibility, and Reward (Keeping them in balance)
A— Awareness (Of the environment and competition)
T— Talk to Each Other (Excellence in communications)
E— Evaluate Impacts on Values (At each step, check motivation and commitment)
G— Grow Your People (Constant attention to selection and training)
Y— Yes, I Can Attitude (Winning attitude that creates the future)

These precepts stressed the creation of a corporate culture devoted to self-discipline, competitive advantage, and excellence in the basics, and they have helped transform the way jobs get done at GM. If they continue to work their magic, they will help the company regain its lost corporate leadership position.

As the culture movement gained speed in the early 1980s, IBM again became the prototype organization. No other large American corporation better exemplified how exceptional performance depended on a strong corporate culture. Building on both the strong sales and service culture created by Tom Watson, Sr., and the technology culture fostered by Tom Watson, Jr., Frank Cary began to mold a "leader" culture that has enabled IBM to dominate most every area of the computer industry. No matter where the information processing industry goes in the future, IBM plans to lead the charge. The impact upon people at IBM has been subtle, yet profound. When John Opel became CEO in 1981, he further attempted to solidify IBM's leadership culture by proclaiming to the world that IBM would match or beat the growth of the information processing industry in all segments. The company honored that commitment even beyond the day Opel stepped down as CEO in 1985.

After Sears acquired Dean Witter and Coldwell Banker, the retail giant plunged headlong into corporate culture development. Knowing it could not afford to operate Dean Witter and Coldwell Banker autonomously, Sears drew a lesson from its experience with Allstate. Allstate had been successful largely because Sears had closely linked the selling of automotive merchandise with the selling of automobile insurance. Could the same pattern work with the new acquisitions? Why not link existing merchandising and insurance operations with the selling of stocks and real estate? Before long Sears was testing financial departments in their stores around the country, and the experiment proved so successful that Dean Witter and Coldwell Banker departments, along with Allstate, became part of the nationwide Sears Financial Network. Despite strong skepticism from Wall Street, the culture building effort seemed to work. However, these improvements were not sufficient to keep Dean Witter and Allstate from suffering financial difficulties, and Sears executives are continuing to struggle to integrate the company's disparate parts in a profitable way.

Era 6: Innovation (1985–Late 1980s)

The concerns of an era, never totally respectful of boundaries, tend to carry over and accumulate in succeeding eras. The concern for superior performance and corporate culture carried over into the sixth era as executives became convinced that creativity lay at the heart of strong strategies and cultures.

In a combined survey of the innovative management practices

of the Fortune Industrial 1000 and the Fortune Service 500, Arthur Young International, the Institute for Innovation, and the ForeSight Group identified "innovation" as a major concern of American executives as they lead their organizations into the last half of the 1980s. In another survey of the most successful midsized firms in America—companies with $25 million to $1 billion in sales—conducted by the American Business Conference and McKinsey & Company, and subsequently published by Don Clifford and Richard Cavanagh in *The Winning Performance*, researchers concluded that "winning companies innovate continuously." The preoccupation with innovation, entrepreneurship, intrapreneurship, personal breakthroughs, and adaptation to change now permeates all aspects of American business. Seminars promising to make executives more creative abound, and almost every company has implemented some kind of formal corporate innovation program.

At the beginning of this era GM moved aggressively to the forefront, attempting to turn the $100 billion company into an innovative leader for the twenty-first century. Chairman Roger Smith presided over the $2.5 billion acquisition of Electronic Data Systems (EDS), the $5 billion-plus acquisition of Hughes Aircraft Company, and several smaller high-tech investments and joint ventures in the fields of robotics and artificial intelligence—Smith's attempt to inculcate innovation into the company's evolving corporate culture through acquisitions. In fact, adapting to change drives Smith's emerging strategy-conscious, innovation-oriented culture. GM's eagerness to harness innovation influences all the company's current activities, from the new Saturn division to a host of new products and continued acquisitions.

In February of 1985 John Akers became IBM's chief executive, and from the outset he set innovation as his top priority, shifting IBM's emphasis from hardware to software development and replacing investments in manufacturing facilities with investments in software laboratories. Knowing that the merging of the computer and communications worlds will radically alter its competitive world, IBM began focusing on the development of new communications software designed to integrate an array of computing and communicating devices. These programs, rather than duplicating the accounting or inventory control software already offered by other firms, will instead drive much deeper to the very operating systems that direct computers to communicate with and control their many components. Backing up this commitment to software innovation, IBM has budgeted $56 billion in capital investment over the next five years. As part of this ambitious program, IBM bought Rolm Corp., the telecommunications equipment company, in 1984, and entered into the joint ownership of Satellite Business Systems with Aetna Life Insurance. In addition, IBM has tried to relate its commitment to innovation to all aspects of its leadership-driven culture. For example, IBM has begun forming partnerships to expand its massive global network and remain at the head of the international pack. The company has also been leading the charge in super-conductivity research, which could further revolutionize the computer industry.

In 1986 Sears celebrated its 100th birthday with a renewed emphasis on the entrepreneurship that made it so successful during the first two management eras. However, today's innovations differ markedly from those of 100 years ago as Sears strives to integrate a spectrum of businesses broader than the company's founders could have imagined. The Sears Financial Network added the Sears Savings Bank to turn the operation into a consumer-oriented, full-service financial institution, and it introduced the revolutionary Discover card, a combination credit/financial service card. Issued by the Greenwood Trust Company of Greenwood, Delaware, a 1985 Sears acquisition, it can buy everything from retail goods to travel services and entertainment, giving customers access to a package of financial products and services that even includes a family savings account. On the merchandising front the company has installed the so-called "Store of the Future" as a primary vehicle for growth. The concept encompasses new and strengthened product lines, with over 150 introduced during Sears's centennial year celebration. Many represent innovative developments or entirely new items: a Ready-to-Roll solid emulsion paint that stays solid until it comes in contact with a roller; a line of contemporary career apparel for women twenty-five to forty-five; a thirty-seven-inch projection TV with a one-hundred-twenty-degree viewing angle, eliminating side viewing distortion; an AudioCruise voice control that allows drivers to control car speed with verbal commands; and a new line of contemporary furniture. The "Store of the Future" also includes new and exciting merchandise presentations, an emphasis on the modernization of existing facilities, and improved levels of customer service at the point of sale.

Our discussion of the history of management has brought us all the way up to the present—which may well be a turning point in American business. Contemporary events contain the seeds of that potential transformation, so in the next chapter we will take a long, hard look at management today.

CHAPTER THREE

Management Today: On the Threshold of Transformation

We live in a moment of history where change is so speeded up that we begin to see the present only when it is already disappearing.

—R. D. LAING

A Turning Point

In the mid 1980s Roger Smith relied on strong leadership to guide General Motors through a major reorientation. As we indicated in the last chapter, GM took bold steps during the culture and innovation eras, reorganizing itself into 170 strategic business units, attempting to integrate strategic thinking and planning into the daily lives of all its workers, acquiring technology-rich companies, and generally moving to reestablish its world reputation. To succeed, GM, like the other Fortune 500 companies, must blend the lessons of the past into an integrated plan for the future. To do this, executives must replace the management of structure, productivity, systems, strategy, culture, and innovation with leadership that constantly coordinates all of the success variables.

For GM, the road will continue to be a difficult one. As hard as the company has tried to push strategic thinking and innovative decision making down through the ranks in an effort to speed up market responsiveness and new product development, progress continues to be slow. Ford, for example, beat GM to the punch with its aerodynamically styled Taurus and Sable models, which have won the number-two automaker great market and financial success. Ross Perot, the outspoken founder and former head of GM's Electronic Data System subsidiary and at one time the company's largest single stockholder, attributes many of GM's current problems to its byzantine bureaucracy. According to Perot, GM's recent attempts to streamline its hierarchical structures have largely failed despite the recent "incentive separation" offer to over 140,000 workers in North America. To achieve a 25 percent staff reduction by 1989, this effort encouraged employees to retire early or otherwise terminate their association with GM. And, despite Smith's aggressive leadership, GM's market share has fallen during the late 1980s from 48 percent to 41 percent.

Although we agree with Perot that GM has not yet fully solved its problems, Smith's leadership may be propelling the auto giant in the right direction. However, with recent plant shutdowns, huge lay-offs, and sagging profits, Smith's job is far from over. Ultimately, success will depend on an even greater emphasis throughout the company on the "synchronizing hand" of leadership.

Recent business and management research has suggested that organizations experience long periods of minor, continuously incremental change followed by short periods of major, discontinuous change. During the former periods, an organization and its executives worry about implementing and refining new management practices, and they work toward sequential and incremental change in one or more of four key areas—strategy, structure, processes, and people. In contrast, during the latter periods, an organization makes radical and simultaneous changes in all four areas. On a macro-scale, will all the comparatively incremental changes that have occurred throughout this century culminate in another major transformation? We think so, but not without a great deal of concentrated effort.

What we call the threshold era will probably continue through the late 1990s, and it may well last longer than recent eras because throughout it executives will be struggling to achieve more than mere refinements of past lessons. By our analysis, management eras since 1910 have tended to grow shorter as executives and organizations found it harder to win competitive advantage with adjustments to existing approaches. In order to make the most of the transformational opportunities the current threshold offers, executives must look beyond incremental changes toward a much more fundamental reorientation, one that involves synchronizing the often seemingly conflicting management responsibilities and practices that have evolved over the past one hundred years.

Synchronicity Through Leadership

Two business concepts have been receiving academic attention lately: the integration theory of management and the attribution theory of leadership. The first suggests that strong, healthy organizations require, to a large extent, the integration, coordination, and synchronization of the myriad variables that contribute to consistent, long-term success. Powerful organizations need more than the pieces of the puzzle—a sound structure, high productivity, tight control systems, an exceptional strategy, a committed culture, and a flair for innovation. They must fit all the pieces snugly into one interlocking and dynamic whole. The growing complexity and uncertainty of the contemporary world, the increasing size and sophistication of organizations, the maturing and leveling of management capabilities, the easy availability of information, the exploding development of technology, and the scarcity of resources all conspire to force business people to become better at managing all the variables simultaneously. Although this century-old evolution has put the necessary material in our hands, we must take care not to overemphasize any one success factor at the expense of the others.

The second concept, the attribution theory of leadership, suggests that leaders can make or break their organizations. To some degree this idea has sprung from the failure of existing management theories to explain, clearly and convincingly, differences in business performance. Even critics who claim that falling back on a nebulous and subjective concept like "leadership" sidesteps the real issue admit that something akin to it can and does make a big difference in organizations.

Business theorists did not pay serious attention to the question of leadership until the qualitative/humanistic eras, beginning with the strategy era of the 1970s, when some began to recognize leadership as something distinctly different from management. At the same time, executives began dealing more strenuously with the broader, qualitative issues of competitive positioning and future direction, which often demanded more than mechanistic managerial maneuvers. And the subsequent eras of culture and innovation also underscored the need for managerial traits beyond the rational and scientific manipulation of structures, systems, and numerical productivity analyses.

But just what *is* the meaning of leadership? To some it means the ability to inspire followers to take action; to others it means setting a good example; and to still others it means influencing people to attain goals rather than simply ordering them to do so. For the purposes of our discussion here, we will use the term "leadership" to mean the visionary perspective, gained through an integrated sense of history, that permits one to know what will work and what will not work, and the passionate persistence to stimulate people to strive toward the peak performances that enhance both individual and collective well-being.

As Clarence Randall once said, "The leader must know, must know that he knows, and must be able to make it abundantly clear to those around him that he knows." To that description we add that the most successful leaders make their sense of purpose abundantly clear to those around them not by force, coercion, or formal authority, but by their sincere devotion to people and purpose, by their vision, and by their patient perseverance in the face of all obstacles.

At the heart of our definition lies the notion of *synchronicity*, the harmonious integration of the six sets of management practices executives have acquired and refined since the beginning of the twentieth century. This has become a hallmark at IBM, and it has also begun to happen at General Motors and Sears. For GM and Sears the challenge will involve integrating their various operations and complex management practices to regain and establish new dominance in their industries, while for IBM the challenge will be to maintain an already existing dominance. GM will have to push even further toward unprecedented reorganization, and Sears will have to continue building upon its enormous customer base and solid retailing experience in new areas as it did recently when it began marketing vacation packages to Florida, California, Hawaii, and Mexico.

Maintaining a dominant position takes every bit as much skill as forging one in the first place, but at this point, IBM executives seem to be doing a lot of things right. With characteristic foresight IBM initiated a leadership-oriented culture back when most companies were just beginning to appreciate IBM's sales and service culture. The new IBM culture, which is still evolving, stresses leadership not only in the industry, but in all aspects of organizational life. Its attention to employees and to management development and training, emphasizing personal and corporate leadership, stands as a model for other corporations, and its concern with marketing and manufacturing continues unabated. IBM recently moved 2,000 people from its headquarters marketing staff into the field to increase direct contact with customers, and, in the midst of a growing number of IBM PC clones, it not only introduced its own inexpensive version of its powerful PC AT, but also pioneered a state-of-the-art plant that produces computers entirely with robots, which could cut the cost of manufacturing PCs in half. However, IBM's short-term financial performance has slipped recently, demonstrating that synchronicity, even for "Big Blue," is a continual quest.

Compressing the Lessons of History

Modern American business history illustrates the penchant of executives for riding with a current set of management practices until something forces them to change. From the structure to the innovation era, executives made every conceivable refinement and modification to each era's primary concern before they felt, through vision or force, mentally, physically, and emotionally prepared to embark on yet another transition. Every company, whether a 100-year-old enterprise or a brand-new start-up, has struggled with overemphasizing one piece of the management puzzle while ignoring others. As business in general has evolved through the changing concerns of the century, so have individual companies, sometimes over 10 years rather than 100. Organizations formed after 1910, and especially those started since 1950, enjoying the benefits of hindsight, can compress the lessons of the past or even rearrange them according to the peculiar demands of their industry or environment.

Consider two companies that began operations in the 1950s and 1960s. One conformed to concerns of the era into which it was born, applying the concerns and lessons of the past eras as it grew, while the other followed the historical sequence of concerns more closely.

Ray Stata founded Analog Devices in 1965 with an MIT classmate, Matthew Lorber. Executives during this systems era designed all sorts of systems to gain firmer control over their operations. Aware of the trend, Stata and Lorber built Analog on a foundation of products designed to improve management control. Their initial products—operations amplifiers, used by equipment makers and the military to take precise readings of real-world conditions such as temperature and pressure in an effort to gain greater systematic control over key variables— supported the systems movement. From the beginning, Analog's management preoccupied itself with management control systems because its market, its product, and its own production requirements demanded them.

Drawing from the existing management philosophy that had evolved through two eras and most of a third (structure, productivity, and systems), Stata was able to compress those lessons into a fraction of the timespan earlier executives needed. Analog was ready to exploit the next era, the one focused on strategy, at the same time that more established American businesses were just beginning to enter it. In 1969, after Stata had scrutinized impending changes in the electronics industry, he strategically foresaw that Analog might sacrifice future growth if it did not become a player in silicon chip production. To enter the semiconductor business, Stata worked out a deal with another young Massachusetts company, Nova Devices, which had the technology but not the capital. By the mid 1970s, Stata could see that more customers who needed to process analog information would be looking for complete systems, not just the components Analog had been making. According to Stata, "The lines between systems and components were beginning to blur." In the winter of 1979–1980, top Analog executives met weekly to brainstorm the challenges facing them. From these strategy sessions emerged a list of diverse fields into which the company might move in order to stay at the forefront of its field.

At this point, Analog experienced rapid, almost simultaneous, evolutions through the eras of culture and innovation, refining structure and productivity practices at the same time. Based on its successful investment experience with Nova Devices, Stata looked for a way to structure an enterprise that could effectively foster the innovative and entrepreneurial endeavors of several companies simultaneously, allowing Analog to pursue a number of technological development paths related to its central orientation—producing products that process real-world signals so computers can understand and use them. When Standard Oil agreed to collaborate by fronting money for Analog to acquire interest in relevant small businesses, Stata found what he believed to be the ideal structure for fostering constant innovation—a sort of corporate incubator that could feed and nurture several ventures simultaneously. His specialized venture-capital type of operation seemed to maximize productivity and innovation. Consequently, with an innovative structure in place, Stata began developing a corporate culture that could attract the best technical talent, stimulate entrepreneurial spirit, offer independent gestation periods for ventures, remove distractions from core projects by separating them from more speculative ones, and allow for the growth of independent subcultures within the company. As the company's several subcultures began to prosper in such diverse, but technologically related, markets as laboratory automation, medical and health care, energy conservation, avionics, telecommunications, broadcasting, and defensive weapons, Analog's overall culture also developed. Today, a mere twenty years after its inception, Analog Devices is poised on the brink of becoming a half-billion-dollar company, an achievement made possible to a great extent by effective synchronization through leadership. Thus Stata may be positioning his company to win a place among the Future 500.

In a quite different industry, W. L. Gore & Associates began business in 1958 when Wilbert L. Gore, the company's chairman until his death in 1986, left Du Pont to pursue a vision his employer did not share. The privately held company now enjoys pretax profits estimated at 20 percent of over $250 million in sales, and it consistently achieves an annual growth rate of 20 to 30 percent. The company's evolution has more closely paralleled the historical sequence of events than Analog's has. However, Gore, like Analog, compressed the lessons of earlier eras and sometimes combined more than one era at a time as it drew from the hard-won lessons of older companies.

Wilbert (Bill) Gore left Du Pont, which had operated on the leading edge of the two eras prior to 1958, when the company rejected his idea to create uses for their new plastic raw material polytetrafluoroethylene (PTFE), or Teflon. Although Gore's first inventions on his own, electrical wire and cable casings, brought the new company instant success, his management and organizational inventions brought even more. Combining insights gleaned from the structure and productivity eras with foresight into the emerging systems era, Gore implemented an integrated structure and system for management that, from the very beginning, maximized the productivity of his people. He coined the term "lattice organization" to describe an approach in which every member of a company should know and have easy access to every other member, without the traditional hierarchical and divisional barriers. The lattice organization, like the criss-crossing of garden lattices, operates on the basis of vertical and horizontal relationships that afford every employee the flexibility to group with others to accomplish a given project. Gore's method of management fostered a highly productive culture of eager, motivated "associates" who invent the products that fuel Gore's phenomenal annual growth rate.

The next three eras at Gore proceeded like clockwork as the company strategically positioned itself for continuous innovation, introducing products such as Goretex, a miracle fiber impervious to sunlight, chemical degradation, heat, and cold. Goretex is now the company's main product, with hundreds of applications ranging from spacesuits to vascular grafts and hiking boots. Bill Gore's lattice organization may have given birth to the company's innovative culture, but the company's real culture era dawned when it began fighting to protect the existing culture against the destructive forces of size and bureaucracy. To do this, Bill Gore focused even more tightly on reinforcing the company's unique philosophy through one-on-one discussions with associates. On the heels of its culture and innovation eras, the company needed to shift attention slightly to ensure the continuous integration of all its success variables. Of course, it had profited all along from Bill Gore's strong leadership, but maintaining that leadership required a great deal of artful balancing. Although Gore has fashioned a highly integrated organization, his company is only one two-hundredth the size of IBM. Can Robert Gore, Bill's son and current president, and his management team synchronize all aspects of the Gore system when the company reaches $1 billion or $10 billion—or will they choose instead to keep the company smaller? Whatever Gore's future holds, its past points clearly toward the metamorphosis of thinking and managing that can emerge under the synchronizing hand of leadership. For Analog, Gore, and other aspirants to the Future 500, we think a successful metamorphosis will hinge on what we call *corporate renewal,* an application of synchronicity through leadership that will help create tomorrow's organizations today.

Corporate Renewal

With the synchronizing hand of leadership, executives of the threshold era should work to renew their organizations with further integration of existing management concepts and practices. While one leader may adjust the ingredients of his company's strategy-culture mix, another may coordinate operational management, and still another may strive to inculcate innovation more fully throughout the organization. In order to gain as much competitive advantage as possible, executives should work diligently to raise the performance standards for all systems, functions, departments, operating units, and managment practices. By elevating the "lowest acceptable standard" for every facet of their organizations, they can send to the entire culture the message that corporate renewal requires the highest possible levels of performance in all areas. We have found that truly excellent companies typically move through three phases in their attempts to raise standards of performance. First they pay general attention to all performance areas, which produces marginal results, until they get results; then they focus on one or two areas then, finally, they address peak performances in all areas once again with greater success.

Corporate renewal may come easily to healthy and growing companies and industries, but what about those that are in decline? Throughout this century management theory has developed around an assumption of continued growth and plentiful resources. Thus, when theorists encounter a declining company or industry, they typically recommend further growth through the addition of units or diversification. However, when such recommendations proved inadequate during the 1970s and 80s traditional theory threw in suggestions for participative management and strengthened corporate culture, without ever really questioning the original assumptions.

Most businesses in decline suffer high levels of administrative stress, low levels of trust, a great deal of secretiveness and centralization of power and authority, rigid reliance on past strategies, leading to conservatism and risk aversion, and a high degree of conflict coupled with a low degree of morale. The result: high turnover and a "cover your backside" mentality. The stress and insecurity that characterize such organizations create a whole new set of crises. Management decisions become increasingly short-term, with a focus on efficiency rather than effectiveness. Trust and communication break down as a focus on personal welfare and organizational survival replaces a focus on corporate purpose and philosophy. Authority and power centralize to limit personal discretion and opportunism at the very time when flexibility and personal discretion would do the most good. The credibility of leaders evaporates just when employee support and confidence would make the greatest difference. Pluralistic viewpoints, normally a benefit for organizational decision making, harden into dogmatic positions. Ironically, during a period that requires intense change, people often recoil at the idea.

Few such companies address conditions of decline with effective leadership. Rather, their executives tend either to deny the situation and delay action or to grasp precipitously at solutions. Denial and delay cause the initial problem to mushroom into a full-fledged crisis, and ill-considered action creates as many problems as it tried to solve.

What should declining companies and industries do? Like their healthier counterparts, they should employ the synchronizing hand of leadership, establishing clear "renewal conditions" that they think can, over the long haul, transform decline into vitality. Such a response to organization decline would require:

- The authority to redirect resources

- Continuity in top management

- Rapid and accurate feedback about the effects of changes on performance

- Budgetary flexibility to allow for fluctuating priorities
- Incentives for conserving resources and increasing productivity
- Discretion to prioritize cuts
- Clear understanding of strategic advantage and distinctive competence

When creating their "renewal conditions," leaders should be aware of certain environmental constraints that may affect their ultimate success. These include lead time (early warning), a clear understanding of the source of the threat, the antagonism of external groups and competitors, the degree to which the organization is restricted by either geography or market, organizational slack (both financial and human), severity of the threat, duration of the threat, and the immutability of the threat. Attention to these external constraints can help executives steer their organizations out of decline and toward the ranks of the Future 500.

For a visible sign of the drive toward corporate renewal in the years ahead, we will be looking for an escalating number of divestitures, mergers, and reorganizations. Already we see companies taking aggressive steps to shore up and fine-tune their operations in order to maximize improved performance and competitive advantage. The business historian writing in the year 2050 may well cite the spinning off of divisions and subsidiaries that didn't fit a company's strategy-culture alloy or its elevated standards of performance as one of the most significant developments of the last quarter of the twentieth century. To be sure, large conglomerates have always tried to unload their "dogs," but many, in the name of renewal, are now divesting themselves of mismatched or substandard units which can then experience renewal on their own, sometimes becoming stars. For example, American Safety Razor, acquired by Philip Morris Company in 1960, did not fulfill the buyer's hope that advertising synergies and the transfer of marketing expertise could make ASR an even better company. When it became clear that the value of ASR as a strategic investment had diminished, ASR's management engineered a leveraged buyout in 1977. Today, despite the heavy burden of high interest payments, the company's profitability has improved substantially, allowing it to acquire a compatible soap manufacturer and candy maker. Ten years ago this sort of corporate renewal by divestiture would have struck students of business as the mere dumping of a dog. Today, enlightened by the lessons of the culture, innovation, and threshold eras, we can view the ASR divestiture as an effective way to focus Philip Morris's business thrusts, raise its lowest acceptable standards of performance, and better synchronize the company's strategy, culture and operations decisions.

In another instructive renewal effort, RCA sold CIT Financial Corp. in 1983, unloaded Hertz Corp. in 1985, then merged with General Electric soon thereafter. All this activity reflected RCA's belief that it could renew itself by divesting unrelated businesses that clouded the company's focus on electronics and broadcasting. With the unrelated businesses gone, RCA made an ideal partner for GE, which has likewise been divesting itself of low-performing, ill-fitting businesses.

On other fronts, Gulf & Western agreed to sell almost half its businesses to Wickes Companies; ITT sold seventy-five subsidiaries in a relatively short span of time; Olin Corp. jettisoned aluminum, paper, homebuilding, barge shipping, pharmaceutical, and firearm businesses to concentrate more on defense, electronics, and chemicals; and B.F. Goodrich planned to unload the polyvinyl chloride and specialty chemical plants that once accounted for almost a quarter of its revenues. Textron Inc., General Mills, Litton, and many others have also pursued renewal by focusing their businesses and refining their overall management practices.

At the other end of the spectrum, mergers will probably continue to create headlines, but we think the acquiring companies will take much more care that they can successfully synchronize the strategies, cultures, systems, and leadership of the combined organizations. ConAgra stuck to basic foods when it acquired and turned around Banquet Foods. The Nabisco and Standard Brands merger also succeeded because such a marriage of equals exploited the relative strengths of each company, achieving a greater competitive advantage for both. To facilitate a smooth union, Nabisco and Standard Brands gave themselves plenty of time to integrate their operations without excessive short-term profit pressure. If Nabisco Brands continues to take similar pains to integrate its more recent merger with R.J. Reynolds, it should enjoy continued success in the future. Other productive mergers include Heinz and Weight Watchers, Dayton-Hudson and Mervyn's, Sara Lee and Hanes, Allied and Bendix, and Philip Morris and General Foods. Each of these mergers demonstrates the wisdom of consciously blending and refining all relevant aspects of combined operations. Other already sprawling corporations such as American Express, Citicorp, and General Electric have embarked on programs to better harmonize existing divisions and subsidiaries so that the resultant unified corporate cultures can pull together and capitalize on one another's strength.

Paradox Management

An expanding knowledge of organizational success factors and the increasing complexity of the business world have worked together to reveal a number of apparent paradoxes. To a great extent, the successful completion of the transformation we foresee depends on the ability of executives to resolve such paradoxes. Learning to manage paradox effectively can greatly extend and enhance leadership skills and abilities.

Paradoxes are not so much realities as products of the human imagination, an attempt to comprehend complexity. We recommend paradox management as an important step toward more effectively managing increasingly complex organizations and their environments. With it, executives can consider the multiple and often contradictory sides of an issue, instead of retreating to the comfort of simpler, single-dimension solutions to problems.

In essence, what we call paradox management means the ability to look at apparently conflicting sides of an issue and manage them both with a "combined with" rather than an "either-or" or "from-to" attitude. For example:

• Unmanaged employees can produce more than closely supervised ones. This seemingly contradicts the current management preference for close supervision. Although organizations do need supervisory relationships, people will achieve the highest possible levels of productivity when they can determine their own directions and commitments. As with all paradox management, attention must be paid to both sides of the issue. W. L. Gore addresses both by equally stressing order and innovation through a flexible, lattice-type organization.

- The best individual business strategies benefit the entire community of competitors. This seems to fly in the face of current competitive positioning theory that pits companies against one another. However, win-win competitive philosophies can allow competitors to meet the demands of different niches and segments to the benefit of all customers without head-to-head battles that may result in temporarily lower prices but ultimately an unstable, unproductive industry. Hewlett-Packard addresses both sides of this issue by letting competitors know through explicit and persistent actions in the marketplace that the company always focuses on higher-end, technically sophisticated products. By doing so, it prods its competitors to serve other markets and avoid wasting valuable resources locking horns with H-P. This doesn't mean competition should stop, but it does mean that the most productive competition can derive from differentiation rather than similarity.

- Seek simplicity and then distrust it. This communicates the idea that simplicity, though ideal, can be misleading. General Electric attempts to manage this paradox by establishing clear, simple strategic positions for its SBUs, while constantly looking for deeper insight and understanding that challenge the established simplicity.

- Less control means more control. This suggests that tight controls stifle creativity but that innovation gives managers a lot of control. Companies like Marketing Corporation of America and Kollmorgen share major portions of their stock and profits with employees, creating an environment in which employees control themselves.

- The safest course can be the most dangerous one. This statement proposes that the risk-free course cannot lead to continuing success. Organizations like Frito-Lay manage this paradox by retaining tension between stability and change, risk and protection.

Walter Wriston, former chairman and CEO of Citicorp, knew more than most how to manage paradoxes. Even in a tradition-bound environment, Wriston found ways to forge change and innovation. In his book, *Risk and Other Four-Letter Words,* he suggests that to manage paradoxes "we must start by telling ourselves the truth." To our list of paradoxes Wriston adds:

- "Information eliminates uncertainty but increases the feeling of insecurity unless that information is converted into knowledge."

- "Because we are bound by what we know, it is difficult to imagine what we don't know."

- "While the details of economic development may be extremely complex, the basic economic principles involved are very simple."

- "Economic interdependence makes national independence even more important."

In the past, most executives have either shied away from paradoxes or tried to hammer them out of existence. Paradoxes can be confusing and even frightening to people who want simple answers to life's complex questions. However, the best answers are simple enough for people to understand, yet complex enough to allow for a rich assortment of nuances and interpretations. During the current era executives should not only welcome paradoxes, they should actively seek them out, forcing themselves to think about every aspect of themselves, their organizations and their leadership practices in terms of seemingly contradictory elements inextricably coiled together.

A group of Stanford Business School researchers led by Kathleen Eisenhardt recently conducted a study to determine the most appropriate mode or posture for organizations in the midst of change. They looked at three categories, each of which included two alternative modes. They labeled the first category, which dealt with planning and action, "Analysis vs. Action," and asked this question: Are business organizations in the midst of change more likely to assume the "analysis" or the "action" mode? The second category, addressing the CEO's role, was called "Commander vs. Coordinator/Coach," and here they posed the question: Is the CEO of a business organization in the midst of change more likely to assume the "commander" or the "coordinator/coach" role? Finally, for the third category, "Entrepreneurial vs. Adaptive," they asked: When an organization is in the midst of change is it more likely to take bold or incremental steps? In their search for answers to these perplexing questions, the researchers studied companies that were wrestling with a variety of environmental and industry changes. Some of these had achieved only lackluster results, while others had turned in stellar performances. After examining the actions of a number of such companies for several months, the Stanford group drew some interesting conclusions.

In the "Analysis vs. Action" category, they found that successful companies in the midst of change practice textbook strategic analysis and planning *combined with* extremely quick action. While both rational analysis and quick action typify successful companies, their less-successful counterparts tend to emphasize one over the other.

In the "Commander vs. Coordinator/Coach" category, CEOs of successful companies in the midst of change set strategy by commanding, but they implemented strategy in a decentralized fashion by coordinating and coaching. Again, the CEOs of successful companies *combine* the commander *with* the coordinator modes, while the CEOs of less successful companies focus on one or the other.

With regard to the "Entrepreneurial vs. Adaptive" category, successful organizations in the midst of change adapt incrementally to change, but they make major entrepreneurial shifts as necessary. Combining the vision of the entrepreneurial mode *with* the flexibility of the adaptive mode brings the best companies their success, while the inability to do so causes weaker companies to falter.

Clearly this research underscores the value of paradox management. Each of the three categories set up by the Stanford team included what executives of the past would have considered opposing schools of thought. In fact much of the current wisdom argues that you cannot expect to be both analytical and action oriented, both commanding and coordinating, or both entrepreneurial and adaptive. But the leaders of successful companies prove the current wisdom wrong.

A New Perspective for the Future 500

The transformation of management that we envision demands a truly ecological perspective that will allow for three important integrations: direct management combined with indirect management, linking and unlinking relationships combined with building relationships, and vertical and horizontal organizations combined with network organizations. These three integrations represent the final stage of metamorphosis on which our theory of complexity depends. In order to better understand how Future 500 companies and their leaders can use the current threshold era of leadership to transform current management practices, let's explore each of these integrations.

First, by direct management we mean all the management activities, both rational and qualitative, that immediately affect the performance of an enterprise. These include capital expenditures, cost reductions, strategic planning, personnel additions or terminations, corporate culture surveys, new products, new technology, acquisitions, divestitures, innovation programs, and so forth. The shift from rational management practices to qualitative management practices in the 1970s represented the beginning of the movement from direct to indirect management. However, at the beginning of the threshold era, most managers still approach qualitative management in a direct way. For example, executives often attempt to change corporate cultures through direct means—new policies, programs or structures—or they try to instill the spirit of innovation in their organizations directly with innovation programs or reward systems.

By indirect management we mean all the management activities that tacitly influence the performance of an enterprise. These include creative strategic thinking, discovering the real needs and wants of people, nurturing the personal satisfaction and career development of each individual worker, accurately anticipating and even creating customer needs, drawing lessons from an organization's history, and promoting a secure, nonthreatening, achievement-oriented environment that fosters growth, learning, and change. Direct management concerns itself with the realm of words and actions; indirect management with the realm of thoughts and feelings. United, these two brands of management unleash the full power of people in organizations. While executives in the late 1980s may enjoy all the resources and skills they need to manage directly, by the end of the threshold era they will need to have assembled the synchronizing leadership skills that facilitate indirect management. To their technical business school educations and on-the-job training they should add such skills as knowledge of history, communication, and sincere concern for people, as well as insight, vision, sensitivity, patience, versatility, and focus.

Northwestern Mutual Life is not just another one of the many insurance companies in America. Dubbing itself "The Quiet Company," Northwestern has already begun to apply some of the skills that don't directly affect the bottom line but do indirectly create an unbeatable environment of productivity and fulfillment. Northwestern allows for flextime hours, an arrangement that lets workers determine when they begin and end their work days, and its nontraditional job definitions offer office employees more responsibility, variety, and flexibility. Under direct management only, such practices would fall by the wayside because they do not produce any immediately measurable benefit. However, combined with indirect management, they directly increase employee satisfaction and fulfillment, thus indirectly affecting productivity and performance. *Best's Review* consistently rates Northwestern first among the nation's seventy-one largest life insurance companies on a number of technical criteria, but its technical achievements stem from its nontechnical expertise, which has helped its people attain record-shattering productivity.

By linking/unlinking relationships we mean forming personal and organizational ties that benefit both parties for a time (linking) but dissolve (unlinking) when mutual benefits no longer exist. These relationships are "disposable." Building relationships, on the other hand, bestow more than conventional benefits, the old standby profits and wages, on the parties involved. Linking/unlinking relationships, like marriages of convenience, are usually short-term, while building relationships, like marriages of mature love, can last. American business people have always been good at linking—merging, acquiring, setting up joint ventures, partnerships and agreements—and then unlinking through divestiture or other means when mutual benefits decline. However, executives have not been so good at forming deeper and more lasting bonds. When linking occurs, the parties invariably worry about the probability of unlinking, and such worries can actually undermine a long-term relationship. Recent years have produced such an explosion of acquisitions and divestitures that it's no wonder courting corporations worry more about the possibility of unlinking than about the details of daily life after the acquisition. By the end of the threshold era executives can add greater value and gain more advantage in the world economy by investing more time and energy in building relationships. Olivetti, the Italian office equipment manufacturer, has entered into a long-term affiliation with AT&T for the mutual benefit of both companies worldwide. The relationship has borne little fruit to date, but both companies seem to be committed to the long-term prospects for the union. Time will tell whether they can resist the normal pressures that often encourage unlinking.

When we talk about network organizations, we're referring to a new type of parent or umbrella organization that nurtures and protects other forms of organizations. A vertical organization, such as a forest products company that buys land, plants and harvests trees, operates sawmills, manufactures wood products, and produces paper, reflects a top-to-bottom or vertically integrated structure, while a conglomerate operating a diverse group of enterprises in related or unrelated businesses displays a side-to-side or horizontally integrated structure. Both types can fall under the network organization's umbrella. You might think of network organizations as mentors, with the skills and resources to provide guidance, nourishment, and protection to the other forms. When a network organization assumes such parental or mentor responsibility, it supports direct and indirect management, as well as linking/unlinking and building relationships. The network organization sits atop the management pyramid, creating an internal and external environment that synchronizes the success factors, promotes corporate renewal, manages paradoxes, and perpetuates itself through the growth and development of other entities. It unites the warring forces of dependence and independence, facilitating true interdependence among units. When interdependent organizations, nurtured by the mentoring network, cry for independence, the network can grant freedom without anarchy. The young organization might in time even mature into a network organization itself by integrating the rules of indirect management and relationship building with traditional practices. When that happens, the network organization orchestrates its own rebirth.

At IBM and AT&T visionary leadership has laid the foundations upon which they can construct network centers for a host of businesses. IBM has already spawned numerous support industries that supply software, hardware components, and peripheral equipment; and it has assumed a mentoring role for companies such as Rolm and MCI. IBM currently works hard at forming the sorts of partnerships and relationships that will help it maintain its network status while at the same time developing other network organizations.

Likewise, AT&T has positioned itself as a potential network by deploying its telecommunication capabilities to exploit every conceivable computing device the future may bring. With its eye on relationship building, it has set up affiliate arrangements with companies such as Olivetti, thus enhancing AT&T's worldwide network influence.

Can IBM and AT&T complete the revolution and remain atop the Future 500 list, or will they falter, letting Sony, Toshiba, or Matsushita steal the lead? Unless they pay strict attention to the subtle yet dramatic changes unfolding at the present time, they could quickly lose their edge to a company like C. Itoh, the $70-billion Japanese trading company that already acts as a network in the worldwide computer market.

While the new emphasis on integration of indirect management, relationship building, and network organizations is vitally important and represents a major milestone, executives must go even further in these directions in the future because the future will become even more complex. Ultimately, executives must arrive at a point where their thinking can cut through complexity. To help them get there we will propose in the next chapter three basic precepts that we believe can turn any executive into an effective complexity manager.

CHAPTER FOUR

Management Tomorrow: Dealing with Complexity

> *Our institutions are failing because they are*
> *disobeying the laws of effective organization*
> *which their administrators do not know about, to*
> *which indeed their cultural mind is closed,*
> *because they contend that there exists and can*
> *exist, no science competent to discover those laws.*
> —STAFFORD BEER

The Search for Deeper Understanding

A number of current or former CEOs have demonstrated their leadership abilities in the present era: Jack Welch of GE, Kenneth Macke of Dayton Hudson, Henry Schacht of Cummins Engine, William Schreyer of Merrill Lynch, Roger Smith of GM, John Akers of IBM, and Edward Telling of Sears. However, we'd like to single out one individual who best exemplifies the way of thinking we recommend for the leaders of the Future 500: John Reed of Citicorp. Moving beyond the precedents set by Walter Wriston, Reed has brought a new management attitude to one of the world's largest global corporations.

From the time Reed took over as chairman and CEO of Citicorp in September 1984, he blended the best of rational and intuitive management skills, approaching a host of strategic and operating issues with an uncanny ability to set both broad and specific priorities. While Wriston had focused on making Citicorp the largest bank in the world through rapid growth and expansion, Reed favored a less obsessive approach that, beginning with a focus on soaring expenses, might bring the burgeoning organization into balance. In a speech to twenty division heads in 1985, Lawrence M. Small, Reed's closest associate and the head of the Institutional Bank (the commercial banking group), stated, "We have too many people doing too much unnecessary bureaucratic activity, too many studies, too many reports, too many management information systems." Small went on to say, "Let's get rid of everything that's unwieldy, top-heavy, and excessively formal." Although aimed on the surface at promoting Reed's cost-cutting measures, Small's words conveyed top management's belief that an innovative organization cannot afford to rely solely on traditional management.

Extending his effort to help Citicorp function in a more harmonious and integrated fashion, Reed launched into a major reorganization, which consolidated all private-banking units within the Individual Bank (responsible for all consumer banking activities). *Business Week* praised the Individual Bank as Citicorp's secret weapon for the future. The new organizational structure reflected John Reed's unique style, distinctly less confrontational, more conservative, and more versatile than Wriston's. During Wriston's seventeen-year tenure as the head of Citicorp, he had stimulated the company to become more entrepreneurial, innovative, and flexible, winning it distinction as the world's most innovative banking institution. However, in a notoriously tradition-bound and bureaucracy-driven industry, Citicorp still suffered from many antiquated practices and procedures. Reed immediately tackled that problem.

In a recent annual report, Reed told stockholders, "As was announced in 1985, we reorganized our three core businesses. We moved our money market and foreign exchange trading activities into the Investment Bank, improving the interaction between the Institutional Bank officers and their Investment Banking colleagues and creating a truly global force to serve our customers. We also structured our Individual Bank to integrate our U.S. branching and card products activities within common units and formed a global Private Banking business which we believe will be of future importance. Even at this early date it appears that this reorganization, which puts Messrs. Theobald, Braddock, and Small in charge of the three core businesses of the Corporation, has opened up new opportunities, brought new strengths to our customers, and will be of important longer-term significance in the evolution of Citicorp."

These decisions represented not a drastic alteration in the long-term strategy Reed himself had helped create years earlier, but rather the conscientious development of better working relationships, both within his firm and between Citicorp and the outside world. His goals were long range, not just encompassing quarterly and yearly milestones, but spanning decades. Under Reed's management Citicorp has strengthened its capital base for long-range returns with what Citicorpers call "bulletproofing," a tactic that allocates hefty percentages of current earnings to beef up loan-loss reserves. With this and similarly forward-looking maneuvers, Reed has taken the broadest possible perspective on Citicorp's future, paying attention not just to tomorrow's bottom line but to the diversity and interrelatedness among all the stakeholders in Citicorp's environment. By contrast Wriston gained a reputation for building an aggressive, perhaps even belligerent organization. Reed, recognizing that he might accomplish more through amicable rather than antagonistic means, has begun improving the bank's relationships not only internally and with customers but externally with regulators and competitors.

The oneness of mind among Reed's top management group has been criticized by some observers as dangerously myopic. However, we view it as a triumph of Reed's innate flair for using guiding principles to unite potentially conflicting viewpoints, and we feel that tomorrow's managers should emulate this approach. Rather than functioning like corporate police, enforcing ever more stringent policies and procedures, wise future managers should encourage different perspectives but pull them together behind unifying principles, grant individuals the freedom to work within those principles, provided they do so responsibly, and nurture mutually beneficial relationships among all the individuals who have a stake in the success of an organization. Such an approach will, we think, allow managers to help their organizations respond fluidly to the accelerating changes that surround modern management. Future organizations that cannot adapt smoothly to change will probably fall by the wayside, either disappearing altogether or being consumed by healthier rivals. Those that do adapt skillfully will satisfy the needs and desires of individuals, enhance the productivity and profitability of the organization itself, create attractive returns to investors, satisfy customers' needs, improve the strength of the industry at large (including all viable competitors), contribute to the well-being of society, and harmonize national interests in the global marketplace.

During the age of the invisible hand of the marketplace, business people preoccupied themselves with "outcomes," focusing their attention on market results. Subsequently, during the age of the visible hand of management, executives became concerned with managerial "actions" that might result in more profitable outcomes. However, we believe tomorrow's business leaders must also develop a deep awareness of the desires and outlooks of all corporate stakeholders, which in turn shape actions and outcomes.

The Three Precepts of Complexity Management

We use the term "complexity" to describe our proposed new way of thinking about management because it suggests the inclusion of all the variables that affect organizational success: the lessons of the invisible hand of the marketplace, all the skills brought to bear over the past hundred years by the visible hand of management, and the current synchronizing hand of leadership.

In the rest of this book we will use "complexity management" to refer to an attitude about managing an organization that derives from three basic precepts: that unifying principles can draw individuals with diverse points of view toward a common purpose, that freedom to act, within the bounds of unifying principles, will empower individuals to work responsibly and effectively, and that the genuine fulfillment of individual needs and desires, which leads to peak performances, depends on strong relationships between each individual and all other stakeholders. We call these three precepts "perspective management," "power management," and "pivot management." Rather than replacing the historical management skills, these three precepts allow business leaders to tap their full potential. Remember, we are not proposing a new set of skills but a new way of thinking about how executives apply *all* their existing and future skills.

Since developing a new way of thinking about anything is an

abstract, theoretical undertaking, we want to examine and discuss these precepts in detail and see how, exactly, they might be applied to the Future 500.

Perspective Management Through Unifying Principles

Perspective management uses unifying principles, or in other words mutually benefitting principles, to harmonize diverse desires and outlooks. It addresses the need to take into account the many and often conflicting points of view held by all those affected by an organization. Successful perspective managers use their understanding of these disparate viewpoints to forge a common understanding of, and commitment to, their organization's overall purposes, without destroying the diversity of desires.

How can an executive maintain a common purpose among conflicting points of view? At Citicorp, John Reed relied on perspective management when he reorganized and consolidated business units in an effort to increase coordination, cooperation, and harmony among a variety of potentially conflicting business purposes. By combining the private-banking units and the branch system within the Individual Bank, Reed tried to differentiate yet integrate the perspectives and purposes of people working in two divergent organizational groups for the benefit of all Citicorp stakeholders. To accomplish this goal, Reed designed a common purpose network, a kind of road map, that could guide all individual and collective efforts.

In order to resolve the apparent paradox inherent in maintaining a common purpose amid a diversity of desires, a leader must be able to design a conceptual road map, a broad set of guiding principles that people starting from different points in the corporate ecosystem can follow to arrive at a common destination. When the full array of stakeholder desires and outlooks are collectively guided by unifying principles that allow for a linking and drawing together of diverse perspectives toward shared purposes, we call the phenomenon a common purpose network.

If executives develop their ability to create such common purpose networks, they can unify individuals without destroying the unique vitality of each. This does not mean that perspective managers need not concern themselves with the market outcomes and managerial actions that have always preoccupied executives, but it does mean that they must blend their concerns with the deeper desires of people and groups. By accounting for multiple perspectives—not only in terms of personal biases, styles, and preferences, but also in terms of functional, geographical, national, organizational, subsidiary, and business-line differences—perspective managers can insure productive actions and profitable outcomes.

By way of illustration, consider the essential role perspective managers could play for a company like Procter & Gamble, with worldwide sales of over $16 billion. As it approaches the next century, P&G must deal with the desires and outlooks of 74,000 employees, 97,975 common stock shareholders, hundreds of competitors, numerous suppliers, government regulators, and millions of customers around the globe. Each of P&G's business segments—from detergents, fabric softeners, cleaners, bar soaps, toothpastes, mouthwashes, deodorants and hair-care products, to paper tissue products, disposable diapers, cough/cold remedies, pharmaceuticals, shortenings, oils, prepared baking mixes, peanut butter, potato chips, coffee, and soft drinks—requires a different perspective, and since almost $5 billion of P&G's sales come from outside the United States, the company must also consider the different perspectives of Latin America, Europe, the Middle East, and the Far East. And let's not forget the multiple functional, technical, and organizational points of view of people working in materials acquisition and handling, supplier relations, manufacturing, quality control, research and development, computer technology, human resources, organizational development, market research, marketing, advertising, distribution, customer service, strategic planning, capital budgeting, financial analysis, accounting and auditing, investor relations, government relations, public and community relations, and environmental impact. On top of all these are added the outlooks of different levels of management, labor unions, clerical staffs, plus regional differences between far-flung plants and field offices and between company headquarters in Cincinnati and sales offices around the world. Clearly, so many diverse perspectives could create a confusing level of complexity for P&G executives. However, a common purpose network, beyond mere adherence to corporate policy, could keep P&G ranking high in the Future 500 indefinitely.

Without perspective management, firms as sprawling as P&G could easily drown in a sea of complexity. The decline of People

Express is a case in point. In its early years employees were encouraged to solve problems at the lowest possible levels because those actually facing a problem had the best perspective for finding solutions. Despite this early respect for employee perspectives, and despite initial high levels of commitment to a common purpose, People Express deteriorated when the company adopted an authoritarian approach in its frenzied attempt to stave off failure. Ironically, its crisis management efforts did nothing but fuel further decline. How different the outcome might have been if executive action had persistently and consistently employed the perspective management that had gotten the airline off the ground in the first place.

In contrast, General Electric has more faithfully adhered to perspective management in recent years. As you will see in Chapter 5, GE has weathered rough seas with constant strategic vision. Within a given GE business unit, a conceptual road map has enabled every employee to coordinate his or her own individual perspectives with all others, and furthermore, the strategic perspectives of the company's many business units function within the overall corporate mandate of market or technology leadership in every GE business.

The best conceptual road maps include mutually benefitting principles, fundamental guidelines and philosophies that can fulfill diverse desires, shape daily actions, and create profitable outcomes. Such principles should form the bedrock of an organization's structures, productivity goals, control and information systems, business strategy, culture, innovation programs, and leadership practices. Sometimes such principles evolve over many years of corporate history, while other times they spring from one person's vision or from lengthy consensus building discussions; but regardless of their origin, they should reside at the heart of every Future 500 firm.

Principles are not simply rules; rather, they set the boundaries within which individuals and groups with diverse desires and outlooks operate to accomplish their own and their organization's purposes. No two organizations will share identical principles. For some, the principles will incorporate certain aspects of information management, for others they will involve marketing philosophies, and for still others they will derive from the development of sophisticated technologies. Regardless of their application in specific situations, guiding principles should accommodate and integrate the diverse perspectives of all who come in contact with the organization.

Almost every business enterprise currently promotes some set of values or basic tenets that more or less rule the actions of people inside the organization, but few of them fully embrace the entire complement of stakeholders. Although the corporate culture era of the early and mid 1980s began to raise awareness of the importance of guiding principles in the management of an organization, no concise, holistic management theory of that era showed executives precisely how to develop and use them in concert with all their other practices. During the ensuing innovation and leadership eras, executives may have learned to manage culture and creativity more adroitly, but they seldom extended their efforts deeply or broadly enough.

The importance of managing by principle was brought vividly home to us recently as we watched a financial services company try to adjust to its new parent corporation. The subsidiary, which for purposes of confidentiality we'll call AFS, was a successful midsized regional financial services company whose extraordinary growth encouraged its executives to form a relationship with a larger, national organization. By doing so they hoped to gain sufficient funding for future growth and expansion into new markets. The CEO at AFS, whom we'll call Max, having sought our advice over the years, kept us abreast of developments. Back in 1985, Max, a majority AFS stockholder, had begun searching for an appropriate merger and parent organization candidate and, at our suggestion, he narrowed the field to companies whose strategy-culture mixes, operating philosophies, and management styles seemed consistent and compatible with his own. After months of analysis and endless meetings, Max found what he considered a perfect match. "As far as basic principles and philosophies go, we are in complete accord," he told us. He cited three specific examples: "Like us, First Financial [not the company's real name] believes in managing individual financial services and products as separate and distinct businesses with a common delivery system; First Financial has given top priority to providing the highest levels of personalized customer service in the industry, as have we; and First Financial is committed, as we are, to compensating its people above the industry average for performance above the industry average." From our own vantage point the merger did seem to promise great benefits to both parties.

When AFS completed its merger in the summer of 1986, the local and national press heralded it as a brilliant move. Unfortunately, over the next twelve months the luster faded as First Financial began requiring strict conformance to corporate policies and procedures. At first AFS accepted the requirements as a necessary attunement to the larger organizational framework. After all, Max and his executive team expected a little bureaucracy as an unpleasant side effect of greater size. However, when First Financial asked AFS to adopt a new management information system that randomly lumped certain categories of financial services and products together, making it difficult to evaluate the performance of separate services and products, Max protested. As he recalls, "This demand from First Financial was a direct violation of one of the principles I assumed would guide the management of the overall organization." He immediately contacted the executive vice president to whom he reported and asked for clarification. "I couldn't believe his response," Max said later. "He told me the new management information system had been under development for two years by the financial accounting department and they had finally worked out all the bugs. Though he didn't like some things about it either, he said headquarters would not allow any more delays in implementing the system because the whole financial reporting structure had been in limbo while waiting for this system to get up and running." The First Financial executive VP attempted to soften the blow by recommending that AFS run parallel systems for the next six months, during which time Max's people might grow comfortable with the new system or find ways to tailor it to their own needs.

In the months that followed, similar dictates from the parent company ran counter to what Max had thought were shared principles and philosophies. Even though First Financial executives continued to espouse the ideas that had brought the two companies together in the first place, they spent much more time worrying about structures, systems, procedures, and other rules and regulations. One evening at a dinner party Max shook his head sadly, saying, "You know, I'm convinced First Financial really does believe in the same basic principles and philosophies I do, but they don't *manage* by them!" The next week, he began preparing to exercise an option, included in the merger agreements, that allowed him to buy back his company.

Many executives, like First Financial's, may pay lip service to managing by principles, but they must in fact place them at the very core of all their thoughts and actions in the future. Consider the following examples of well-articulated principles. An architectural design firm states, "We surpass the expectation of our employees; they in turn surpass our [management's] expectations; together we surpass our customers' expectations; and our customers remain exceedingly loyal." A manufacturer of household appliances subscribes to this principle: "The kind of innovation that leads to loyal customers, committed employees, and satisfied investors flourishes when we value risk taking and intuition as much as analysis and corporate policies." And finally, an international management consulting firm articulates this principle: "Demanding adherence to the most rigorous standards of thinking, analysis, and writing in the industry brings us the most capable and committed people and the most sought-after clients, which in turn provides our people and the firm with the rewards of profit, influence, reputation, and growth." Ideally, statements of mutually benefitting principles should be concise, simple, yet powerful. And they should provide all stakeholders (including even competitors) with a clear conceptual road map.

How do competitors benefit? If a company's principles come across clearly and powerfully enough to spur that company's people toward a common purpose that results in superior performance, then competitors can more clearly see where they might carve their own profitable niches in the market. Given such principles, even head-to-head competition, so frequently a wasteful and counterproductive undertaking, can result in an expanded total market and gains for both competitors, as we have seen during the "Cola Wars" between Coke and Pepsi.

With mutually benefiting principles in place, self-management becomes a realistic possibility, allowing people to arrange formal and informal common-purpose networks that encompass diverse perspectives. If some people reject an organization's carefully stated principles, those people would do well to remove themselves because they would probably not succeed within that particular environment. However, assuming the organization has hired the right sort of people, most will rise to the challenge of unity amid diversity. In the case of First Financial and AFS, the parent company preached principles, but when it did not manage by them, it fell back on rules and regulations that forced strict conformity without recognizing divergent perspectives. As a result,

AFS could not practice self-management because, in reality, First Financial managed by systems, structures, procedures, and controls, not by principles. W. L. Gore & Associates, discussed in the preceding chapter, does achieve self-management based on principles because Gore executives preach and teach that people can and should manage themselves. Gore calls it "un-management," under which newly hired associates have already weighed the correlation between their own perspectives and those of the firm before they arrive; then, once aboard, they are encouraged to begin joining, under the tutorship of an informal sponsor, that part of the common-purpose network that seems to suit them best.

Mutually benefiting principles in a self-management environment perpetuate themselves. As the principles become more entrenched, those who remain with the organization grow more committed, applying the principles in ever more flexible and creative ways. Building such a dynamic principle-driven organization takes time and patience, and we think McKinsey & Company, the prestigious management consulting firm and advisor to many Fortune 500 companies, provides a striking example of how well it can work. By adhering to the principles of rigorous thinking, painstaking analysis, and high standards of verbal and written communication, by hiring people with superior intellect, capability, and commitment, and by assuming the posture of "thought leader," McKinsey & Company has achieved unequaled respect in the management consulting industry. Those who join McKinsey's elite ranks have already been indoctrinated into the company's remarkable history, begun by the visionary leader James O. McKinsey and continued by Marvin Bower and others. Yet the principles that guide McKinsey & Company allow for substantial individual initiative and contribution, and like all good common-purpose networks, they permit mutually benefitting results for all concerned.

Power Management Through Freedom to Act

Power management gives individuals the freedom to work and act within the boundaries of an organization's unifying principles. In essence it means affording stakeholders the freedom to influence and determine actions and outcomes. This applies to employees, managers, suppliers, customers, shareholders, citizens, governments, and competitors. Power managers allow individuals and groups to acquire and exercise maximum power, based on their demonstrated capability to direct such power for the benefit of all stakeholders.

John Reed at Citicorp offers a good example of power management in action. Reed and Citicorp know how to exploit their wealth of management talent by letting people know that all channels for improvement and innovation remain constantly open. Individuals who thrive on the freedom to try out new ideas and make an impact on an organization flourish at Citicorp, and they do so not in isolation, but in groups. Believing that no one person can offer all the solutions to all the problems all the time, Citicorp empowers work groups to develop and to implement strategies, giving individuals strong voices but encouraging them to work within common-purpose networks. Acting as an effective power manager, John Reed encourages the executives who report directly to him to afford their own managers the freedom to formulate strategies, structure organizational relationships, and set operating priorities. Citicorp's "Five I's," which include the three core businesses, Individual Bank, Institutional Bank and Investment Bank, as well as the company's planned forays into the insurance and information fields, form the primary spheres of power inside the organization. Additionally, Reed has striven to manage the power of stakeholders outside the company, such as regulators and industry affiliates, through closer relationships and cooperation.

Any power manager's effectiveness depends on integrity, competence, and the ability to instill trust. Most have built a quality track record with their firms, so they can rely on their recognized expertise, often in a functional or technical area, to reinforce credibility. They attune their own diverse and highly individualized desires to the common purposes of the organization, thus making their influence widely pervasive.

Transcending their functional or technical backgrounds, power managers display an intimate understanding of and enthusiasm for a wide range of business approaches, skills, and behaviors; and they feel comfortable with a variety of perspectives. This sort of flexibility allows power managers to develop more than one constituency base in an organization and, as a consequence, to unleash and coordinate power among diverse constituencies. Such positioning helps them understand and overcome resistance to change inside and outside an organization. The power manager utilizes, yet transcends, rational thought, and develops an intimacy with the extrarational feelings, emotions, and strivings of all stakeholders.

Successful power management depends on mutual trust, because without it people tend to view an executive as a representative of some special-interest group rather than as a concerned, caring, and just purveyor of power. Power managers gain the trust of all stakeholders by giving them appropriate opportunities to gain power themselves in accordance with the firm's mutually benefitting principles.

At 3M, for example, managers continually strive to reinforce and champion the positive attributes of the corporation while minimizing or eliminating the negative. Despite their firm belief in the need for organization, they also realize the tendencies of an organization to produce unproductive bureaucracy. To offset this tendency, 3M managers, much like the power manager we have described, help workers resolve conflicts, solve problems, and restructure working relationships and environments without having to cut undue red tape. At 3M, power management speeds innovation of new ideas and products.

At Arthur Young's Management Consulting Group the firm's broad client contacts and its understanding of organizational power dynamics allow its most adept consultants to serve as power managers within the Arthur Young environment as well as for client firms. Strong track records of empowering people and groups to get results enable these consultants to marshal and deliver resources effectively, quickly, and informally. The best ones, convinced that dedicated people will become extremely productive and innovative if given the appropriate organizational support and work environment, constantly champion the empowerment of people toward change. In the end they hope to train other Arthur Young consultants and key managers in client organizations to become effective power managers and change agents themselves. This is an important point. Productive, successful change requires risk and confidence, but many managers almost instinctively seek ways to minimize risk and avoid uncertainty. This tendency toward risk avoidance makes people fear change. In such situations, power managers, like those at Arthur Young, can perform a vital role by clearing the way for creativity, innovation, and change. If the power manager can reduce risk avoidance and fear of change among employees who possess intimate knowledge of a particular business, market, or technology, and if those employees themselves, in concert with management, promote change, the results can be astonishing, because whenever employees become the agents of change, others in the organization accept the changes more readily. Of equal importance, employee change agents provide management with fresh approaches to solving problems.

To business people accustomed to thinking in terms of controlling their organization's structures, processes, and people, the use of the word freedom might be alarming. However, true freedom goes hand in hand with the responsibility to work in accordance with fundamental principles. Otherwise, an organization invites anarchy and chaos, not true freedom. To grant genuine freedom to individuals, an organization must set forth principles that do not impede the growth of individuals, groups, or the structures and processes they adopt to get results. Nor should an organization coerce individuals into accepting principles that simply do not fit with their particular desires, values, and beliefs. This applies not only to employees and managers, but to stockholders, customers, and the community as well. All must feel free to accept, reject, praise, or criticize the principles that form an organization's common purpose. A business organization cannot be all things to all people, but it can expect the best results from allowing people the freedom and resulting power to shape and change the corporate environment in accordance with mutually benefitting principles. When stakeholders do accept and embrace an organization's principles of their own free will, management does not need to resort to any sort of coercive controls.

Compliance never equals commitment. No future manager should ever try to rob people of the freedom to choose how they will respond and react mentally, emotionally, and spiritually to a situation. No matter what physical constraints, controls, or limitations a misguided leader may place upon a person, that individual will inevitably retain the final control over his or her mind and spirit. We are reminded of the old saying, "a person persuaded against his will is of the same opinion still."

Ms. Steve Shirley, founder of F International, offers an interesting example of how freedom can empower people. Her company is a consulting organization that specializes in designing integrated office information systems, evaluating hardware and software, converging existing systems, creating internal documentation systems, providing programming services, and helping management apply micro- as well as personal computers to business operations. Launched by Shirley out of her own need and desire for the freedom to work from home as a freelancer, F International now employs more than a thousand freelancers in the United Kingdom, the Netherlands, and Denmark.

F International differs from similar types of organizations in that all of its employees, including the CEO and the salaried senior management people, work out of their own homes. However, with a 30 percent annual growth rate and service-generated sales of $10 million, the company is a far cry from the usual home-based business. As in the case of all growing companies, management must wrestle with the thorny issue of control. The way Steve Shirley manages this far-flung and unconnected group of people offers some insight into how other companies might use power management. Shirley resolves the control issue at F International by having its 1000 people work in teams, within which the individual members audit each other's work for the good of the entire company. Parceled into regions composed of approximately 100 people each, the firm empowers individuals within each region to exercise a great deal of freedom in terms of organizing their own teams to meet their own and their clients' needs. When a region grows beyond 100 people, it splits up to ensure that the regions don't become too impersonal and end up stifling freedom and flexibility. Project managers (a position open to anyone desirous and capable of fulfilling the role) lead the teams and obtain support from regional and corporate officers. Shirley claims, "We control products, productivity, and quality—not time spent. Once you give up the idea that you must see somebody sitting at a desk, you're free to look at the product."

Addressing the issue of communication in an organization composed of independent workers, Shirley goes on to say, "An office building implies dependency. It's got all these people in a box together. What we do is create a different structure that emphasizes communication and interdependence and that puts people in a structure that is important for them to do their work. It replaced the office building in a way." At F International the effective management of freedom increases productivity as well as common purpose and interdependence, thus improving personal and organizational performance.

Sally Partmore, a former employee at 3M (not an enlightened company), describes her experience after working at F International for nine months: "The main benefit for me is that I'm much more responsible for my work than I would be in a normal company. I haven't got a boss breathing down my neck all the time."

The first step toward the management of freedom involves a commitment to the notion that management should not exert any compulsory means to get individuals to act, think, or feel in a particular way, but instead should foster self-management in accordance with mutually benefitting principles. Free agency does not imply that executives and managers should never give direction, advice, or counsel, or that they shouldn't persuade and encourage. They should do so, actively and aggressively, but such advice and persuasion should never go so far as to exclude personal choice. Rather, the effective power manager unlocks all the possibilities for employees, customers, suppliers, investors, or affected citizens, then helps them sort through the advantages and disadvantages of each. For their own part, the stakeholders influencing or creating organizational arrangements or relationships must accept corresponding responsibility for weighing all consequences of a given action.

Under the leadership of power managers, individuals choose their own groups, career paths, associations, contracts, and relationships. Once executives and managers begin operating on the basis of free agency, they must prepare themselves for a proliferation of organizational arrangements, structures, processes, and subcultures, each uniquely tailored by their individual architects. We think such a proliferation will, paradoxically, cause more coherence than confusion among fulfilled groups.

Those organizations empowering people to form the richest assortment of organizational arrangements will attract the best people, and those people, in turn, will create a remarkable assortment of productive subcultures. Already General Electric, Corning, and AT&T are attempting to encourage the creation, sponsorship, or acquisition of new organizations or partnerships that offer alternative working environments in which people can develop new products and services. Though most such activity to date has been directed at fostering innovation and entrepreneurship, we believe that future executives should extend the effort to all aspects of the corporate environment. To do so they must encourage managers to help individual workers design flexible structures and processes that facilitate customer input and feedback, enhance supplier relationships, address community or environmental concerns and, generally, maximize the freedom of responsible stakeholders to act or influence action in accordance with the mutually benefitting principles that govern the company as a whole.

Structuring for freedom comes fairly naturally to a firm, like F International, that operates in an industry as innovative as software engineering and consulting, but it's also possible to accomplish in a steel mill. Consider the example set by Chaparral Steel in Midlothian, Texas, where managers don't interfere with workers to encourage them to do their work by whatever methods they deem best to meet customer needs and shareholder expectations. Chaparral's people even implement their own quality and safety control programs. When decision-making power resides with those who do the work, they must enjoy the freedom and flexibility to organize themselves appropriately. Foremen, acting as power managers, hire all their own people, then let them know they can talk to anybody in the company about how to make Chaparral a better company and a better place to work. People can organize teams, task forces, or other internal and external groups as long as they add value or fulfill genuine needs. In such a way, the organization simultaneously satisfies employee, company, customer, and other stakeholder needs. With only four levels of management, compared to General Motors' seventeen, the real organizing of the work environment takes place on the mill floor where remarkable levels of productivity have been achieved. In the American steel business, average annual production per worker seldom surpasses 300–400 tons. In Japan the average rises to 800–900 tons. But at Chaparral, it soars to 1300 tons. Obviously, using freedom to empower people can produce results for even an old-fashioned smokestack industry.

In the end, power managers facilitate both individual and collective well-being. No one individual can enjoy material and spiritual well-being at the expense of others, nor can a collection of people maintain lifestyle and workstyle success if other people suffer as a consequence. In the final analysis, power extended or limited for the purpose of amassing gain for a single individual or group, while disregarding the desires and needs of other individuals and groups, leads to oppression, not freedom. We doubt that such abusive power can survive among the Future 500.

A "survival of the fittest" philosophy may have served business organizations in the past, but in the future we think the corporations that embrace a "well-being of all" philosophy will reap rewards far beyond those available to the survivalists.

Pivot Management Through Individual Fulfillment

Pivot management involves the nurturing of formal and informal relationships to help individuals achieve fulfillment, which leads to peak performance. It means establishing and maintaining a network of relationships, from the formal to ad hoc, through which individual workers and managers can strive to harmonize perspectives, unleash power, and help each stakeholder gain fulfillment at his or her best. We call these relationships pivots because actions and outcomes revolve around individual stakeholders. At higher levels of management, the network of pivotal relationships consists of senior and middle managers (opinion leaders), who influence managers and individuals at lower levels in the organization. At the lower levels, each worker influences each other worker. The principle even applies at the international level, with governments influencing business organizations and vice versa. Effective pivot management insures that every individual stakeholder constantly relates to others. A field salesman interacts with a sales manager as well as with individual customers and thus becomes a pivot. Likewise, an investor relations specialist forms relationships with individual investors and investor group representatives, and, at the same time, with a Chairman and CEO, who in turn form relationships with each individual member of the management team and with each individual board member.

Again, we believe John Reed has emphasized pivot management at Citicorp. Soon after assuming his position, Reed, hoping to find a way to keep Thomas Theobald, who had been a contender for the top job, from leaving Citicorp, and wanting to ease the growing tension between two key areas of the company, invited Theobald to move from his position as head of the Institutional Bank to head of the Investment Bank, with its newly added treasury operations. The suggestion appealed greatly to Theobald, who could draw upon his Institutional Bank experience to bring the two units closer together. Reed's sensitivity and attention to the individual fulfillment of Theobald and two important subcultures allowed him to turn around a potentially damaging situation. Tom Theobald is now one of Reed's primary allies, working through his own network of pivot managers to fulfill individual stakeholders in the Investment Bank environment.

Since peak performance and increased productivity come from the workers who believe their managers have their best interests at heart, pivot managers take special care to relate to everyone around them with honest affection and patience. By doing so, they inspire their people, win loyalty and satisfaction from their customers, enjoy the respect of competitors, and gain support and praise from the citizens of their communities. Investors grow more confident about making long-term investment in the company, and government watchdogs turn their attention toward companies or industries where insensitive self-interest has caused harm.

Since individual fulfillment depends on so many elusive factors, from concrete achievements and rewards to satisfying relationships and feelings of security and emotional and spiritual well-being, the pivot manager pays attention to the whole person and not just a few aspects. However, such concern should not reflect the sort of benevolent despotism that characterized business owners and their managers earlier in this century. When individual stakeholders understand and embrace an organization's unifying principles, enjoy the appropriate freedom to take action that will produce individual and collective benefits, and believe that corporate executives and managers truly care about the personal welfare of all, we believe they will become far more self-initiating, self-correcting, and self-actualizing than ever before.

In the future fight for competitive advantage, no amount of money will be able to buy one key success factor: a talented and loyal group of managers who know and effectively manage their businesses and their people and who constantly prepare their successors. To appreciate how pivot management can produce this key to success, consider the way former CEO Frank Cary paid attention to the individual development and fulfillment of executives at IBM. When a group of researchers tracked Cary's activities over a period of four months in an effort to determine his priorities, they found that attracting, developing, and retaining the next generation of leadership at IBM was at the top of the list. IBM, it turns out, retains its executives by making sure they obtain maximum fulfillment in their professional lives. A similar

study of GE's former CEO, Reginald Jones, led to a similar conclusion. All this individual training, development, and counseling
should give IBM and GE clear shots at the top of the Future 500.

What, exactly, must executives do to become pivot managers?
Above all, they must learn to manage through the individual. As
became apparent during our discussion of the history of modern
management, only recently have executives and companies truly
begun to treat workers as distinctly individual human beings
rather than as organizational components or units. Even after the
culture era, they still tended to think of the "people" collectively.
We urge executives to take the next step, thinking *first* in terms of
unique individuals, then in terms of groups of individuals. While
an organization certainly consists of a collection of individuals,
effective management by principle and effective management of
freedom require attention to each unique person. Placing the
individual squarely at the center of management concern turns
the current collective approach upside down, reversing the traditional flow of a leader's concern from the largest to the smallest
organizational issues.

Our study of leadership has taught us as much about "follow-
ership" as anything else. We found that researchers, seeking to
learn how organizations evolve and change over time, have been
delving into so-called "adaptation theories." One of the more interesting and perhaps cynical of these is the population ecology
theory, which suggests that we view organizations as populations
containing three types of people: experimenters, centoids, and
laggards. Experimenters bring about change, centoids maintain
the *status quo*, and laggards cling to the old ways of doing things.
This theory suggests further that people inside the organization,
not management, determine how and when the organization
adapts, and that in the long run management's efforts to create
change do not matter in the least.

While it may seem extreme, this theory did help us clarify our
views about complexity management. People are a company's
most valuable resource, but management through a collection of
people and management through the individual require entirely
different orientations and skills. A good example of the difference comes from Analog Devices, where Ray Stata's managers
spend a great deal of time ensuring that individual contributors
receive the attention, recognition, and rewards they deserve.
While more traditional companies would lavish the lion's share of

recognition and financial rewards on line and staff managers, Analog has consciously constructed a parallel career ladder designed to promote highly competent technical contributors without necessarily giving them line management responsibilities.

Executives and managers who wish to manage through the individual must become good coaches, mentors, and counselors. Where executives previously viewed "people development" as a by-product of organizational performance, now they should reverse that view, seeing organizational performance as a by-product of individual development. But remember the need for "combined with" thinking, and don't think of this reorientation as a "from-to" shift, for organizations need both. Current trends in human resource management point toward high-commitment work systems in which the interests of an organization and its people coincide. According to Harvard Business School professor Richard Walton, indications of this profound change abound: "Jobs are defined more broadly, management is leaner and more flexible, ambitious and dynamic performance expectations replace minimum work standards, compensation systems place more emphasis on learning and collaboration, employees exercise more voice, union-management relations involve more joint problem solving and planning, and employment assurance becomes a high-priority policy issue." Heeding this trend toward responding to the needs of individuals, innovative companies throughout the world such as Motorola, Herman Miller, and Kollmorgen have begun implementing quality of worklife, employee involvement, innovative work structures, participative management, joint ownership, and consensus building programs.

When executives and managers assume mentoring roles, they make it possible for individuals to evaluate, correct, and improve themselves. However, a genuine policy of self-evaluation will not come easy to a manager schooled in the traditional practice of playing evaluator and taskmaster. Too often executives grow impatient with the often lengthy self-actualizing process and try to push an individual too fast or too hard, but that can actually retard a person's progress. W. L. Gore has done a good job of resisting this temptation. When new associates join the company, they are encouraged to look around until they find something they would really like to do. When they do get excited, they feel free to communicate their interests to a senior associate, in effect a pivot manager, who can help them become quickly involved in that activity, provided it coincides with the company's guiding principles.

With all the research being conducted on change in organizations, one key fact has surfaced: organizations don't change unless the individuals within those organizations want to, feel the need to, and actually decide to change. Given this fact, managers should stop trying to *force* people and organizations to change and start orchestrating environments in which individuals feel responsible for, and free to make, changes that fulfill their needs in line with the organization's principles. In our research we have admired the effects of self-evaluation, self-correction, and self-improvement stimulated by leaders like Carlo Maria Giulini, conductor of the Los Angeles Philharmonic Orchestra, Irwin Federman, president of Monolithic Memories, and William Hewitt, a past CEO of John Deere. These men lead by *pulling* rather than pushing, by *inspiring* rather than ordering. Instead of manipulating people, they allow individuals to create their own achievable, though challenging, goals. Such leadership skills encourage individuals to rely on their own initiative and experiences rather than on the constraining prescriptions of management.

Obstacles on the Road to Complexity Management

Applying these three precepts of complexity management will take a tremendous amount of energy and patience, and it will require a deep and genuine commitment no one can feign. If the precepts are not used sincerely, an organization's stakeholders will see complexity management as just another manipulative technique that "uses" people for personal or organizational gain. With that thought in mind, we'd like to review what we think could be the biggest obstacles on the path toward the future.

First, a failure to integrate the management practices and "disciplines" of the past hundred years will make it difficult for a leader to adopt the "combined with" mind-set complexity management demands.

Second, a failure by top management to accept unconditionally the outlooks of others, the need for freedom, and the integrity of the individual could compromise future success.

Third, a failure to address abuses in the application of complexity management will offset its effectiveness. Some individuals may find it hard to add responsibility to the exercise of their freedom, and some employees, managers, customers, investors, competitors, government agencies, or community groups will inevitably abuse the freedom granted by complexity management. When that happens, executives must take swift action, realigning the violators or removing them from the corporate environment.

Fourth, executives will find it hard to abandon simple, one-sided answers to the apparent paradoxes that will flourish as the business world becomes ever more complex. The new answers need not be overly complex, but they must be sufficiently comprehensive and integrative to fulfill all stakeholders.

Fifth, executives must resist the inclination to treat their people with the corporate paternalism of the past. The once-hallowed "manager knows best" attitude will be especially hard to shake, while many may go to the other extreme, becoming afraid to speak their own minds for fear of imposing their beliefs on others.

Invitation to the Future

While developing our ideas about complexity management, we spent a great deal of time studying both the past and the present states of business, but we spent an equal amount of time thinking about the future because, if our ideas are to have any impact, executives must be able to apply them to the very real problems they will face in the coming years. In the following chapters we will test our ideas about complexity management and the characteristics of the Future 500 against eight pressing issues of the future: increasing globalization, business-government partnerships, collaborative competition, creative capital financing, ethical leadership, dynamic organizational forms, integrated subcultures, and fulfilled employees. In so doing, we will outline the histories of these issues and show how some actual corporations are addressing them. Then we will project the issues into the future to see how complexity management might finally resolve them.

PART II

EIGHT DIMENSIONS
OF THE
CORPORATE FUTURE

CHAPTER FIVE

Vanishing Borders: Managing Global Markets

> *The new electronic interdependence recreates the world in the image of a global village.*
> —MARSHALL MCLUHAN

Global Electric or General Electric?

The world has changed dramatically since 1900, and international business has changed with it. As advances in transportation and communication have drawn the residents of the global village closer together, businesses both here and abroad have faced a growing dilemma: how to profit from the homogenization of markets in an increasingly specialized world. In the years and decades ahead the futures of all major corporations will depend more than ever on solving this dilemma.

When Jack Welch began his term as chairman and CEO of General Electric, he must have asked himself some hard questions about GE's future in the global village: Could the company's acclaimed sector and SBU structure accommodate projected long-term growth and diversification? Would its so-called "arena system" for strategic planning produce truly integrated strategies across sectors and SBUs? Are there better ways to achieve international integration than through existing management approaches? International business represented more than 40 percent of GE's earnings in recent years, and, though it is only one of the company's six designated sectors, it shouldered more than its share of responsibility for GE's future, both as the focal point of planning for the company's overseas affiliates, and as the integrating mechanism for all of GE's international endeavors.

For example, if the consumer sector were to design a new iron for the U.S. market, the international sector would have to decide whether or not it should encourage the SBU to produce the iron in several other countries as well. By doing so, it might help the company improve the cost effectiveness overall, at the same time enhancing the global market position. To do this, the international sector might form an internal joint venture with the SBU, sharing both the risks and the rewards.

During his first few years of leadership at GE, Welch promoted a compelling vision that every GE business should dominate its field in terms of market share or technological leadership. Such a lofty goal led to the acquisition and divestiture of many businesses. In a five-year period, GE spent over $10 billion on 70 acquisitions, new businesses, and joint ventures, and during that same period it sold 190 businesses, a staggering $6 billion worth, that Welch felt did not match his vision. Welch's continuation of his predecessor's repositioning efforts gathered momentum as GE moved into robotics, factory automation, information network services, and a host of other high-tech areas. Internationally, GE made similarly aggressive moves, among them cogeneration facilities in China, increased investment in Singapore, expansion into world plastics markets, Yugoslavian coproduction of engines, joint ventures in India. GE's merger with RCA and its acquisition of Kidder Peabody attracted a good deal of press coverage and seemed to many observers brilliant steps toward future positioning. However, not everyone agrees. Earnings in recent years have increased only slightly, and the company's factory automation gamble lost over $120 million over three years. In a *Fortune* article, GE executive vice president James Baker called the company's original projections for the factory of the future "flaky."

Can the company transform its management practices quickly and thoroughly enough to take advantage of global homogenization in a specialized world? Having led the way in strategic business planning for so many years, can it find a way to become Number 1 or Number 2 in every global segment it serves? Success will require even more of the flexibility the company displayed when it formed a joint venture with Mitsubishi or when it set up coproduction in Yugoslavia, and it will depend on supreme patience in developing long-range markets such as the factory of the future. But we think it will also take skillful complexity management.

Other multinational companies—among them Nestle, Black & Decker, and Parker Pen—must also solve this problem. At Nestle, the issue arose as early as World War II, when the company gave local managers throughout the world a significant degree of autonomy to avoid disruptions in Europe during the war years and to facilitate international expansion after the war. Today the company is trying to effect tighter marketing coordination of its global strategies. The task involves convincing executives in various countries to accept standardized product and marketing ideas, and to accomplish this task Nestle has transferred many successful local managers to headquarters, from which they might influence other country executives to participate more fully in coordinated global strategies.

The same issue has confronted Black & Decker, which has dominated the European consumer tool market for so long that many of its European executives resist a more coordinated and integrated approach. Recently, however, strong Japanese competition has made a more unified global marketing strategy more critical than ever. To overcome resistance to change, Black & Decker replaced several uncooperative key European executives.

In the early 1980s the Parker Pen Company cut in half the number of pen styles it marketed, and it closed over half of its plants worldwide. The company's foreign subsidiary managers accepted the changes until executives at Parker headquarters demanded that they also adhere to standardized advertising and packaging programs. After the foreign subsidiary managers refused, Parker scrapped its highly publicized globalization campaign and suffered the loss of several senior executives.

Not every company will succeed on the international front, but those who deal effectively with the complexities of global issues will greatly increase the odds in their favor. Before considering how perspective, power, and pivot management can help executives address and resolve these issues, let's examine the historical evolution of international business.

100 Years of International Business

If only in the form of rudimentary trading, international business has existed for thousands of years, but it took the twentieth century's advances in transportation and communication to make it one of the most powerful forces in the global village.

Like the eras we identified for modern management, the following divisions represent less of an ironclad reality than they do a useful way to think about world trade. Note how the eras of international business parallel those of modern management.

Before we try to predict what the future may hold for international business, let's examine these modern eras in a little more detail and see how one company, General Electric, responded to them.

Market Expansion (1890–1920)

The first international enterprises emerged in the late 1800s. Many of them came from the shores of America, and in most cases the Americans simply sold overseas the goods originally manufactured for domestic markets. Given the rapid expansion of business early in the twentieth century, it comes as no surprise that business owners and managers focused on increasing their "market stakes" or sales overseas. This approach led to the creation of international sales and marketing organizations by General Electric, Coca-Cola, Swift, Du Pont, U.S. Rubber, National Cash Register, Gillette, and others. To oversee their foreign empires, these and similar organizations developed the multidivisional management structures that dominated large corporations throughout the structure era (1910–1935).

Meanwhile, established European industrial giants, who had largely ignored the relatively small, unstable, and chaotic U.S. markets throughout the 1800s, began making forays here in the late 1800s and early 1900s. These exploratory expeditions into American industrial markets sometimes prospered, and when they did, they usually resulted in the incorporation of the largest American firms into worldwide cartels, which partitioned markets among themselves. Some American firms, such as Du Pont, used

International Business Eras

Market Expansion	Supply Orientation and Retrenchment	Multinationals	Globalization	Global Strategy Implementation	Global Homogenization in a Specialized World

1890	1910	1930	1950	1970	1990	2010

Structure — Productivity — Systems — Strategy — Culture — Innovation — Leadership — Complexity Management

Management Eras

cartels to create mutual patent licensing arrangements, thus gaining a variety of the Europeans' advanced technological processes.

Several factors contributed to this phenomenon. With the first big surge in domestic American business expansion during the early 1890s, many firms not only grew larger at home, they extended their influence abroad. When depression hammered the American economy between 1893 and 1897, causing domestic demand to plummet, business owners looked to foreign markets to unload surpluses, and exports rose during this period. This early depression also brought such a great general "shake-out" in business that many companies disappeared entirely, while many of the survivors grew to dominate the next hundred years.

Between 1897 and 1914, U.S. direct foreign investments more than quadrupled, from $635 million to $2.7 billion. In order to penetrate foreign markets with exports, American companies typically set up sales organizations abroad. However, when tariff barriers and foreign governments' insistence on local production made this arrangement increasingly difficult, the Americans tried to maintain their hold on foreign markets by building factories abroad.

During World War I many of the production and distribution facilities of the European giants were disrupted, and the biggest American firms with strong capital and production capacity filled the void, coming to dominate the international business scene.

By the end of the international market expansion era, the most successful and durable international endeavors had established clear-cut relationships with foreign operations, either through partially owned affiliates or wholly owned subsidiaries. Firms that took on a "local" guise prospered more than those who simply "invaded" foreign turf.

General Electric nicely illustrates how an American enterprise used the affiliate approach to its advantage. Formed in the early 1890s, GE began developing a sophisticated worldwide network of affiliates, each of whose marketing and manufacturing efforts were restricted to a specific geographic area. Since GE had not yet grown large enough to cover the whole world with its own management organization, it profitably served foreign markets via these "local" GE companies. By 1914, GE had associated firms in Canada, England, France, Germany, and Japan. Investments ranged from strong controlling interests of 97 percent to small, minor holdings. GE also operated wholly owned subsidiaries and sales branches in other parts of the world. Taking a markedly different approach to moving into foreign markets in a big way, Westinghouse Electric Company built its own manufacturing plants in many countries. However, despite its huge foreign assets, Westinghouse did not prosper abroad as much as General Electric with its affiliate approach.

Supply-Orientation and Retrenchment (1920–1945)

Between 1919 and 1929, Americans nearly doubled their direct foreign investments, going from $3.8 billion to $7.5 billion. However, more of this money went toward supply-oriented investments in raw materials as manufacturers who were expanding at home and abroad needed increased, steady supplies for subsequent processing, manufacturing, and distribution. By 1929, expenditures on such investments as mines, oil wells, and agricultural plantations accounted for more than half of all direct overseas investments. Although companies did continue some market-oriented investments during this era, their emphasis steadily shifted to the supply side.

The international environment prior to and during World War II forced firms with overseas operations to retrench. In some countries, extreme nationalism gave rise to discrimination against foreign firms. In Germany, for example, American businesses could not operate unless they could prove that they were not under foreign, Jewish, or Marxist control, that they were, in fact, pure German. Germany's preparations for war, rising militarism in Japan, social unrest in France, Italy's aggressions in Ethiopia, and civil war in Spain created a general climate of global uncertainty. As a result, many American firms began to divest themselves of their operations abroad, until, by 1940, the book value of U.S. direct foreign investments fell below 1929 levels, to $7 billion. Foreign firms operating in the United States came under similar pressure. By now American internationals were competing around the world against British and other foreign-based firms. For example, the American Viscose Corporation, one of the world's largest rayon producers, was once part of a British conglomerate that sold its interest in the American company in 1941 after tremendous pressure from the U.S. government.

During World War II international businesses with units or subsidiaries abroad lost touch with those units who fell under the control of occupying forces, and foreign business units in territory controlled by the Allies often switched to wartime work. As a result, the international business picture became extremely fragmented. By the end of this era direct foreign investment had still not risen above the 1929 level.

The General Electric Company's history during this era ran slightly counter to the experiences of most American internationals. In 1919, GE created an international corporation called International General Electric Company (IGEC). A wholly owned subsidiary of General Electric, IGEC acquired all of GE's foreign holdings, and under the direction of its president, Gerard Swope, it sought to make inroads into electrical industries around the world. Before long, Swope had established a strong presence for IGEC in England, Germany, and other parts of Europe. GE formed IGEC for three reasons: to provide and concentrate the special knowledge needed to handle the complexities of international trade and payments; to administer the different policies and structures required by various countries; and to take advantage of the skills and experience of Swope himself, who had left Westinghouse after gaining valuable experience about what would and would not work overseas. While IGEC took 100 percent control of some foreign affiliates, such as manufacturing facilities in Brazil, it only held a minority interest in some European affiliates. In the more advanced, industrialized countries, IGEC affiliates operated under almost exclusively local management; in less-developed countries they borrowed the expertise of American management. During the prewar years, while many U.S. internationals were retrenching, GE remained surprisingly strong because its approach to international business did not offend increasingly nationalistic concerns.

Multinationals (1945–1970)

As international enterprises acquired and reacquired whatever foreign business units they could during the decade following World War II, the modern multinational corporation began to take shape. The institutional frameworks for international business remained much the same after World War II, but international markets grew faster than at any time since the late 1800s. Jet travel and worldwide communications were shrinking the planet and making effective coordination of worldwide organizations more feasible. It became almost as easy for a New York-based business to operate a branch plant in Frankfurt or Lagos as in Dallas or Los Angeles.

A series of trade agreements, most notably the General Agreements on Trade and Tariffs (GATT) and the Havana Charter (never ratified by the U.S. Senate), provided uniform trading structures that furthered the worldwide integration of firms. Meanwhile, at home, legal complications provided an extra incentive for multinationals to integrate their operations. Between 1945 and 1952, the United States Justice Department actively prosecuted firms involved in international cartel agreements, making it unsafe for U.S. companies to divide the world into segmented markets with foreign firms and affiliates. Once again, since companies with 100 percent ownership of business units abroad did not risk anti-trust violations, direct investment became the best way to penetrate and maintain foreign markets. American investment in Europe doubled between 1957 and 1962 and again between 1962 and 1967. During the 1960s, European firms, in turn, made more and more direct investments in the United States. By 1970, U.S. direct investment abroad had reached $78 billion.

In general, investors preferred those countries with relatively high standards of living, healthy economic growth rates, rich natural resources, and a favorable political climate. In the wake of communications and transportation advances between 1945 and 1970, a trend toward interrelated plants among several nations developed, thus propelling worldwide integration even further. Now, instead of building factories to supply local markets, multinationals could begin to economize and gain efficiency by integrating all economic activities on a worldwide basis, a foreshadow of genuine globalization.

America's influence on international business became more and more apparent during this era. American executives and companies had developed management structures, efficiency, and productivity methods, and management and financial control systems that allowed them to compete aggressively and effectively throughout the world. In his 1968 book, *The American Challenge*, J.J. Servan-Schreiber wrote: "Fifteen years from now it is quite possible that the world's third-greatest industrial power, just after the United States and Russia, will not be Europe, but American industry in Europe. Already, in the ninth year of the Common

Market, this European market is basically American in organization."

Across the sea, European executives were quickly incorporating the management practices of American firms. By 1970, McKinsey & Company had consulted with over half of the 100 largest British industrial companies, helping them reorganize their management structures and systems along American lines, in most cases replacing the traditional holding company structure with the modern multidivisional one. The same adaptation of American management structures and systems occurred to a lesser degree in Germany, but it strongly influenced the Japanese, who adopted and improved upon the quality, inventory, and other control systems developed by the Americans. All this imitation, though flattering, eroded the American competitive advantage as non-American executives and their companies embraced our management practices with a zeal and freshness that helped them catch, and in some cases, even surpass their mentors.

During this period GE, building on its already extensive international base, expanded aggressively. Departing from the tendency toward centralization that characterized the previous period, GE increasingly decentralized during the early years of this era. At the same time, it made diversification a watchword both domestically and internationally. By 1968 GE, now widely diversified and decentralized around the world, had evolved into a prototypical multinational corporation, organized into ten groups, forty-six divisions and one hundred ninety departments competing in no fewer than twenty-three of the twenty-six two-digit SIC industry classifications. Internationally, rapid growth allowed GE to draw component parts of businesses together, then reconfigure them into whole businesses, until by the end of this era, GE had decentralized operations in every major country.

Globalization (1970–Late 1980s)

In the early days, American firms venturing abroad segregated their foreign from their domestic operations by creating international divisions or subsidiaries. However, this practice began to change as the divisionalized modern multinationals sought to integrate their international and domestic operations. As early as the mid to late 1960s, many large corporations began centralizing their operations around the world, reorganizing themselves into so-called "worldwide," "cosmopolitan," or "global" structures. Throughout the 1970s and the early 1980s, some firms created worldwide product divisions, while others retained their foreign subsidiaries but awarded them equal status with domestic units, with both falling under central control. These developments led London-based business historian Christopher Tugendhat to say in 1971, "A characteristic feature of multinational companies is that their subsidiaries operate under the discipline and framework of a common global strategy and common global control."

Yet in the mid 1980s, debate continued over the emergence and centralizaton of the "global" corporation. Some predicted a continued trend toward global marketing, while others argued that global corporations would have to become true insiders in major foreign markets, particularly Europe and Japan. According to a prominent McKinsey & Company consultant, success in the globalization game would depend on an executive's and a company's ability to assume a global perspective, eliminating the boundaries, both physical and mental, between domestic and international operations. All aspects of an organization, from its people to its structures and systems, must reflect this perspective.

By the end of this era more and more companies and industries had become global, with events and actions in one country strongly affecting those in others. By making Coke a worldwide brand, Coca-Cola pioneered the globalization of the soft drink industry. Since then several other industries, including televisions, cars, telecommunications, and semiconductors, have followed suit. More will surely follow, and as they do, the problems and opportunities associated with globalization will preoccupy U.S. and foreign business leaders.

Beginning in 1969, GE embarked on a massive restructuring effort that it hoped would bring consolidation and centralization, particularly in the area of strategic planning. By collapsing its 190 departments into 43 strategic business units (SBUs), each of which reported to the CEO for planning purposes, GE took an important step toward globalization. In the early 1980s GE introduced what it called the "sector level" of management between the CEO and the SBUs. One of these six sectors, the international sector designed to oversee and coordinate all international operations, moved GE even further toward globalization.

(Late 1980s–Late 1990s)
Global Strategy Implementation

Contemporary executives are wrestling with the formulation and implementation of global strategies, and they will surely continue to focus great attention on the different roles that corporate divisions and organizations in different countries can and should play. Globalized corporations struggle with the need for central control of global strategies and the equally important need for freedom, flexibility, and effectiveness within and among separate countries. The market opportunities and demands from country to country display both similarities and differences. Since some markets contain more advanced competitors, more sophisticated consumers, and more readily available technologies than others, finding a way to implement a global strategy while allowing for country-by-country differences presents the foremost challenge of the future.

Addressing this problem, two professors at the Harvard Business School, Christopher Bartlett and Sumantra Ghoshal, have introduced a new way of thinking about international business. They suggest that international executives consider two dimensions when determining the roles and responsibilities of country-by-country organizations: the strategic importance of the local environment (classified according to large market, home market for a competitor, or sophisticated market) and the internal competence of the local organization (in such areas as technology, production, marketing, and sales). According to this model, only after rating these dimensions can an executive select the appropriate posture for a country organization, be it a Strategic Leader (high strategic importance and high competence), a Contributor (low strategic importance, high competence), an Implementor (low strategic importance and low competence), or a Black Hole (high strategic importance, low competence). Ideally this kind of analysis should help global corporations guide country organizations toward precisely determining their roles and responsibilities in implementing global strategies—a global strategy could remain intact while the unique characteristics and capabilities of specific country organizations are protected.

At General Electric great changes have taken place during the 1980s. Chairman and CEO Reginald Jones had previously sought to reposition the "new GE" for what he liked to call a "technological renaissance." Jones had forcefully informed the financial community that "General Electric is embarked on a course of large-scale innovation, productivity improvement, and business development for the 1980s, and we have built up the financial resources to bring that bold entrepreneurial strategy to a successful conclusion." Jones passed his mantle of authority to Jack Welch, who continued the revitalizing that Jones had begun. However, to say that Welch simply inherited a company in the midst of major change would be a gross understatement, because Jones left him with several concrete visions of GE's new business opportunities: the factory of the future, the office of the future, the house of the future, the electric car, and synthetic fuel.

For planning purposes, always a top priority at GE, the company pinpointed six broad business areas it called "arenas": Energy, Communications/Information/ Sensing, Energy Applications/Productivity, Materials and Resources, Transportation and Propulsion, and Pervasive Services. Since such broad arenas often cut across traditional organizational boundaries, how could GE's famous SBUs (strategic business units), which had been organized into six major sectors themselves (Consumer, Industrial, Technical, International, Resources, and Power) best exploit them? Daniel Fink, senior vice president for Corporate Planning and Development, partially answered that question when he said, "Sometimes the solution is to reorganize and collect those synergistic businesses under single management. But there are too many opportunities out there. We'd have to reorganize every three days just to keep up with them."

Precisely how should GE and other multinationals set about solving the problems associated with global strategy implementation? In the following sections we will try to answer that question.

Global Homogenization in a Specialized World

Paradoxically, the needs and desires of the customers of the Future 500 will simultaneously become more universal and more specialized. While the demand for specialized products and services by an increasingly diverse customer base will grow, these specialized and distinct market segments will become fairly uniform around the globe. Clear-cut differences will remain from country to country, but international suppliers will try to satisfy them with adjustments to standardized products and services. Such homogeneity plus specialization will allow for greater global interdependence as well as greater diversity, distinctiveness, and uniqueness in customer preferences.

Will executives and their companies try to take advantage of global homogeneity and specialization or will they fall prey to destructive national retrenching and protectionism? The latter course would, of course, prevent the sort of transformation we predict for the future and it would undoubtedly plunge world business into the nationalization of industries, brutal trade wars, tariff battles, import restrictions, embargoes, sanctions, and other misguided acts of self-interest that could eventually lead to war. As it has throughout history, the search for competitive advantage will propel international commerce, but unless business leaders recognize the opportunities inherent in homogenization/specialization and global interdependence, corporations could make the mistake of seeking competitive advantage by reinforcing differences and stressing independence.

The Wall Street Journal recently reported that although European governments are scrambling to attract foreign direct capital investment, training grants, and low-interest loans to ensure jobs, obtain advanced technology, and guarantee economic growth, many observers suspect that such activities may damage rather than help a client country. The article, entitled "Europe's Investment Incentives: Who Reaps the Major Benefits?" quoted critics who suggest that financial incentives may hurt local companies if foreign companies take undue advantage of the arrangement. On another front, the continuing controversy over how the U.S. should structure trade relations with Japan keeps open the possibility of a breakdown in communication and cooperation that could lead to retrenchment rather than transformation. Can complexity management enable us to manage this dimension of the future effectively? Let's take a look.

The Role of Complexity Management

Our study of the history of international business has highlighted increasing globalization—the world is becoming a homogeneous marketplace in which multinational companies can simultaneously introduce diverse and specialized products and services. The distinctiveness among foreign markets in the early part of this century has been gradually disappearing, until today, executives and managers face the challenge and rewards of implementing truly global strategies. The increasing complexity of the future will bring more specialization—a proliferation of market segments and the products and services designed to meet their needs—and the homogeneity of global markets will make it possible for even the smallest companies to penetrate the global arena from the start. Companies that learn how to manage global markets quickly and effectively will lead the Future 500 in this dimension of the future.

Looking at the issues facing General Electric, Nestle, Black & Decker, and Parker Pen, we concluded that the overriding concern facing global corporations today is the pursuit of integrated and coordinated globalization strategies through internationally dispersed divisions, subsidiaries, and affiliates whose respective managements, owners, domestic governments, and other stakeholders may prefer conflicting agendas. At Nestle, for example, executives must determine whether or not the local executives recently transferred to headquarters can sufficiently influence country executives to embrace integrated and standardized product-marketing strategies. If they cannot, country executives may view them as self-interested manipulators.

Black & Decker must figure out how to get middle managers and employees in European plants and offices to welcome a unified global strategy. Black & Decker forced compliance in the ranks of its European senior executives by firing the resisters, forcing other workers and middle managers to act more circumspectly, perhaps withholding their true feelings and commitments, and making it even more difficult for the company to harmonize conflicting agendas.

Can Parker Pen successfully determine where the common

ground lies between too little or too much standardization? The company thought it had found the answer when subsidiary managers accepted company-wide product changes, but corporate executives misread their willingness to buy standardized advertising and packaging programs. Did the Parker Pen executives at headquarters demand too much standardization, or did they simply fail to implement their plans properly?

Finally, in the case of General Electric, can it continue to be a leader in international business? Will GE create the model of global marketing as they have usually managed to do in the past or does the company have its hands full with the domestic cares of RCA, Kidder Peabody, and a host of other companies? If it can remain an international leader, it will definitely reap profits but, more importantly, it will gain global clout, an intangible asset executives have only recently begun to appreciate.

We think the precepts of complexity management can help multinational companies resolve these and similar issues, but only if executives and managers go beyond the skills and approaches of the past hundred years and start thinking about global markets in a radically new way.

Applying Perspective Management

Perspective management, which allows for multiple points of view while promoting unifying and mutually benefitting principles, can help executives harmonize the diverse agendas of corporate executives, country managers, owners, governments, and international workers. These are some steps an international executive might take to apply perspective management to global homogenization in a specialized world:

- Create an international forum for openly discussing conflicting agendas between and among crucial stakeholders—corporate executives, domestic executives, foreign executives, government leaders, domestic and foreign managers and employees, and corporate-subsidiary-affiliate boards of directors. Such forums should include all those directly and indirectly affected by global decisions, and they should be conducted at all levels and in all important geographic locations. Ultimately they can culminate in a senior-level forum that has been given responsibility for finding ways to address and resolve concerns and issues. For example, GE could establish an annual international conference designed to open up channels of communication among key international stakeholders.

- Incorporate into the strategic planning process a preliminary step in which relevant stakeholders can jointly analyze and resolve questions of global standardization and differentiation before individual business units proceed with their own strategic planning processes. For example, Black & Decker could hold preliminary strategy sessions with all European subsidiaries before embarking on business unit planning processes.

- Increase the communication level among and between related domestic and foreign business units through electronic mail systems, sophisticated telephone networks, teleconferencing, video presentations, retreats, or other conventional means. For example, Nestle could incorporate an E-Mail system that would transmit and translate any message from one country to any other country within minutes.

Applying Power Management

The power manager can empower appropriate individuals and groups to implement global strategies with maximum freedom earned through consistent performance. We suggest the following specific steps:

- Give the marketing executives in strategically related domestic and foreign businesses the opportunity and responsibility to devise integration and standardization plans and programs. Then, allow them to implement their plans and programs freely. For example, Parker Pen could establish an international marketing council to develop such plans.

- Thoroughly and constantly communicate the benefits of developing integrated global business strategies, then allow domestic and foreign divisions, subsidiaries, affiliates, and other business entities to decide when and how they will respond. Listen closely to the reasons for resistance. For example, GE could extend its leadership position by encouraging executives in all its international SBUs to articulate the benefits of global integration of business strategies in speeches, memorandums, press releases and interviews, and even in published books and journal articles.

- Separate globally standardized and integrated business units from the rest of the corporation, operating them as a single global division. For example, GE's international sector might group together those SBUs that seem particularly poised for global marketing and allow them to function as a separate sector.

Applying Pivot Management

With pivot management executives find new ways to tap the talent and influence of pivotal individuals throughout the company. The application of pivot management in international business might include these efforts:

- Find out exactly where each country executive stands on issues of globalization, then determine how each executive and respective business can specifically benefit from global strategies. For example, Nestle might use its transferred executives as pivots for making sure key country executives get the opportunity to influence and commit to global plans.

- Determine precisely all stakeholder agendas. Whether dealing with the desires of corporate officers, country managers, local workers, government leaders, foreign shareholders, or local citizens, never ignore conflicts but deal with them to achieve a collectively beneficial resolution. For example, Parker Pen could interview all country executives to determine exactly where they stand *vis-à-vis* the recent difficulties.

- Avoid getting blind-sided by an individual's or group's desires, values, beliefs, or biases that might eventually undermine global implementation strategies. Don't worry about "over-communicating" with individuals. For example, GE might conduct worldwide monthly reviews of global strategies, identifying implementation problem areas and requesting immediate response from affected SBUs.

With the U.S. suffering huge foreign trade deficits, and with more and more domestic firms trying to market their goods and services overseas, issues surrounding international business will undoubtedly multiply in the coming years. In few other areas will executives be more hard pressed to deal with complexity, because global enterprise includes so many stakeholders from vastly different economic, social, and governmental systems. Perspective management will obviously play a major role in resolving these issues, but so will power and pivot management, with which business leaders of all countries can extract the benefits of increased specialization in an ever more homogenized world. Here, more than ever, the success of the Future 500 will depend on unifying principles, respect for individual freedom, and the nurturing of relationships that replace nationalistic antagonism with better understanding and cooperation.

CHAPTER SIX

Partners on Purpose: Building a New Kind of Alliance Between the Private and Public Sectors

> *Tyranny is the normal pattern of government. It is only by intense thought, by great effort, by burning idealism and unlimited sacrifice that freedom has prevailed as a system of government.*
>
> —ADLAI STEVENSON

Striving Toward Meaningful Alliances

On the morning of January 28, 1986, excitement turned to horror when the space shuttle Challenger exploded, killing seven Americans. In the weeks that followed, scientists, government officials, and the aerospace industry tried to figure out what had gone wrong, and, ultimately, some of the blame fell on Morton Thiokol, the manufacturer of the space shuttle's rocket boosters and on the company's relationship with NASA, the government agency responsible for America's space program.

At the time of the disaster Morton Thiokol's space shuttle contract was worth $350–400 million a year. In the wake of the Challenger disaster, the company's reputation and its very livelihood lie in jeopardy. It could end up losing millions in fee reductions and incentive pay for its contribution to mission failure; find itself overwhelmed by lawsuits brought by the astronauts' families; see its precious NASA contract awarded to a second source supplier; and suffer damaging drops in the value of its stock.

The NASA-Morton Thiokol relationship is not the only alliance between the private and public sectors in the late 1980s that faces a serious threat, and although the NASA-Morton Thiokol relationship stands as unique among such alliances, a close study of it can shed important and dramatic light on an opportunity for change.

In the aftermath of Challenger, Morton Thiokol and NASA pointed fingers at one another while the Rogers Commission, appointed by President Reagan to investigate the accident, tried to pinpoint responsibility and accountability. Air Force General Donald Kutyna, a key member of the Rogers Commission, thought the problem stemmed from the fact that "the whole adversary nature of NASA questioning the work of one of its suppliers just disappeared." William P. Rogers, former Secretary of State and chairman of the commission, primarily faulted NASA's "flawed decision making systems." However, Representative James Scheuer, a New York Democrat and member of the congressional committee that oversees the space program, said, "What Thiokol's management did, before the launching and then to the engineers who told the world about it, was utterly repugnant, just disgraceful." He went on to conclude, "There is a lot of blame to go around, but Thiokol deserves a fat share of it."

Similar finger pointing has characterized much of the dealings between government and business in recent years, but some companies and government entities have to some degree overcome that tendency. Consider three recent examples that cover a wide range of different kinds of government-business alliances: Citicorp and the state of Maryland, Southland Corporation and the government of Venezuela, and Bristol-Myers along with other pharmaceutical and biotechnology companies and the FDA and the U.S. Congress.

For years Citicorp has been attempting to provide full-service banking throughout all fifty states, but interstate banking laws prohibited out-of-state banks from providing all but the most minimal services. Citicorp was forced to establish industrial lending, savings and loan institutions, and consumer finance operations to skirt banking laws. Needless to say, the resulting relationships were less than harmonious. Recently, however, Citicorp took a landmark step to resolve the issue, becoming the first out-of-state full-service bank in Maryland when it designed a mutually benefitting partnership arrangement that included a major credit card center located in Maryland. The center would employ a thousand white-collar workers on property purchased from the state for $1 million. As a result Citicorp won its fight to operate as a full-service bank in Maryland, while the state furthered its image as a healthy business environment.

Addressing a similar issue outside the United States, Southland Corp. found a way to succeed in the oil refining business by selling 50 percent of its Citgo oil refining and marketing operation to Venezuela for $300 million, with an additional $250 million going into working capital. Again, both parties benefited—the Venezuelan government gaining a captive market for its crude oil, and Southland obtaining a long-term supply of crude oil for its Louisiana refinery.

Bristol-Myers and other pharmaceutical companies want the FDA to approve pending legislation that would allow them to license and sell drugs in foreign countries before seeking FDA approval for domestic distribution. Ralph Nader, the American Public Health Association, and other groups oppose the idea, claiming it would set an immoral double standard, but a liberalized law could increase drug exports by more than $500 million annually, creating in its wake thousands of new jobs. While the watchdogs worry that the FDA is not strict enough, the industry worries that it is too strict. Whichever may be true, a better working relationship between government and business might help resolve the issue in a way that would save consumers, corporations, legislators, and government agencies from endless arguments and wasteful maneuverings.

Although we do favor an improved working relationship between the private and public sectors in the future, we also think both sides should take great care to insure that greater cooperation and coordination do not compromise the free enterprise system, but rather support the orchestration of business environments. In the case of Morton Thiokol and NASA, the two organizations must ask some hard questions. How do we develop economic policies that will promote free enterprise but also minimize the costs associated with the aerospace program? How can we increase NASA's control and accountability while increasing aerospace contractors' control and accountability? Who should test equipment and monitor facilities' functions?

Some of these questions will be easier to answer than others, but we think complexity management can provide many of the answers. Before we examine how perspective, power, and pivot management might help companies and government entities form a cooperative rather than adversarial alliance, wherein each party seeks to control the other, we should first review the historical development of such relationships.

The Evolving Relationship Between Government and Business

The relationship between the public and private sectors in this country has always been an uneasy one. Notice how the eras of government-business relationships parallel those of modern management.

Establishing Government Control (1900–1940)

By 1900 American business had plunged into ambitious experiments with monopoly capitalism, some of which prompted the most intense merger and acquisition activity in the history of our economic system. In some industries monopolies had, in fact, existed for quite some time, but these typically involved the major producers forming a trust to partition the country's markets among themselves, thus forcing smaller producers to sell out or perish. Around 1900, however, powerful individuals began consolidating trusts into single companies. Standard Oil and Du Pont, for example, virtually controlled the nationwide production of oil and explosives.

With the balance so clearly tipping toward monopoly, government, fearing an erosion of the principles of free enterprise, intervened by enforcing antitrust legislation against the most blatant and powerful monopolies. Where government had once feared to tread, it now became a strong presence, forcing both the Standard Oil and Du Pont monopolies to disband in the early 1900s. Government was sending a clear message: it would not tolerate business practices that threatened the very principles of free enterprise.

Government-Business Eras

1890	1910	1930	1950	1970	1990	2010

Establishing Government Control

Protecting Free Enterprise

Government-Business in Crisis

Searching for a New Model

Differing Roles in a Holistic Environment

Structure

Productivity

Systems

Strategy

Culture

Innovation

Leadership

Complexity Management

Management Eras

On the international scene, where large French, British, and American manufacturers controlled vast trusts and cartels, monopolistic practices continued unabated until World War I, after which the allies and their major firms used victory as an excuse to plunder German firms' technologies and ignore international patent restrictions.

At home, American business leaders, having received a clear signal that government would prohibit monopolistic practices, invested their war profits in diversification, growth, and widespread technological advances. Of course, the subsequent enlarged sense of prosperity and unlimited opportunity opened the door to a new set of abuses. Highly speculative and risky maneuvers, such as interlocking directorates and ownership holdings among industries, became commonplace, as did extremely questionable financial practices, fraudulent transactions, and unsound credit arrangements. Banks routinely approved huge loans for the purchase of stocks and bonds, which they themselves sold, thus collecting both interest and substantial service fees on transactions. But when the bubble burst in 1929, the system self-destructed, plunging the nation into the Great Depression.

The government, with only a weak and decentralized Federal Reserve System, found itself struggling to manage this crisis and to insure that it would never recur. Subsequently, through the Glass-Steagull Act and the Banking Act of 1933, the government formulated strict standards of acceptable conduct for bank officers. These new standards separated investment banking from commercial banking, compartmentalized trust and commercial banking functions within banks, prohibited banks from owning substantial equity in businesses, and created the Federal Deposit Insurance Corporation, the Securities and Exchange Commission, and a newly centralized Federal Reserve System. With these and other measures the government increasingly defined itself as a champion of free enterprise and an enforcer of good business practices.

During this first era of government-business relations the aerospace industry felt the expanding influence and control of government. Although the first successful flight occurred in 1903, no "aircraft" or aerospace industry *per se* existed until World War I. Between 1917 and 1918, however, production of airplanes soared from 2,148 to 14,020. While production prior to the war had been privately financed, the war effort required the government to abandon its usual procurement process of buying from competing bidders; needing quick delivery of war machines, the government was now willing to obtain them with cost-plus profit agreements. Despite the fact that such an approach undermined the principles of free enterprise, the U.S. could do little else when it became clear that other countries had taken an early lead in the "air race" by removing their aircraft industries from the hands of squabbling private concerns.

After the war ended, the government curtailed aircraft purchasing and sold its surplus in 1919, causing many aircraft manufacturers to reorganize or declare bankruptcy. Then, in the late 1920s, the first passenger airlines began operations, and airplane manufacturers began competing for this new market. By 1935, Douglas and Lockheed were struggling for dominance in the fledgling industry, with Douglas emerging as the leader with its technically superior DC-3s. In 1939, the government enacted a law to encourage the building of airplane prototypes by buying those not ultimately chosen at a percentage of their cost. Now government had taken a new turn as it tried to use its power to reduce financial risk and keep an entire industry alive.

One small company, Thiokol, entered the aerospace industry near the end of this era when it began developing a liquid polymer that would one day be considered the best solid propellant for rockets. In 1925, J. C. Patrick and Nathan Mnookin, two Kansas City chemists, were searching for a cheap antifreeze when they accidentally created a new form of synthetic rubber. Because of its smelly and indissoluble nature, they named the material "Thiokol" after the Greek words for sulphur and glue. Unable to market the material themselves, they formed an arrangement with Standard Oil of Indiana in 1927 to develop the new product. When Patrick and Mnookin grew disenchanted with Standard Oil's participation, they enlisted the help of Bevis Longstreth, a salt merchant from Kansas City, who helped them persuade a New York investment firm to kick in $75,000. Two thirds of the money would buy out Standard Oil's interest and the remainder would be put to work developing Thiokol. In 1930, Thiokol, with Longstreth as president, incorporated and moved to Yardsville, New Jersey. Not much happened at the new company during the 1930s, but a technique was developed to lessen the product's foul odor. By 1938, Thiokol had turned over manufacturing to Dow

Chemical, who took a 31 percent interest in the company. Not until 1941 did the company realize its first profit, $89,000

Protecting Free Enterprise (1940–1970)

For three decades business and government more or less honored a cease-fire as they grew comfortable with the way the principles of free enterprise were working, but although government enacted legislation favorable to business, it still felt no compunction about intervening whenever it thought business was acting unfairly or against the public interest. In essence, government maintained its established role as the protector of the free enterprise system.

For American business, this era brought unprecedented growth and world dominance, especially in the period following World War II. Competition, though fierce, confined itself almost exclusively to the national arena as the Americans enjoyed a seemingly unbeatable worldwide advantage in both technology and managerial expertise. Given such advantages, American business grew smug, and even during the 1960s, when international competition began to pose a real threat, neither government nor business abandoned their complacency.

Financial organizations also felt more and more comfortable with their defined roles as increasingly sophisticated financial analysis techniques and overall conditions of prosperity allowed them to assess credit risk and managerial competence more confidently than ever.

The government not only protected the nation's free enterprise, it also defended its freedom during this era, leading the public sector toward more aggressive planning, direction, and coordinating of industries important to national security. In the aerospace industry, government sought a balance between its desire for competitive suppliers and the speed and economy of working with a single firm to accomplish gargantuan undertakings. This was a paradox that foreshadowed a coming government-business crisis.

During World War II, the American aviation industry went from a 1939 production of 5,856 planes to a 1944 production of 96,318 planes. This war-generated expansion meant building new facilities and converting automobile plants into aircraft assembly plants, most of which the government financed.

The aviation and aerospace industries differed from most other enterprises because their colossal and costly endeavors involved a single buyer and few sellers. Since the country needed a broad industrial base to ensure the survival of an industry upon which its national security rested, the government tried to forestall bankruptcies by spreading the business around. It strove, as best it could, to strengthen both its defense capabilities and its time-honored free enterprise system. But after World War II competition in the aircraft and aerospace industries usually took place only at the beginning of the procurement process. From then on a single firm would develop and produce a needed system.

Aerospace industry sales declined rapidly from a wartime peak of $16 billion to $1 billion in 1947, and although growth in civilian demand partly compensated for the decline in military aircraft sales, it took the Korean War, which began in 1950, to spur the construction of advanced aircraft production facilities. Again, the government provided most of the necessary funding.

In 1959 the government created the National Aeronautics and Space Administration (NASA) and opened the gates for a wave of incentive contracts. Until then most contracts, especially for research and development, had been cost-plus-profit based, but such arrangements gave suppliers little incentive to contain costs. Facing alarming cost overruns, the Defense Department and NASA turned to incentive-based contracts, and contractors doing business with the space agency soon found government watchdogs constantly peering over their shoulders. To help provide NASA with the management expertise to supervise its aerospace contracts, the agency began to hire management companies, such as GE's and AT&T's Bellcomm on the Apollo project. Bellcomm prepared systems specifications and mission assurance, while GE tracked engine reliability factors.

In his book *The Space Dealers*, Edwin Hoyt observed that "all the way through, the American space business has been notable for: its rivalries and differences of opinion, some of them very costly to the country and to science in general; the struggle of the existing aeronautical companies to dominate the field; the dichotomy between government advance and private industrial control; and the military-industrial idea that given enough money, given enough willingness to spend and duplicate and make mistakes, the country (and American business) can accomplish anything."

In 1946, Thiokol's West Coast sales manager, Walter Boswell, alerted the company's president, Joe Crosby, to the fact that Cal Tech's Jet Propulsion Lab had become a steady buyer of Thiokol's liquid polymer. While the lab ordered fairly small amounts of the substance, Crosby foresaw a potential windfall there. When he learned that the Jet Propulsion Lab had found Thiokol's liquid polymer the best existing fuel for solid propellant rockets, Crosby began directly promoting his product to the Army. Unfortunately for Crosby and Thiokol, however, the Army stuck with its own "pet" products, forcing Crosby to take the next step into the manufacture of solid rocket engines, despite the fact that the company had no prior experience in rocketry. The Army provided $250,000 a year in funding, a paltry sum by industry standards, but enough to enable Crosby to launch his mission.

After Crosby secured a contract from Army ordinance to pilot-plant Cal Tech's case-bonding technique in 1947, he rented a building in Maryland, hired a six-man engineering staff, and officially entered the rocket business. By 1949, Thiokol's twenty-seven-man staff had transferred to the Army's missile center in Huntsville, Alabama. The case-bonding process had struck pay dirt and Thiokol began to secure many large contracts, one especially big one from Hughes Aircraft. Still, since most of the early contracts came from the Army, Thiokol won the dubious distinction of being an "Army baby." The close association with the Army undoubtedly helped Thiokol in the long run, but over the short term, procurement red tape hampered corporate growth. The Navy and Air Force, not keen on having their work done for them in the Army's facilities, seemed to offer alternative markets for Thiokol, so with this in mind Crosby built a small, separate facility in Elkton, Maryland in 1952. As a result, by 1956 Thiokol owned 70 percent of all solid rocket development business, although it lost the Navy's Polaris IRBM contract to Aerojet because Thiokol's small Elkton plant could not easily satisfy the needs of the large rocket. While Crosby had wanted to construct a larger solid engine plant as early as 1955, the company couldn't afford the investment. However, in 1956 he raised $1,950,000 through a stock offering and began construction on an 11,000 acre site near Brigham City, Utah.

Over the next few years competition among solid rocket fuel firms intensified. When a number of suitors, among them General Dynamics, Union Carbide, Curtiss-Wright, and Lockheed, began expressing interest in merging with Thiokol, Crosby declined all offers.

In 1963 Thiokol sales hit a record $271 million. However, government space planners' choice of liquid-fuel boosters over solid-fuel rockets led to losses of $95 million in Thiokol sales within two years. Management coped with the loss by implementing cost-cutting programs, reorganizing the company, and focusing on diversification activities, particularly in the area of commercial projects. Forty-five hundred employees lost their jobs.

A year later, Crosby moved up to chairman and was succeeded as president by Dr. Harold W. Ritchey, a rocket fuel scientist characterized by *Business Week* as a "hard-headed businessman." Under Ritchey's direction Thiokol's previously informal organizational structure and communication network became much more formal and, since the company's survival seemed to depend on non-aerospace business, Thiokol's emphasis turned more and more toward its chemical division.

In the late 1960s, still under Ritchey, Thiokol acquired Afa Corp., a producer of specialized packaging devices, and the fibers operation of W. R. Grace and Co. The latter turned out to be one of Thiokol's winners. In 1968 sales had stood at less than $10 million domestically, but by 1976 total domestic and international sales crested at $100 million.

Government-Business in Crisis (1970–Late 1980s)

When OPEC held the world for ransom in the early seventies, American business received quite a jolt to its complacency. Foreign competition was savaging international markets formerly dominated by American firms and, more seriously, was carving out an increasingly large share of domestic markets. Much of this conquest resulted from foreign governments carefully supporting and protecting their industries, a competitive advantage many traditional U.S. industries, such as steel and textiles, could not overcome. Increasingly severe crises throughout American industry highlighted the inadequacies of the finance and systems-oriented management styles of American executives, as well as the shortcomings of national industrial policy.

While financial institutions could rely on traditional quantitative analysis tools to make sound capital investment decisions in a relatively stable business environment, such tools proved inade-

quate in light of intense international competition, rapidly changing global markets, new technologies, and wildly fluctuating costs
of natural resources. Clearly, investors needed more timely and
more detailed information on which to base their decisions, but
the kinds of arrangements that could produce such information
were usually banned by legislation originally aimed at curbing
abuse. In the absence of such information, costs of capital became
as unstable as the markets serviced and the resultant high levels
of all-around risk in doing business dramatically drove up costs.

All of these new problems caught the government off guard.
While it had done a good job of protecting free enterprise in the
preceding era, it found itself almost completely unprepared to do
so in the new high-tech world. Could government and business
find better ways of working together? Unfortunately, the answers
would not come quickly and the crisis would deepen until it
reached a climax in the late 1980s.

Writing of the aerospace industry during this era, Herman
Stekler, in his book *The Structure and Performance of the Aerospace
Industry*, said, "The salient features . . . are: a high concentration
of sales; the absence of competition; a failure on the buyer's part
to impose economic incentives on the sellers; and high entry barriers." These and other characteristics of the industry, including
cost overruns, overoptimism, and fluctuating demand, greatly
tested this alliance of government and business.

In November 1973, NASA picked Thiokol over Aerojet and
United Technology Center to develop the solid rocket motors for
the space shuttle booster. The cost of the six-year research and
development phase could reach as much as $106 million. Two
factors influenced the selection of Thiokol: it didn't need to train
any new workers, and it operated existing facilities that could
handle the job. The shuttle contract, ostensibly the last major
solid rocket award for a long time to come, created a virtual monopoly for the winner, while it visited dire consequences on the
losers, with staff reductions from minimal at Aerojet to painful at
United Technology Center. In June 1974 the Government Accounting Office recommended that NASA reconsider the fifteen-
year, $1 billion award of the shuttle solid motor to Thiokol in
light of a change in the predicted cost differences between
Thiokol and the other bidders. Richard Davis, Thiokol's CEO,
defended the award by saying, "The shuttle was an absolute ne-
cessity in order to maintain stability in Thiokol's aerospace busi-

ness over the long term." Despite the GAO's protest, Thiokol retained its contract.

Negotiations between Charles S. Locke, chairman of Morton-Norwich and Robert E. Davis, chairman of Thiokol, both of whom worried about the possibility of hostile takeovers, led to the merger of the companies in June 1982. Locke would serve as chairman and CEO of the combined operation, with Davis becoming president and chief operating officer. When Morton-Norwich bought Thiokol for $540 million in cash and stock, Morton Thiokol was born. Thiokol Corporate Development vice president Edward Kearney remarked, "We think the combination will result in a very strong company. There's a lot of compatibility between the specialty chemicals businesses of both companies but little overlap." In the merged company, specialty chemicals would play a major role and account for approximately one third of sales. Specifically, the breakdown would be: Specialty Chemicals, 33 percent; Aerospace and Defense Products, 29 percent; Morton Salt, 22 percent; and Texize Household Products, 16 percent.

In March 1983, Robert Davis and at least eight other key Thiokol executives left Morton Thiokol, not boding well for a business dependent on long-term personal contacts. In 1984, Dow Chemical Company began buying into Morton Thiokol, spending $72 million in April to acquire 8 percent of the target's 16.8 million shares. Dow claimed that it had simply made an "investment," but Morton Thiokol's Charles Locke, skeptical, responded by selling the Texize division to Dow. The division, Locke felt, would perform much better with Dow's other household products and would benefit from the purchaser's deeper pockets. After all, shouldn't aerospace and specialty chemicals form the basis of Morton Thiokol's growth?

In January 1986, when the space shuttle Challenger's rocket boosters exploded seconds after liftoff, the tragedy focused national attention on the government-business relationship as never before in history, and the painstaking postmortem of the catastrophe raised more questions than it answered. For Morton Thiokol, the answers could spell the difference between life and death.

An extremely disturbing realization about the relationship between NASA and Morton Thiokol came to light after the disaster. Until then the company had enjoyed a monopoly on the supply of solid rocket boosters for the shuttle programs, and while NASA had implicitly assured Morton Thiokol of a contract renewal, there was always the threat of a second source bidding process. The *Washington Post* reported, "Last December [1985], responding to congressional complaints that the Thiokol monopoly was resulting in higher costs, NASA proposed moving to second source bidding on purchases of booster rockets, opening the booster contract to competition for the first time."

Of proposed new bidding Senator Donald Riegle of Michigan, the ranking Democrat on the subcommittee that oversees NASA, said, "You can say suppliers should ignore this kind of pressure, but that's like ignoring the laws of physics." Even Thomas Russell, Morton Thiokol vice president of Corporate Development, "acknowledged that because Morton Thiokol is a major NASA contractor, it is difficult for the Chicago-based company to contradict the space agency." Mr. Russell commented, "We're certainly not adversarial with NASA; we're part of the team, as are all contractors in the program to explore space with NASA. But I don't think that kind of situation prevents us from doing what's right."

The press reacted strongly. *The New Republic* offered this analysis: "The relationship between NASA and the contractor Morton Thiokol was also a problem. In the Mercury, Gemini, and Apollo programs, NASA chose its contractors not by competitive bidding, but by NASA's judgment of which company could best do the job. A company held on to the contract as long as it performed its assigned task. In the shuttle program the rules are different. Indeed, in a few weeks Morton Thiokol stood the chance of losing part of its multi-million dollar contract simply because other companies had been asked to submit bids. The NASA officials testified they did not believe that economic considerations influenced the company. Such statements are naive at best. It was unforgivable for Morton Thiokol managers to overrule their engineers when the engineers were expressing deeply felt safety fears. But it was also inexcusable for the NASA officials not to understand the power they held because of the new economics of manned space when they asked Morton Thiokol to reconsider its recommendation not to launch."

And *The New York Times* provided this critique: "Both NASA and Morton Thiokol, each for its own reasons, became afraid to raise questions that could grind the shuttle program to an immediate halt. Exacerbating the problem was Thiokol's status as NASA's sole supplier of booster rockets. Had two companies been building rockets, some experts contend, the problems with the O-rings' seals might have surfaced much earlier, as a competitor sought to steal away Thiokol's business by pointing out failings in Thiokol's design."

Apparently, NASA and Morton Thiokol, among other related organizations, deserved blame for both judgmental and quality control lapses. The Presidential Commission's study of the disaster concluded that quality control had become a game of "Russian roulette," and Richard P. Feynman, the Nobel Laureate physicist and a member of the commission, stated, "Each time the shuttle flew and nothing happened, someone suggested that the risk wasn't as bad as they first thought. So they kept lowering their standards, bit by bit, until the situation got so bad that Thiokol was flying in a condition no one would have tolerated a few years ago."

This swirl of controversy raised serious questions about the roles of government and business and their proper relationships. Who was monitoring and controlling potential abuses of power? Who was protecting free enterprise? Who was responsible? When questions like this arise we believe the parties must answer with a new model of cooperation. Otherwise, similar crises, possibly of much greater consequence, could undermine the vitality of the entire economic system.

Searching for a New Model (Late 1980s–Late 1990s)

Faced with so many complex and competitive business conditions, American businesses naturally turned to the government for help. Could the two overcome their traditional adversarial relationship and ad hoc approach to decision making and find a way to hammer out a coherent industrial strategy? Over the years a sort of industrial welfare aimed at helping declining industries had developed, with most legislation, tax breaks, and other aid designed for the needy rather than the affluent corporation. But what about lending a hand to developing industries that might be destroyed by foreign competitors?

Given heavyweight competition from overseas where some governments often do develop coherent and successful industrial policies, American business has found itself increasingly disadvantaged. Bruce Scott, a Harvard Business School professor, has compared America's industrial policy approach to the fielding of a tough team of independent athletes who, over the years, ran up a string of winning seasons. But with other countries putting together tough teams, too, and providing them, in many cases, with better governmental "coaching," America has found it harder and harder to remain undefeated.

The Business-Higher Education Forum, in a report entitled "America's Competitive Challenge," summarized the problem confronting American government-business relationships when it said, "We stand at the hinge of history, with an unprecedented opportunity to combine the lessons of our past with the resources of our future to revitalize the economy, create more jobs, and increase our standard of living. American society, through its seeming addiction to adversarial relationships, has created a formidable barrier to restoring the nation's competitiveness."

From the business viewpoint, laissez-faire capitalism dictates that the government that governs best governs least. Government's perspective, however, holds that businesses left unchecked will quite likely abuse their freedom. As a result, most Americans view government intervention as a necessary evil to be applied when crises occur. Unfortunately, when two factions with different points of view attempt to respond to a crisis, their response is often uncoordinated and confrontational.

America's major competitors, especially Japan and Germany, have avoided this dilemma by letting their governments target promising industries for development, while shifting capital and labor away from declining ones. By protecting industries in targeted areas until they can compete internationally, and by securing substantial funds for ongoing investment, especially in research and development, such governments provide their enterprises with more stability and opportunity for sustained growth than their American counterparts enjoy. Sadly, American business is at the mercy of unstable, cyclical economic fluctuations that hamper long-term research, development, and capitalization.

In this one area, at least, American enterprise has failed to achieve a proper balance between freedom and responsibility. The strong American belief in individual rights has led the nation to guarantee those rights with a large safety net of social programs, and to create an industrial safety net to help formerly productive companies to survive hard times. Unfortunately, we have not paid equal attention to the nurturing of those upcoming industries that will guarantee a successful future.

Increasingly, critics have suggested that the costs of such an industrial welfare system will outstrip our ability to provide it. But if other countries continue to allocate subsidies according to an industry's possible future, rather than to its past, contribution to the economic well-being of their nations, American industry will find itself falling further and further behind.

The free market economy of capitalism rests on the assumption of vigorous competition and lack of centralized controls, which, when applied to specific firms, once gave owners unilateral power to operate as they pleased, with the market rewarding the strong and penalizing the weak. In modern times, this power resides in the hands of managers primarily responsible for maximizing stockholders' equity. As society began to recognize that unbridled power could lead to abuses, it tried to hold businesses accountable for the consequences of executive actions. Thus, legislation now dictates proper corporate conduct concerning businesses' interactions with customers, competitors, employees, and the social and natural environments. In addition to maximizing stockholders' interests, business people must now worry about the far-ranging impact of every major decision.

For government, this development poses a thorny problem. While on the one hand society demands greater involvement of regulatory agencies in the operation of business, on the other hand it mistrusts the resultant relationships as potentially corrupt. However, to inaugurate a strong national industrial policy, the two traditional opponents *must* cooperate. According to the Fowler-McCracken Commission, a group charged with improving government-business cooperation in the conduct of U.S. international policy, the only solution to the problem involves ending the "outmoded, counterproductive . . . even crippling . . . adversarial concept between government and business." If executives accept such a recommendation, they must initiate a long-term campaign to reevaluate some basic assumptions about free enterprise and strike a better balance between freedom and responsibility. The line between the two will not be easy to redraw, because greater government-business cooperation brings with it greater potential abuses as well as benefits.

The Challenger disaster underscores the pain that can attend a breakdown in communication, cooperation, and trust between government and business. Before the catastrophe, the NASA-Morton Thiokol relationship seemed to offer hope for a new model for cooperative government-business endeavors many other industries might adopt. Afterward, the whole nation became aware of the dangers inherent in that model. Can we seize this opportunity to learn more about and improve the ties between government and business, or will we revert to our deepseated suspicion that the two always make unsuitable bedfellows?

A New Perspective for a New Alliance

Since we think complexity management can benefit governments as well as corporations, we urge government leaders to join corporate executives in using principles to create and maintain sounder, more productive relationships between the two sectors. In our view, one-on-one communication between individual companies and government agencies can resolve more paradoxical situations than all the procedural and legal battles in the world.

In the global economy of the future, the principles upon which various nations' economic systems operate will differ markedly, and the U.S. should not abandon the principle of protecting individual rights and minimizing abuses. However, instead of legislating specific practices or procedures, we think that the U.S. government should act more flexibly in its alliance with business, allowing the balance of freedom and responsibility to differ from industry to industry.

The government should not automatically assume that business is abusing power. Industries, companies, and other stakeholders in the economic system should enjoy greater freedom to determine courses of action within the limits laid down by overriding principles. If and when a company or group of companies abuses the privilege of greater freedom, the individual companies involved, not the entire industry, should be penalized and controlled. In this way, all fair-playing stakeholders can win.

Traditionally, despite this nation's tremendous business and economic diversity, it has developed no elaborate central planning program for the private sector. Intensified global competition and greater interdependence between global trading partners will demand better coordination in the future. But by coordination we do not mean control. The control that comes from central planning may work for Japan, but the United States must take care that coordination efforts do not undermine the freedom of its institutions to plan and coordinate among themselves. Nevertheless, a democratic government can set forth principles within which joint planning and coordination can occur. By permitting new levels of discussion, interchange, planning, and coordination among private institutions while protecting the rights of individuals and institutions, the American government can enjoy the best of both worlds. Success, of course, depends on the parties paying as much attention to the rights of others as they do to their own.

Government can become more flexible, and business leaders can become more fully aware of the larger context in which they exercise their freedom to pursue profit. If government's perspective broadens to focus more on the equilibrium of the entire system, and if the perspective of business can widen to include collective concerns heretofore relegated to government, all stakeholders will benefit.

History, and particularly recent history, proves that the increasing complexity of the world makes it more and more difficult for one organization to solve all its problems itself. Consequently, organizations need to form new, encompassing alliances with other organizations. Unfortunately, whenever such alliances have lacked legitimacy and accountability in the past, they have stimulated legislation. A successful future will require elected and appointed political and government leaders who recognize the value of business forums for joint planning and coordination, and it will demand business executives who can attune themselves to issues once considered the domain of government.

The future of the partnership between business and government will depend on self-control and self-monitoring. Otherwise, the two cannot expect to balance superior business performance with political freedom. The worst problems of our society occur when one individual, group, or institution overextends its power and freedom in an attempt to garner for itself an inordinate amount of the benefits that the whole community should share. The leaders of the future should not tolerate that sort of selfish shortsightedness but should promote principles and practices whereby everyone wins. Otherwise, everyone loses.

Government leaders and the executives of the Future 500 should view the years ahead as a time for learning and applying new political and collective leadership skills. If political and gov-

ernment leaders gain a greater appreciation of the business management process that creates wealth, if they allow the private
sector to redistribute that wealth, and if business executives develop a deeper understanding of the complex task of keeping the
freedom of individuals and the collective well-being of a nation
alive, all stakeholders will win.

The tensions between government and business will never vanish because the roles and tasks of the two do and should differ in
a genuine way. However, tension between the two should spur us
toward improved understanding of their respective roles. That's
where the precepts of complexity management come in.

Government-Business Relations and Complexity Management

Our analysis of government-business history has convinced us
that the earlier eras of control, intervention, and protection can
no longer meet the demands of the global marketplace. We believe the future will demand more from both sectors. Government must learn to orchestrate environments more effectively,
and 'private industry must learn to exercise more self-monitoring
and self-disciplining. Only then can coordination and cooperation
replace control and intervention.

The overriding issue facing companies like Morton Thiokol,
Citicorp, Southland Corp., Bristol-Myers, and the government
entities with which they interrelate involves achieving true alliances without compromising the free enterprise system.

The banking industry, more than most, has invited strict regulation and control because of past abuses, but its future, more
than most, hinges on increased deregulation and heightened coordination. Can Citicorp continue to convince federal and state
governments to become even more flexible and exert less control
over interstate banking laws?

Southland Corp. faces the difficult task of making sure that the
lines between government and industry remain clear. In its current relationship with the Venezuelan government the overlap in
roles will surely produce unforeseen conflicts as both the govern-

ment and the company attempt to set corporate policies and priorities. Can Southland keep the corporate and government roles differentiated, yet complementary, when these conflicts arise?

Can and should Bristol-Myers and other pharmaceutical manufacturers control and monitor themselves in the global marketplace without abusing their power?

Finally, in the case of Morton Thiokol and NASA, how can the two work together to develop a relationship that promotes competition, minimizes costs, increases accountability, and allows both partners to coordinate cooperative decision making with mutually beneficial results?

Let's consider how executives of the future can apply complexity management to answer these and similar questions.

Applying Perspective Management

Perspective managers in both the private and public sectors must learn to appreciate the diverse and at times seemingly conflicting viewpoints. Doing so should help both parties come closer together. Among other measures, perspective managers can:

- Create coordinated lobbying efforts. For example, Southland Corp. might initiate an association of all U.S. and foreign corporations with joint ownership positions in Venezuela, enabling participants to better define their respective roles and avoid potential conflicts.

- Constantly communicate success stories of mutually beneficial government-business relationships. For example, Citicorp could disseminate news of its experience with the State of Maryland inside and outside its own industry in an attempt to further government-business relationships across the board.

- Budget more funds for meetings between corporate and government entities that go beyond the parties merely advocating their own interests. Such get-togethers could begin erasing long-standing adversarial attitudes. For example, Bristol-Myers might sponsor a series of such meetings with the FDA and consumer groups to begin the long process of blending perspectives for the benefit of all affected stakeholders.

Applying Power Management

Power managers in both sectors would grant individuals and groups the freedom to act in the name of improved government-business relationships. They could:

- Distinguish between policy and operational interaction with government entities, then afford lower management levels the power to improve working relationships. For example, executives at Morton Thiokol and NASA might attempt to increase integration and coordination within the space program through decentralization of day-to-day operations and centralization of key areas of responsibility. Under such an approach NASA's central operations and Morton Thiokol's top management would focus more on overall policies and less on operating procedures, allowing NASA to develop closer and better working relationships with Morton Thiokol and other aerospace contractors at lower organizational levels.

- As an interim or permanent solution, require independent third parties in the private sector to monitor and guide government-business alliances and partnerships. For example, Morton Thiokol and NASA executives together might encourage independent engineering, consulting, or other qualified firms approved by the government to test and monitor NASA's facilities and the aerospace contractors' products.

- Convince government regulators to experiment with self-regulation. For example, Bristol-Myers could promote an experiment with the FDA that would allow it and other pharmaceutical companies to establish and monitor their own drug licensing and selling activities in selected drug categories. Then, the FDA could closely monitor this self-regulation, quickly removing from the experiment any companies that abused their privileges. Successful self-regulators would win even more freedom.

Applying Pivot Management

Pivot managers should focus on individual relationships in an effort to produce higher performance and greater fulfillment. They could:

- Strengthen one-on-one relationships with influential individuals within government and consumer groups at all management levels. For example, an influential Bristol-Myers executive could develop a close relationship with someone like Ralph Nader. If such relationships were based on a genuine desire to achieve mutually benefitting results, consumer activists could further their causes without compromising their integrity and the company could gain valuable grassroots insights into the ways in which its actions and products affect its reputation.

- Locate advocates of better government-business alliances and partnerships in relevant government agencies, establishing a network of pivotal relationships that could enhance industry-government relationships. For example, Citicorp could further extend its local, state, and federal networking efforts to help loosen interstate banking laws in many other states.

We think complexity management can help all levels of business, from small local entrepreneurs to large global corporations, construct more mutually productive relationships with all levels of government, from local zoning commissions to federal agencies and even with the governments of other nations. Before it can happen, however, business and government leaders alike must reexamine their roles and rethink their relationships.

CHAPTER SEVEN

Cutthroat Teammates: Balancing Competition with Collaboration

All competition is in its nature only a furious plagiarism.

—G. K. CHESTERTON

Enlightened Competition

Throughout the twentieth century, American industry has prided itself on its competitive spirit, not only in the international arena but also on the domestic battlefield, where deadly head-to-head struggles for competitive advantage have strengthened some companies' positions while damaging or even ruining others. And nowhere has the fight been more bitter or ruthless than in the computer business. However, one company has tried to balance cutthroat competition with greater industry-wide collaboration.

By its own definition, Control Data Corporation, a worldwide computer and financial services company, engages in the business of providing solutions to problems through the innovative use of technology in the fields of computing-related hardware and computer-enhanced services. On the hardware side Control Data designs, develops, manufactures, and markets a complete line of supermini and large-scale computer systems. Its customers include engineering, educational, and scientific organizations, who use Control Data systems for university research, student instruction, weather forecasting, engineering design, energy management, petroleum exploration and production, and aerospace and defense. Through ETA Systems, Control Data markets one of the most powerful computer systems in the world, and in the peripheral products area, the company offers a broad line of computer data storage devices, which are compatible not only with Control Data systems but also with those manufactured by other computer companies. Its data storage products come both from its own facilities and through a number of joint ventures with Honeywell, Sperry, Bull Systems, NCR Corp., and N.V. Philips of the Netherlands.

In the field of computer services, Control Data offers a wide range of products, including business data processing, complex scientific and engineering problem solving, information services such as ARBITRON, transaction processing for financial institutions, Integrated Computer-Aided Engineering and Manufacturing (ICEM), engineering services for computer equipment maintenance, consulting and software development, education and training programs (including a joint venture with WICAT Systems to market computer-based education products and services), medical information systems, business and technology centers, and various other computer application services. The company owns and operates Commercial Credit Company, a wholly owned subsidiary that provides consumer financial services from personal loans, second mortgages, and life and health insurance to vehicle leasing and fleet management, international leasing, factoring, business credit insurance, and credit counseling and collection.

Currently Control Data's vision of providing solutions through the innovative use of technology continues to prove exceptionally effective in a highly competitive industry. Its innovations, particularly in the area of computer-enhanced services, have generally kept the company's bottom line healthy despite some annual fluctuations. As a second-tier mainframe computer producer, Control Data has struggled along with the rest of the "BUNCH" (an acronym for the collection of major second-tier companies—Burroughs, Univac or Sperry, NCR, Control Data, and Honeywell) to compete with IBM's 76 percent share of the mainframe market. To date, however, the BUNCH has failed to make striking inroads into IBM's turf. Control Data has tried to stake out its niche by aiming its mainframes at scientific and engineering applications; and Burroughs and Sperry have merged into Unisys in an effort to gain competitive clout, but their mainframe lines remain separate businesses (many mergers are simply a conventional way of creating permanent competitive cooperation). Many observers believe that the ultimate survival of all the second-tier firms will require their joining forces in some creative fashion. In response to that belief, Control Data's chairman and CEO initiated an interesting collaborative venture whereby smaller computer companies might cooperate in the area of microelectronics research. The result, the Microelectronics and Computer Technology Corporation (MCC), has established an early model for balancing competition with collaboration.

With MCC, Control Data and the BUNCH are trying to solve a number of competitive interaction issues. Substantial legal barriers as well as ones created by management attitudes have afflicted all the rival computer companies. From a legal standpoint, U.S. antitrust laws make it easier for companies to grow large through internal and external expansion (mergers and acquisitions) than to develop clout through collective action. On the attitude side, the right of management to act in its own interest within the bounds of the law rules the free enterprise system, and executives fear that trifling with such a fundamental principle could invite disaster. Nevertheless, the free enterprise system provides ways of selective cooperation. Recent mergers in the airline and financial services industries have shown how competitors can cooperate without destroying free enterprise by grouping previously separate entities. The computer industry itself has witnessed the merger between Burroughs and Sperry and a number of joint ventures besides MCC. Mergers, acquisitions, and joint ventures have always held the promise of competitive collaboration. The self-regulation of the chemical industry through a type of industry cartel, CIIT, aimed at insuring the safety of employees and society exemplifies one of the most promising ways competitors can legally cooperate.

The overriding issue raised by collaboration involves direction, organization, and control. Can rivals forge a consensus in these areas, which have for so long provided the basis for differentiation and conflict? IBM and GM have done so to some degree. Since the early 1980s IBM has formed alliances with several firms in the United States alone—Rolm, Intel, Merrill Lynch, Aetna Life and Casualty, and MCI to name a few; and General Motors had been weaving its own network by joint venturing with Toyota and Fanuc (a Fujitsu-operated robot manufacturer), forming ties with Suzuki, Isuzu, and Daewoo (a Korean conglomerate), and establishing key suppliers and research groups.

Other companies, such as Coca-Cola, B. F. Goodrich, and Delta Airlines have tried to attain greater collaboration the old-fashioned way, with mergers and acquisitions. Coke has been merging its company-owned bottling operations with JTL Corp., its largest independent bottler. Goodrich and Uniroyal, two fierce rivals in the tire industry, have been linking up their tiremaking facilities to create the Uniroyal-Goodrich Tire Company. Delta bought Western Airlines in an effort to combine resources and enhance market share. As we pointed out in Chapter 3 the merger, acquisition, and divestiture game is being played for bigger stakes than ever. We believe all this activity signals a trend toward resolving the problems inherent in head-to-head competition. Companies seeking greater collaboration while maintaining free enterprise will face more complex issues in the decades ahead, so we again propose that executives use perspective, power, and pivot management to resolve them. To see exactly how American enterprise has gotten to the present turning point, we want to review the history of business competition.

The Saga of Corporate Combat

The language and images of war have often been used as metaphors for trade. References to hostile takeovers, invasions of turf, pirating, scorched earth policies, aggression, and defensive tactics appear in the business press every day, but a close examination of the evolution of competition during this century actually reveals a decline in all-out warfare.

Here again, it is interesting to compare the eras of competition and corporate combat with the eras of modern American management, as shown in chart on page 135.

The Rise of the Competitive System (1890–1920)

Toward the end of the age of market mechanisms, and at the beginning of the age of modern management, business leaders,

Competition Eras

Competitive System	Competition Through Size	Growth Through Marketing	Competitive Warfare	Indirect Competition & Nichemanship	Competitive Collaboration	Win-Win Competition

1890	1910	1930	1950	1970	1990	2010

	Structure	Productivity	Systems	Strategy	Culture	Innovation	Leadership	Complexity Management

Management Eras

investors, and financiers began creating this century's large industrial enterprises, and as they flexed their muscles a lot of head-to-
head battles erupted. Some of the new enterprises blatantly tried
to control or destroy competition, others attempted to manipulate
securities, while still others combined production and distribution
to gain clout or relied on technological innovations to create
brand-new industries. Regardless of their approaches, however,
most of their efforts essentially tested the parameters of the free
enterprise system. Mergers, acquisitions, associations, and cartels
flourished, particularly in those industries that had adopted qualities of the modern business organization early on. Although the
Sherman Anti-Trust Act became law in 1890, the Supreme
Court's interpretation of it came much later, in 1899. Once the
Supreme Court eventually decided that government could pursue legal action against a company combination if it restrained
trade, business organizations could no longer control competition
through monopolies, cartels, trusts, or other trade associations
that controlled price, production, and distribution.

A subsequent upsurge of mergers in 1899 occurred as corporate America established legal holding companies. However, even
these invited prosecution under the Sherman Anti-Trust Act if
they actually fixed prices or assigned markets. For example, in
1903 Northern Securities Company, a combination of the Northern Pacific and Great Northern Railroad companies, was ordered
by a circuit court to dissolve its combination, and the Supreme
Court concurred in 1904. Corporate attorneys began advising
their clients to organize themselves into single operating entities
without constituent or subsidiary units to avoid prosecution. A
similar trend toward consolidation and centralization in large
industries such as railroads, oil, cotton, and food commodities
ushered in the age of modern business management. As company
combinations moved from trade associations to trusts to holding
companies and finally to integrated and centralized operating
entities, they increasingly required sophisticated management
hierarchies.

In the following years companies and their managers devised
ways of conforming to the restrictions of America's free enterprise system until, by 1920, the economic and legal infrastructure
that would shape competition in the U.S. and throughout the
world for decades to come stood firmly in place. Some newer
industries, such as office machines, learned some valuable lessons

from watching other industries attempt, and fail, to control competition. Office machine makers chose to control markets by building national sales organizations. Remington Typewriter, National Cash Register, Underwood Company, Wagner Typewriter, A.B. Dick & Company, and, later, Burroughs Adding Machine Company and Computing-Tabulator Recording Company (later to become IBM) quickly learned that they could use national sales forces to move mass produced products in great volume. The competitive philosophy of the day—control or destroy the competition—played itself out in the emerging office machines industry in an interesting way. Because the industry didn't really start rolling until after 1899, when the Supreme Court gave the Sherman Act its teeth, business combinations already looked like a losing bet. Soon creative leaders like John Patterson and Tom Watson at National Cash Register put their money on a new way of destroying competition. As you may recall from Chapter 1, Patterson roped an unwary Tom Watson into setting up ostensibly independent cash register outlets next to competitors' locations for the sole purpose of undercutting their prices. Eventually, the Sherman Act caught up with NCR and closed off this innovative way of skirting the parameters of free enterprise.

With the rules of the game becoming clearer, the office machines manufacturers, learning from the mistakes of firms like National Cash Register, decided to grow by extending their sales organizations nationally and internationally.

Competition Through Size (1920–1945)

After World War I more and more companies wanted a bigger slice of the American and worldwide business pie. With the prospects of manipulating and controlling competition and markets reduced to "fair" competitive practices, the players increased the size of their organizations to make them less vulnerable to competing firms, changing markets, and fluctuating economic conditions. Management looked inward, developing effective structures that could handle the increasing size of integrated organizations and increase overall efficiency and productivity. Sheer size was one of the few remaining legal ways a company could control competition. If a company could get big enough through acceptable mergers and acquisitions, it might be able to dominate its markets. National networks of branch offices, national sales forces, and national distribution agreements all helped firms achieve the size they needed to remain competitively viable. These approaches were particularly attractive to the capital-intensive manufacturing companies, because the very nature of their markets brought greater rewards to larger firms than smaller ones as volumes rose, unit costs fell, and specialized scheduling, advertising, and other centralized services added to the bottom line. In addition, the larger firms could more effectively structure, coordinate, and administer production, distribution, and marketing functions. Consequently, the manufacturing companies set the tone for less capital-intensive industries like retailing and service, and most enterprises assumed that efficient, well-managed production operations provided the key to survival, with distribution and selling determining the difference between mediocrity and excellence. While the concept of marketing did come into play during this era, selling commanded far greater attention.

The conventional wisdom of the day suggested that bigger was always better, and when the Depression struck, this wisdom was reinforced because only individuals or companies with enough wealth could survive the crisis. Eventually, World War II also reinforced the advantages of size and strength.

The office machine industry, the forerunner to the computer industry, eagerly joined the competitive scramble for size. The Underwood Company and Wagner Typewriter merged to form Underwood Typewriter, then Underwood merged with Elliot Fisher, a manufacturer of accounting and bookkeeping machines, calculators, cash registers, and typewriters. National Cash Register, on the other hand, failed at the size game after John Patterson's son, Frederick, succeeded him. By 1920 NCR seemed ideally poised to continue dominance of the industry, but Frederick Patterson took an overly cautious approach, avoiding the bold moves necessary to retain NCR's primary position. While other companies expanded through acquisition, merger, and innovation, NCR hesitated to diversify out of cash registers. When it eventually did so in the late 1920s, it was too late; by 1928 Remington Rand had become the largest business machine company in the United States, with $60 million in sales and $6 million in profits.

James H. Rand, Jr. had developed the Kardex tabulating system, establishing the Rand Kardex Company in 1915. A few years later along with a group of Wall Street bankers and promoters, he put together a conglomeration of companies to create the

Remington Rand Company. The companies that made up Remington Rand were Remington Typewriter (owned in part by Rand's father, who had acquired it from the Remington family before the turn of the century), Dalton Adding Machine, Rand Kardex, Powers Accounting Machine Corporation, and several smaller office equipment and supplies firms. James Rand was bound and determined to outmaneuver his competitors by getting bigger, faster. The company's strong and effective sales organization helped the newly combined companies set sales records. Unfortunately for Remington Rand, during the late 1930s and early 1940s the company began losing the size battle to the rapidly growing IBM. By 1945, Remington Rand's sales of $133 million lagged behind IBM's $142 million, and, more important, its profits were only half of IBM's.

Growth Through Marketing (1945–1970)

After World War II, size, manufacturing capacity, the strength of national sales organizations, and other measures of production output or sales volume still contributed to corporate growth, but marketing effectiveness increasingly became the overriding concern. Demand for a greater diversity of products and services exploded after the war, as the populace sought to put the sacrifices of the war behind them and enjoy the enhanced production capacity it had created. In this climate, marketing seemed to spell the difference between success and failure. Product differentiation, new product and service development, packaging, advertising, merchandising, pricing, and other marketing techniques began to guide the decisions of management, even though most executives still thought bigger was better and more competitive.

As marketing fueled growth, growth in turn fueled control systems, and by the mid 1950s executives and their companies were installing the control systems described in Chapter 2. Even though the business environment was becoming more complex during this era, marketing problems seemed relatively uncomplicated. In those days marketing simply meant finding new customer needs and meeting those needs, matching a competitor's unit costs through capital improvements, or entering a previously unserved new market. However, this simplified approach invited certain hazards. In a classic 1960 *Harvard Business Review* article, "Marketing Myopia," Theodore Levitt suggested that at one time *all* industries were growth industries, but that some now faced decline, not because of saturated markets, but because of poor management caused by marketing myopia, the shortsighted assumption that marketing alone could create competitive advantage.

During these postwar years James Rand foresaw the growth potential of electronic computers and attempted to position his company to take advantage of the opportunity. Ironically, despite his anticipation of what would turn into an earth-shattering phenomenon, Rand never regarded his computers as more than a sideline, a mere extension of his company's tabulating business. This odd blend of anticipation and underestimation stemmed from Rand's orientation toward growth, particularly short-term growth, during this era. When Remington Rand bought Eckert-Mauchly Computer Company, founded by computer pioneers John Mauchly and Presper Eckert, developers of ENIAC and UNIVAC, Rand was marketing everything from office equipment to electric shavers, but when it sold the Eckert-Mauchly Division's UNIVAC I to the U.S. Bureau of Census in 1951 the company seemed destined for success in the computer industry. However, Rand never mustered the management or marketing depth necessary to build upon this initial advantage.

During this period Engineering Research Associates, Inc., (ERA) had been developing one of the first computer systems, Atlas, for the National Security Agency. ERA's success at winning large government contracts and the technical prowess of its people attracted the attention of James Rand. In December 1951, Remington Rand bought ERA for $1.7 million in Remington Rand stock. With its Eckert-Mauchly Division, its own computer development laboratories in Norwalk, Connecticut, and now its ERA acquisition, Remington Rand had assembled the strongest computer capabilities and talent in the world, propelling it clearly ahead of IBM, Burroughs, National Cash Register, and other emerging rivals. In the early fifties, John Parker, William Norris, and Howard Engstrom, principals of ERA, along with Eckert and Mauchly, kept Remington Rand well ahead of IBM, its nearest competitor; Rand was selling computers to such lucrative accounts as General Electric, Westinghouse, U.S. Steel, and Metropolitan Life. Soon, however, Rand's rapid growth could not overcome its opportunistic and shallow approach to marketing, financing, and organizing, until in the mid and late 1950s, particularly on the marketing front, IBM began to dominate the market.

Rand's financial weakness made it more difficult to match IBM's ability to finance the renting of computer systems. To overcome this disadvantage, James Rand resorted to opportunism once again in 1955 by selling his company to a larger, more financially capable firm, Sperry Gyroscope Company, which he assumed would give Remington Rand the financial muscle to fund more aggressive computer marketing. The new Sperry Rand Company consolidated all its computer operations into one division. William Norris, who had come to Remington Rand by way of ERA, became the new Univac Division's general manager and a vice president of Sperry Rand. With General Douglas MacArthur as Chairman of the Board of Sperry Rand and Bill Norris as the head of the Univac Division, the future looked bright again.

Although 80 percent of all U.S. computers came from Bill Norris' division, Norris felt uneasy about Sperry Rand's ability to maintain its lead. He realized that future greatness depended more on sales to the commercial sector than to the government, which would require aggressive marketing and growth beyond Sperry Rand's capabilities. Norris' superiors, not sharing his reservations, failed to give him the support, funding, and authority he needed to maintain competitive leadership. In his book *New Frontiers for Business Leadership*, Norris recalls, "We sat there with a tremendous technological and sales lead and watched IBM pass us as if we were standing still." Frustrated with his own firm's lack of commitment to aggressive marketing, Bill Norris and eight associates resigned in 1957 to start Control Data Corporation.

When Control Data sold 600,000 shares of common stock at $1 per share, it became the first computer company to be publicly financed. Led by Norris, Control Data turned into a giant almost overnight. Although Norris now admits that he followed no particular plan to grow big, he acknowledges that competitive advantage depended on size and growth. Norris, more of a marketer and entrepreneur than a technician and engineer, brought to his fledgling enterprise a sense of marketing that would allow Control Data to soar in those early years. His book's introduction claims, "Control Data was a very small fish in a sea of very big predators, but that did not worry Norris because he had picked a different place to swim." Norris and his associates directed their company's efforts toward a segment of the market that would allow them to take maximum advantage of their technical and professional expertise: large-scale computer systems designed for engineering and scientific applications. Effective market positioning, a notion just beginning to be recognized as a vital part of marketing management, fueled Control Data's early growth. Despite a constant shortage of cash, Control Data managed to acquire other companies through the exchange of stock, until, by 1970, the company, with $1 billion in sales, had 40,000 employees.

Competitive Warfare (1970–1980)

The marketing thrust of the previous era gained speed during subsequent years as corporations and their executives devised complex strategic plans for desirable market positions and competitive advantages. Along with competitive positioning came a proliferation of strategic planning techniques and processes that led to all-out competitive warfare in most industries.

Those who devised the best competitive strategies won the war of the seventies, especially in the computer industry. Control Data's Bill Norris, a master at competitive positioning and a fanatic when it came to long-range planning, did not think twice about battling the giants. Earlier Norris had demonstrated his strategic vision and marketing savvy by carving out and dominating an unserved market niche, and now, in the 1970s, he would sharpen his and his company's competitive positioning skills while engaging in head-to-head combat with his rivals.

In the early 1970s Control Data identified another unserved market: peripherals, memories, printers, disk drives, tape drives, and other paraphernalia needed by the computer industry to run large mainframe machines. Later Norris found another one: small businesses and organizations that could not afford to purchase computers but that still needed them occasionally to process data. Control Data's service bureau beautifully fulfilled the needs of these customers, and the company quickly attacked IBM's dominance with an antitrust suit that the two companies eventually settled out of court in 1973, giving Control Data an estimated $100 million in benefits plus IBM's Service Bureau Corporation (SBC). The acquisition of SBC tripled Control Data's service bureau business, broadened its market, and infused the company with needed management talent. Ironically, Control

Data's acquisition of SBC made Control Data one of the largest single users of IBM equipment. By 1977 Control Data was recognized as the undisputed leader in computer services and peripheral equipment, and by 1980 it boasted revenues of $3.8 billion, earnings of $260 million and almost 60,000 employees.

Indirect Competition and Nichemanship (1980–Late 1980s)

Since intense head-to-head competition often left even the winners wounded and weakened, most companies gradually began searching for less damaging, less wasteful, and more efficient means of winning competitive advantage. At the beginning of this era, companies began looking for differentiation opportunities, underserved customer segments, new markets, and other less competitive niches. After all, Davids like Control Data had taken on and thrashed Goliaths like IBM on certain battlefields, proving that size alone cannot guarantee success.

Nichemanship meant carving out and dominating a distinctive and often small market segment or constantly creating new products, services, and markets that could push a company ahead of its competitors. To forward the cause, consultants and academics alike attempted to categorize the different positions competitors could assume in an industry or market, and much of their advice boiled down to some form of indirect competition. The conventional strategic marketing wisdom of the day urged "market leaders" to defend their turf, "market followers" to find and exploit the leader's weakness, small firms to discover and defend a market niche the big firms hadn't satisfied, and start-ups to create new products and services that fulfilled needs in a previously uncontested market. In every case, the message was the same: avoid butting heads with your competitors unless you are Goliath, and even if you are Goliath, you'd better watch out for David.

A few enlightened market leaders during this era actually fostered a competitive market environment in which companies could comfortably compete directly with the market leader in a way that benefited both the industry and its customers. Rather than stifling competition, this loosely collaborative approach actually expanded product service offerings, produced fair rather than artificially low prices, and allowed all competitors a profit. For example, market leaders in the hotel industry, like Marriott, didn't attempt to dominate all market segments, but allowed competitors, like Holiday Inn, to create their own differentiated images. This approach may have been the exception rather than the rule during this era, but it nevertheless presaged the changing pattern of competition.

The pursuit of niches and indirect competition became a way of corporate life at Control Data. During the previous era the company had relied on indirect competitive strategies just to survive, but in this era it consciously perfected the art. In an industry where its rivals were building large, integrated systems, Control Data focused on applications and services. While Control Data's competitors talked about applications, Control Data actually delivered them in the form of "knowledge services," applications that fulfilled some basic needs of society. By 1981 over 40 percent of Control Data's revenues came from services, a share it hoped to enlarge to 50 percent. Control Data had clearly claimed a position as the world's largest data services company.

Control Data also attacked areas competitors would never even dream of entering. For example, the company began Rural Venture services, helping Alaskan Eskimos grow potatoes in the permafrost, and it supplied wellness and nutrition services to the Rosebud Indian Reservation in South Dakota. Not as far afield from its competitors, but still indirectly competitive, Control Data also offered remote scientific and engineering data processing on six continents through CYBERNET. Other specialized data services included ARBITRON, the world's largest radio and TV ratings system, TICKETRON, a nationwide computerized box office, CYBERSEARCH, a nationwide computerized employment agency, and TECHNOTEC, an international technology exchange service. In addition, Control Data continued its heavy commitment to sophisticated computer-based education systems such as PLATO. Under Norris' leadership, Control Data continued to grow and develop by creating markets that hadn't previously existed, until the company shone as a prime example of how a Fortune 500 company can compete without waging war on its rivals.

Competitive Collaboration (Late 1980s–Late 1990s)

By the mid to late 1980s, while many executives continued to pursue indirect competition with strategic positioning, some forward-looking leaders saw the opportunities inherent in more formal cooperative and collaborative relationships with competitors. Motivated by the desire to reduce waste, inefficiency, and duplication, some competitors began exploring ways to work together to fend off foreign competition and government regulation and to extend the horizons of corporate accomplishment. As companies like General Motors cast their gazes toward the future, they began to realize the handicaps brought about by excess manufacturing capacity, and service-oriented industries like the Big Eight accounting firms began seeing the disadvantages of the duplication of expertise. If they continue this sort of thinking, such companies may come to appreciate the largely untapped capabilities of countries such as Korea, Taiwan, Brazil, Saudi Arabia, Malaysia, the Philippines, Thailand, and China. We think increasing globalization, redesigned relationships between the private and public sectors, and the benefits of differentiation over imitation should stimulate executives of the Future 500 to transform the ways their organizations compete with one another. Although corporate America should never abandon its dedication to a free enterprise system, executives of the future can creatively incorporate competitive collaboration into their repertoires. Doing so will, we believe, result in greater freedom.

Some of the best academic minds at the Harvard Business School and other respected institutions point out that another ten years of conventional competition could very well destroy many of today's most admired corporations. The Future 500, we think, will learn how to exploit unconventional competitive arrangements such as joint research consortiums, orderly marketing agreements, and, in some cases, cartels. If they do, once-antagonistic competitors can cooperatively restructure old industries and create new ones.

Control Data's Bill Norris is a visionary corporate leader who initiated a promising path to the future when he made a shockingly unorthodox proposal that he hoped would help flagging U.S. microelectronics and computer firms. Norris wanted to see such companies overcome problems of high capital costs, scarce capital resources, increased pressure to develop new technologies, short supplies of scientific and engineering talent, wasteful duplication of research and development efforts, and declining positions vis-à-vis already collaborating Japanese competitors through the Microelectronics and Computer Technology Corporation

(MCC), the research joint venture or consortium mentioned in Chapter 7. Ten companies—including Control Data, Honeywell, RCA, and Sperry—provided initial funding of $600 million for MCC, giving MCC creative muscle with scores of their brightest scientists and engineers. Bill Norris and collaborators chose an unusual individual as the first head of MCC: ex-spy chief Bobby Inman. As a former National Security Agency Chief, number-two man at the CIA, Naval Intelligence Director, and four-star Admiral, Inman seemed an unlikely candidate to head a bold experiment in competitive collaboration. However, he brought to the job a track record of forging agreements among rivals, which would help him in persuading competitors that collaboration and cooperation could win them long-term gains. At the NSA and CIA he developed an unequaled reputation for mediating among warring factions within the U.S. intelligence community and getting them to rally around common causes. Putting the mission or common purpose ahead of self-interest, he mastered the art of consensus building, a skill sorely needed to marshal MCC's jealous competitors behind a cooperative arrangement that could help them create the information-handling technologies of the future. If the plan worked, MCC would be inventing the opportunities, but supporting members would be developing specific products. In this way, all participants might enjoy equal access to research and development findings, then subsequently develop those findings independently for three years. After this "ceasefire" they could sell the results to companies outside the consortium.

Can such an unprecedented experiment actually be successful? It seems to be. The number of MCC affiliates has risen from ten to twenty-one, as newcomers like Kodak, 3M, and Bellcore (the research arm of the twenty-two Bell operating companies) have come aboard. Now approximately 300 MCC scientists are working on projects in a number of areas, including semiconductor manufacturing, computer architecture, and computer-aided design. Inman's Washington contacts and access to Congress aided lobbying for a bill that would protect companies involved in joint research endeavors from antitrust suits, a bill President Reagan eventually signed into law. MCC's facilities in Austin, Texas have received a steady stream of visitors, as corporate representatives from companies in the steel, machine tools, defense electronics, and other industries have come to study this new "model" for competitive collaboration. While MCC's achievement cannot be fully evaluated for many years, it has set an important precedent. In fact, the Department of Commerce has recently been negotiating with the Anti-Trust Division of the Department of Justice to protect still other types of corporate cooperation.

Winning Through Collaboration

As we have seen, American enterprise has steadily evolved the market economy model of freely trading production and consumption units that intersect and change almost daily, until a large number of loosely collaborating entities have come into being, from huge organizations operating multiproduct and multinational firms to agricultural coops, trade associations, banking consortiums, labor unions, stock exchanges (which are nothing more than cooperatives operating according to a set of rules that permit constructive competition), and professional licensing. Clearly, business has relied more and more on cooperation without unduly damaging free enterprise. If we continue in this direction toward mutually productive collaboration, all stakeholders will benefit.

We think research joint ventures, negotiated marketing arrangements, coordinating trade associations, resource pooling cartels, consortiums, unions, coops, and a myriad of formal and informal collaborations will increasingly characterize corporate competitive behavior, allowing formerly hostile organizations to achieve the broader perspective that self-success comes from the success of all. In recent years Japan and other countries have proven that the coordination of research and development and the subsequent sharing of findings and information among all stakeholders in an industry make it possible not only to reduce the overall costs of technological advancement but also to accelerate the introduction of new products to the marketplace. Does this mean that Americans should replace free markets with planned markets? Not at all. But business leaders should begin practicing *selective* coordination. Not all industries will require the same level of coordination. In some small or highly specialized fields, win-win competition can come about with little or no coordination, while in more complex international industries, intense collaboration is needed. In the future, competitors, not governments, should resolve the thorny problems of negotiation, coordination, or planning to avoid the debilitating bureaucratic red tape that government involvement invariably creates. Free market environments will depend on all stakeholders—competitors, customers, suppliers, governments, communities, and nations—striving for mutual benefits.

If cutthroat teammates devise strategies that gain them competitive advantage without needlessly damaging or destroying each other, win-win competition can become the global norm. This does not mean that businesses will not fail in the next millennium, because every business should retain as much right to fail as to succeed. However, the combative, competitive mentality based on a "survival of the fittest" philosophy should give way to a more enlightened view that everyone *can* win. Such an encompassing strategic mind-set would cause executives to consider competitive overlap (areas where competitors' products, services, customer segments, or markets compete directly) and competitive interdependence (areas where interdependent relationships among competitors will benefit all stakeholders in the industry) as much as they once considered conventional competitive advantage. By avoiding competitive overlap and developing competitive interdependence, the Future 500 can enhance their competitive advantages. Central to this new mentality will be an extensive broadening of the success spectrum. The differences between marginally and exceptionally profitable organizations should increase dramatically, creating every imaginable gradation and hue of success and profitability. However, we think those who fail won't do so at the hands of ruthless rivals but as a result of their own inability to practice complexity management.

The transformation to win-win competition cannot occur magically or overnight. Rather, it will depend on the completion of all the other transformations discussed in this book. However, as in the other areas, applying the precepts of complexity management to this specific dimension of the future will reap great rewards.

Win-Win Competition and Complexity Management

Our review of competitive history reveals a steady evolution of the means with which business men and women gain advantage over competitors. In the early eras they operated through monopolies or cartels, which the government eventually prohibited in order to protect free enterprise. Perhaps had the monopolies and cartels behaved in a genuinely benevolent fashion and displayed concern for the well-being of all stakeholders, including their smaller rivals, U.S. antitrust laws would not have come into play. While some form of collaboration and cooperation has always offered a means for increasing efficiency, removing waste, and eliminating unnecessary duplication, it has also allowed certain individuals and firms to gather personal gain at the expense of others. Win-win competition requires a higher level of moral and ethical responsibility and a vigilance against the abuse of power. Recently, collaborative competition has begun as a response to an increasingly interrelated world, but for it to succeed, executives must remain ever alert for abuses that could prompt additional legislation.

As we discussed earlier, we believe that the growing interdependence of companies and countries argues against rugged individualism, which can turn into an expensive and wasteful indulgence. Yes, free enterprise and the rights of individuals should permeate our corporate way of life, but so, too, should innovative and mutually benefitting competitive arrangements that further the purposes of all members of the corporate system.

As we stressed at the beginning of this chapter, the overriding concern of executives desiring to collaborate with competitors will be how to direct, organize and control such efforts. While the legal restrictions governing various forms of collaboration seem to be loosening, most executives, raised in this century's climate of aggressive head-to-head competition, will not find it easy to cooperate with competitors, nor will they always be able to avoid potential abuses. However, Control Data's push to establish MCC, the chemical industry's creation of CIIT, IBM's host of alliances, GM's joint ventures, Coke's connecting with bottlers, Goodrich's joint tiremaking facilities with Uniroyal, and Delta's merger with

Western all point to the fact that companies can balance competition with collaboration to the benefit of their entire industries.

We expect such activities to continue and even proliferate in the future. If they do, several specific issues will arise. For example, Control Data and MCC will probably face the difficult issue of equitably sharing the benefits of a major breakthrough, because tremendous new opportunities can easily destroy previously collective-minded motivations. In the chemical industry, how far can and should CIIT go toward fostering self-regulation? At IBM, how can the company bring order to its complex alliances for the benefit of all those affected by them? For GM, what lies beyond the current round of worldwide joint ventures? When Coke has bought all the available bottlers, will it still wage the "cola wars"? Should Goodrich share other kinds of facilities or functions with Uniroyal? Can Delta, along with the rest of the airline industry, resolve the sticky issues of deregulation?

We offer complexity management as a partial answer to these sorts of questions. Let's consider how a perspective, power, and pivot manager might address this dimension of the future.

Applying Perspective Management

Perspective management allows an industry or group of competitors to uncover a common purpose without sacrificing individual distinctiveness. Below are a few of the ways executives might apply perspective management to competitive issues:

- Work to formulate a set of mutually benefitting principles at the industry or market level that all industry or market participants can heartily accept. For example, the chemical industry's CIIT could coordinate the development of such a statement of industry principles for review by each participant.

- Begin communicating, within the limits of existing laws, more frequently and in more depth with executives from competing companies to determine areas of potential collaboration or cooperation that would benefit all affected stakeholders. For example, Goodrich might communicate with other tire industry competitors to determine whether other joint endeavors might be appropriate and beneficial.

- Analyze the potential advantages and disadvantages of greater competitive collaboration in an industry, summarize findings and conclusions in an industry white paper, and circulate it as a catalyst for further discussion. For example, Delta could undertake a study of airline competition to analyze areas of benefit and areas of waste and negative factors.

Applying Power Management

Power management awards people freedom to devise their own methods of collaboration within predetermined guidelines. Consider the following suggestions for applying power management:

- Lobby for legislation that will empower industry and competitor associations to assume more of the burden and responsibility for setting and monitoring competitive practices. For example, Delta might lobby for the creation of an airline industry association like CIIT to begin self-monitoring activities.

- Exploit the existing freedom to experiment with different types of collaborative arrangements, within current legal bounds, such as joint ventures, industry councils, company alliances, cooperative research, shared facilities or functions, long-term contracts, etc., to further the awareness and appreciation of win-win competition. For example, IBM could assume a leadership role in experimenting with a variety of collaborative arrangements, sharing the pros and cons of each with companies inside and outside its industry.

- Promote a freer sharing of ideas by establishing a corporate clearinghouse for ideas that will foster win-win competition and encourage competitors to do the same. Join forces to create a similar sort of clearinghouse at the industrial level with the participation of appropriate government agencies. For example, MCC could begin soliciting such recommendations from industry participants as a way of diffusing potential battles over future technologies.

Applying Pivot Management

Pivot management emphasizes key individuals networking to improve the competitive environment for the greater collective well-being. Pivot managers might:

• Encourage individual competitors to avoid wasteful head-on competitive battles. Competitive advantage does not have to come at the expense of other stakeholders. In fact, the healthier all the companies in a given market become, the healthier the entire economy becomes. For example, GM might lead the way in the auto industry by continuing its search for high-tech personal transportation alternatives for the future and by working to establish an atmosphere of greater differentiation throughout the industry.

• Develop a network of relationships with competitor, industry, government, and community opinion leaders who share common perspectives on win-win competition. Work together in accordance with legally acceptable practices to find ways for all stakeholders in an industry to reap the benefits of superior performance and maximum fulfillment. GM might lead a worldwide networking effort with auto industry companies designed to find ways to make cars better, safer, and more efficient through certain forms of collaboration.

• Make sure their own companies eliminate any competitive practices that promote abuses of power, position, or knowledge. For example, IBM might share research and development findings more freely with the industry in an effort to assist competitors as well as allow for alliances that will benefit IBM.

In the final analysis, win-win competition will come about when executives and managers recognize that a commitment to collective well-being within a free enterprise economy can raise the level of any one company's well-being. Although attempts to achieve such a goal have historically involved replacing free enterprise with a controlled economy, the Future 500 must forge cooperation without compromising freedom.

CHAPTER EIGHT

Creative Capitalists: Drawing Investors into the Corporate Environment

Wall Street: A thoroughfare that begins in a graveyard and ends in a river.
—H. L. MENCKEN

Patient Capital

In 1985 Merrill Lynch celebrated its 100th year in business, and it used the occasion to create a new statement of purpose, one that might see it successfully through another century: "Our mission is to be a client-focused, worldwide financial services organization, striving for excellence by serving the needs of individuals, corporations, governments, and institutions. Our objective is to be the acknowledged leader in the value we offer our clients, the returns we offer our shareholders, and the rewards we offer our employees. This then will be our legacy of leadership."

This new mission statement has stimulated far-reaching changes at Merrill Lynch. For example, in the past, the firm's broker incentive system rewarded brokers for selling clients the financial services Merrill Lynch had targeted for them, not necessarily those the clients really needed. Basically, Merrill Lynch paid little more than lip service to the idea of getting to know customers and identifying their needs. Then, in February, 1986 Merrill restructured its broker compensation system to reflect a genuine attempt to develop strong long-term client-firm relation-ships, even if it attained that goal at the expense of client-broker relationships.

The new compensation plan reflects the firm's increased em-phasis on marketing: Merrill wants to get across the message that it exists to help individuals and businesses solve problems, not just to sell them financial products. With the competition between investment houses heating up, Merrill hopes to stake out a repu-tation as the most concerned manager of a client's total financial needs.

The company also intends to excel in both retail and capital markets. While Merrill Lynch has historically offered a model of the strong, stable, and sizable financial institution, with an exten-sive retail network catering to the small investor, now it wants to carve out a larger piece of the institutional market. *Business Week* said of Kenneth H. Miller, head of Merrill Lynch's Capital Mar-kets: "Miller makes no bones about his desire to prove that he can pull off a major takeover as successfully as such other investment bankers as First Boston Corp.'s Bruce J. Wasserstein. . . . Capital Markets is also trying to prove that Merrill Lynch can pull off a leveraged management buy-out as cleanly as the acknowledged leader, Kohlberg, Kravis, Roberts & Co."

Merrill Lynch's current chairman and CEO, William Schreyer, explained the company's decision to establish Consumer Markets and Capital Markets as two stand-alone business units by saying, "Having a two-organization set-up is the only way, if you're going to focus on the two major customer groups. But it's absolutely vital to have a linking mechanism. In our set-up, that's got to be the parent company. The separate but joint efforts, with each group lending strength to the other, must underlie the drive to demonstrate decisively that a firm can be tops on both the retail and capital markets side of the Street."

We think that Merrill's ranking among the Future 500 will de-pend on its ability to meet the changing needs of a broad base of investors and corporate clients while setting a new direction for Wall Street.

At a time when the typical portfolio of an institutional investor experiences an annual turnover rate of 50 percent and the port-folios of smaller investors experience a 200 percent-plus annual turnover rate, American business must find new ways of getting the kind of long-term, patient capital it needs to develop long-term corporate strategies for competing in the global market-place.

By both direct and indirect means, firms like Merrill Lynch have caused corporations throughout the world to search for better ways of financing their enterprises. Unfortunately, the majority of such endeavors have come up short, leaving executives and their companies thirsting for new answers. Consider three cases in point: Fred Meyer, Eastern Air Lines, and Honda.

Fred Meyer, Inc., a national discount retailing chain, went private a few years ago with the help of Kohlberg, Kravis, Roberts & Company, a leader in the field of leveraged and management buyouts. Taking the company private could supposedly bring new incentives to management, increase employee productivity, improve service to customers, and achieve measurable gains in asset utilization for all stakeholders. Unfortunately, it did not, because going private simply turned out to be just another financial manipulation that distorted the picture of real performance. Kohlberg, Kravis paid a 92 percent premium over market price in the Fred Meyer buyout. Afterward, interest expense went from $1 million to $29 million over a two-year period, store operating costs increased 155 percent because the new Fred Meyer no longer owned the real estate on which it operated, and tax deductions skyrocketed (a major motivation behind the transaction), placing the company in a net loss position from a tax standpoint. The financing of the buyout was accomplished in large part through tax-generated cash flows. Now, the new Fred Meyer wants to go public again. Millions of dollars changed hands in this transaction, but no one assumed any additional risk, and store operations didn't change. In the end, financial maneuverings created a false sense of progress, but no real added value.

Eastern Air Lines has pursued another contemporary financing gambit, employee ownership, as a means to increase productivity, build commitment to a common purpose, and integrate investor and company perspectives. Employees at Eastern, owning almost 25 percent of the stock, have seated four representatives on the board, but their presence has not prevented new labor-management fights, short-sighted decision making, and a tearing apart of the corporate culture at Eastern.

At an Ohio assembly line, American workers build Honda Accords as good as or better than Japanese-made equivalents, demonstrating that American workers can out-compete anyone in the world. However, the profits earned at the Ohio plant belong to Japanese, not American, investors. The Japanese, willing to invest time and money to engineer improved cars, have proven the value of patient capital. In fact, Japanese institutional portfolios turn over at rates one-half to one-fourth of American rates. In general, Japanese investors often forego current earnings in favor of future expansion and longer-term gains.

In light of the continuing struggle to find better ways of helping investors develop longer-term investment outlooks that permit managers to formulate and implement longer-term corporate strategies, let's consider the history of equity financing. That perspective will reveal how complexity management might benefit company-investor relationships.

The Historical Influence of Investors on Business

At the beginning of the twentieth century, investors and managers functioned as two separate and distinct groups. Prior to this period their inseparability had made communication and coordination simple, particularly since most businesses were relatively small enterprises. But with the beginning of the century, the skills and interests of the two groups began to differ.

In the diagram on page 157 you can compare the management eras presented in Chapter 2 with the eras of corporate financing.

Owner-Manager Separation (1890–1935)

Before the rise of the large firm, owners usually managed their businesses directly, but as organizations became larger and more complex, and as incorporation replaced sole proprietorships and partnerships, management became the domain of professionals rather than owners. Firms growing large through vertical integration didn't need to sell stock for capital because they generated sufficient income to support all of their fixed and variable costs through high-volume output. In these cases, the entrepreneurs who created the firms, their families, and their close associates retained stock ownership and continued to exercise full control over operational decisions. However, firms that grew large

Corporate Financing Eras

1890	1910	1930	1950	1970	1990	2010
	Owner-Manager Separation		Wall Street's Rise Through Public Ownership	Corporate Manipulation and Short-Term Investor Expectations	Redirecting Wall Street	Long-Term Investor-Company Relationships
	Structure		Productivity	Systems · Strategy · Culture · Innovation	Leadership	Complexity Management

Management Eras

through horizontal mergers found their ownership dispersing at the outset. When merger "trusts" or holding companies began consolidating into single corporations in the 1890s, they began issuing stock to raise necessary capital. As a result the New York Stock Exchange became a central player in the capitalization game. The success of industrial securities between 1890 and 1903 enhanced their acceptance among investors, and before long all large merger corporations had investors, financiers, and speculators sitting on administrative boards along with the founding entrepreneurs.

Owners in all of the large firms, whether vertically integrated or horizontally combined, lacked many of the new management skills needed to control all aspects of operations, and salaried managers, who seldom owned much stock, quickly filled lower and middle management positions. As organizations continued to grow in the early 1900s, ownership became ever more widely scattered, until the stockholders exercised very little influence over daily administrative decisions. Managers now ran the big companies.

The decade from 1910 to 1920 brought an end to the era of mergers and acquisitions. Unstable economic conditions and the growth of national monopolies such as Standard Oil and Du Pont had resulted in such high levels of merger and acquisition activity that government increased enforcement of antimonopoly legislation. Denied the prospect of monopoly markets, companies turned to diversification and new product development, a thrust that intensified when America emerged as a world power after World War I. Although firms still could find readily available financing, many of the new investment arrangements proved highly risky and speculative. Those risks became painfully apparent during the Great Depression, after which legislation demanded greater fiscal responsibility in the management of stock transactions.

In 1907 Charles E. Merrill came to New York after studying at Amherst and the University of Michigan Law School. While working at a textile firm in New York, young Merrill exercised at the Twenty-third Street YMCA, where he met Edmund C. Lynch. At the time, Lynch, a Johns Hopkins graduate, was working as a salesman for Liquid Carbonic and just happened to be looking for a roommate. Merrill and Lynch shared a boardinghouse room for a short time.

Merrill gained his first Wall Street experience in 1909 with George H. Burr & Co., a commercial paper firm, where the young Merrill served as *the* bond department. During his years at Burr, Merrill began formulating his own ideas about the investment business, and in a November 1911 article in *Leslie's Weekly*, addressed to "Mr. Average Investor," he stressed the need for a broker to consider the customer's circumstances and objectives when recommending investments. He also emphasized the importance of appealing to a greater number of investors: "Having thousands of customers scattered throughout the United States is infinitely preferable to being dependent upon the fluctuating buying power of a smaller and perhaps on the whole wealthier group of investors in any one section." After Merrill set up his own offices at 7 Wall Street, he persuaded his friend, Ed Lynch, who had been filling the bond position at Burr & Co., to join him.

In 1915 Merrill Lynch & Co. hung out its shingle. Taking advantage of the increasing separation between investors and managers, the company specialized in the distribution of new securities for growing companies. According to a company publication, *A Legacy of Leadership*, "The partners made a powerful team with complementary strengths." And one biographer observed: "Merrill could imagine the possibilities; Lynch imagined what might go wrong in a malevolent world. Lynch put his hands to the wheel of every proposal and took it on a verbal shakedown cruise. He would accept no airy generalities and his uncanny legalistic instinct was a terror to captious corporation lawyers. Merrill would evolve the principles of an agreement. Lynch would exact a hidebound contract."

In 1919 Ed Pierce, a partner with A. A. Housman & Co. and an eventual partner of Merrill, Lynch, spent a great deal of time trying to get his firm into the "wire business," the long-distance selling of securities. When Pierce's logic prevailed, he found four brokers in the midwest who agreed to subscribe to the new wire service, and within a few years A. A. Housman became the biggest wire house in the nation. Soon Pierce struck out on his own.

Back at Merrill Lynch, according to corporate historians, "More than half of the seventy-two underwritings Merrill Lynch brought to the market in the postwar decade were for retailers . . . the concentration was on new growth industries not yet quite accepted by the financial establishment." And another chronicler added: "The firm was not recognized by the panjandrums of the

Street as being important enough to participate in syndicates for the blue chips in heavy industry." Setting its sights on "Mr. Average Investor," Merrill Lynch advertised more than any other Wall Street brokerage house. In 1928, according to the firm's corporate history, "Charles Merrill was among those who sensed the oncoming storm. Worried about the speculative excess of the stock market boom, he advised his customers on March 31, 1928, 'Now is the time to get out of debt. Sell enough securities to lighten your obligations or pay them off entirely.' He made it plain: 'We do not urge that you sell securities indiscriminately, but we do advise in no uncertain terms that you take advantage of present high prices and put your own financial house in order.' Merrill invited President Calvin Coolidge (a fellow Amherst man) to join the firm after his term in office ended. The former president's duties would consist of voicing warnings against excessive speculation and overextension of credit.

In 1930 Merrill Lynch sold its brokerage business, including offices, partners, and employees, to E. A. Pierce and Co. The remaining portion of Merrill Lynch & Co. would focus strictly on investment banking. In the early 1930s, E. A. Pierce and Co. took over more than a dozen other firms. According to an old Wall Street joke, "Germany's on the verge of collapse—but don't worry, E. A. Pierce will take it over." In 1934, President Roosevelt signed the Securities Exchange Act, designed to bring needed order and control to Wall Street finagling. However, by this time the investor-company-management-broker-investment banker machinery that would shape the financial future of an age had been set in motion.

Wall Street's Rise Through Public Ownership (1935–1960)

This era established the traditions of conservative corporate financing associated with scientific rational management. Since American business faced no serious foreign competitors, had built unbeatable technological advantages, and enjoyed cheap natural resources, it could afford more conservative strategies. Steady expansion and growth reinforced relationships between investors and managers that involved little more than measuring return on investment. In light of the advantages American industries had created, no one could see any excuse for poor returns.

As corporations continued to prosper, decentralized control structures became necessary, and these structures strengthened the emphasis on short-term financial indicators by encouraging the evaluation of each division as a profit center. Consequently, measures of managerial performance took return on investment strongly into account.

At the end of this period, the majority of large industrial corporations in the United States were publicly held. By 1963 neither individuals and their families nor any other small group owned more than 80 percent of the stock of any of the 200 largest non-financial corporations. In only 5 did a family or group own 50 percent of the stock, and in another 26, a family or group maintained minority control by owning 10 percent to 50 percent of the stock. Of the 200 corporations, 169, or 85 percent, were publicly owned and controlled by management. Investors in these firms generally demanded such short-term performance that a quarter-by-quarter earnings-per-share mentality shaped virtually every management action.

In 1939 the house of E. A. Pierce nearly collapsed, and a partner, Winthrop Smith, urged his partners to invite Charles Merrill to join them. When Merrill did so in 1940, the company reorganized itself under the name Merrill Lynch, E. A. Pierce and Cassatt. Alpheus Beane joined the company soon thereafter, prompting yet another name change to Merrill Lynch, Pierce, Fenner & Beane. After Charlie Merrill reviewed the results of a public opinion survey on financial markets that showed stockbrokers to have gained a general reputation for dishonesty, he began designing a blueprint for a new company, catering to a new mass of investors, that would take Wall Street to Main Street.

As he had earlier in his career, Merrill spent a lot of money advertising this new philosophy. The first announcement heralded a Statement of Basic Policy, otherwise known as the firm's "Ten Commandments." The first commandment stated that "The interests of our customers MUST come first." Another, putting forth the firm's commitment to supplying research information and market education, proclaimed: "Investigate—Then Invest." Years later, business historian Robert Sobel would write in *The Big Board:* "Merrill Lynch was the creation of Charles Merrill, who, along with Jay Cooke and J. P. Morgan, Sr., was one of the district's most important figures. Cooke pioneered the distribution of large issues, Morgan made the Street the center of the nation, and Merrill was able to accomplish something the New Deal attempted and could not carry through; he brought Wall Street to the nation. More than any other person, Merrill made the purchase of securities 'respectable' after the lean thirties. He introduced the Street to the small investor, and was the best symbol of what was later to be called People's Capitalism."

Merrill Lynch, Pierce, Fenner & Beane provided the model for other securities retailers. Committed to providing solid research so investors could make knowledgeable decisions, Merrill Lynch led the way by establishing a large fact-finding and research operation. However, "Mr. Average Investor" could assimilate only a small amount of information on a company, so Merrill Lynch and other brokerage houses directed their fact finding and research at the easiest to comprehend of all corporate data: the bottom line.

In the mid to late 1950s the New York Stock Exchange fueled Merrill Lynch's growth by becoming an enthusiastic advocate of broader stock ownership. In fact, the president of the NYSE launched his own campaign to get more of the public to "Own Your Share of American Business."

When Charles Merrill died in October 1956, Winthrop H. Smith took over as Directing and Managing Partner. The next year Alph Beane withdrew from the firm, and the remaining partners decided to pay tribute to Win Smith by replacing Beane's name on the masthead. In 1959, Merrill Lynch, Pierce, Fenner & Smith, with its 6,500 employees, came into being.

Corporate Manipulation and Short-Term Investor Expectations (1960–1980)

The 1960s saw a new kind of investor gain prominence: the corporation itself. Instead of expanding by creating new product lines, many firms started buying companies in different industries and were soon creating the new-style conglomerates. Mergers and acquisitions offered a quick and acceptable way for corporations to manipulate their earnings, net worth, and stock price, giving the appearance, not always accurate, of continued growth and development. Usually, the acquired firms continued to function as before, although sometimes the owner company would introduce its own management techniques.

As foreign competition effectively penetrated traditional

American markets, as business conditions grew less stable and predictable, and as the cost of resources skyrocketed in the 1970s, many American firms responded by expanding their portfolios, trying to rejuvenate flagging American strategic advantages. Dominated by executives with financial or legal skills, these companies hoped mergers would hedge their bets, because diverse businesses operating under one corporate aegis might offset each other: an upturn in one industry could theoretically compensate for a downturn in another. Harvard Business School professors Robert Hayes and William Abernathy, writing in the *Harvard Business Review,* commented on this trend, "In 1978 alone there were some 80 mergers involving companies with assets in excess of $100 million each, in 1979 there were almost 100. This represents roughly $20 billion in transfers of large companies from one owner to another . . . There are perfectly good reasons for this flurry of activity. It is entirely natural for financially (or legally) trained managers to concentrate on essentially financial (or legal) activities. It is also natural for managers who subscribe to the portfolio 'law of large numbers' to seek to reduce total corporate risk by parceling it out among a sufficiently large number of separate product lines, businesses, or technologies. Under certain conditions it may very well make sense to buy rather than build new plants or modernize existing ones. Mergers are obviously an exciting game, they tend to produce fairly quick and decisive results, and they offer the kind of public recognition that helps careers along." All this merger and acquisition activity, with its emphasis on quick returns for investors, further entrenched the expectation of quick financial gains.

At the same time, brokerage firms developed, packaged, and arranged ever more creative financial deals, continuing the flow of commissions to brokers and revenues to the brokerage houses while spurring corporations to bend over backward to achieve short-term returns. Their success further increased the near-sighted expectations of investors, which led in turn to even more outlandish corporate manipulations. Unfortunately, the short-range perspective did virtually nothing to curb or reverse the erosion of American businesses' global competitiveness. In fact, management's preoccupation with Wall Street games, more respectfully referred to as capital-market practices, actually contributed to the erosion. Instead of focusing on product/market needs, long-term strategy, or organizational effectiveness, executives chased Wall Street's standards for immediate returns to share-holders with financial manipulations that never addressed the roots of their problems.

During this era stock trading volume escalated rapidly, and the complexion of financial markets began changing as institutional investors became increasingly important. The national mood—exacerbated by John Kennedy's assassination, Viet Nam, and a restless younger generation—shifted from optimism to cynicism. To overcome such cynicism, corporations renewed efforts to make good on their promises of continued growth and profitability, but they did so in the usual superficial and manipulative ways.

Merrill Lynch responded to the economic and social climate of the day by aggressively expanding internationally and domestically, improving its business development strategy through an organized system of calling on corporate prospects, and increasing the variety of services offered to customers.

Mike McCarthy became chairman and CEO in 1961. One senior executive, John Fitzgerald, recalls the period in the company's own account of its history: "McCarthy's idea of taking advantage of the broad market that was out there, pushing aggressively to get Merrill Lynch into the smaller cities and at the same time adding second, third, and fourth offices in major cities, was very key to what later developed in terms of profitability." Thanks to the company's distribution prowess (159 offices) Merrill Lynch became, in terms of volume, one of the largest under-writers.

The company had positioned itself beautifully to take the glamour and growth stocks of Wall Street to middle America, and in keeping with financial practices of the era, it saw mergers and acquisitions as a quick route to both glamour and growth. By 1968, acquisitions represented 44 percent of the total investment in American business, up from 9 percent a decade earlier. At Merrill Lynch, net income rose to $55 million by 1967. The company itself continued to acquire other companies, such as Lionel D. Edie & Company, which added investment counseling, economic consulting services, and two mutual funds to the mix. In the next few years Merrill Lynch would go from zero sales in mutual funds distribution to the leader in the industry with $217 million in sales.

In its 1969 annual report, Merrill Lynch described the firm's future plans: "We have decided to grow by offering additional services to the investor while at the same time strengthening our traditional brokerage and underwriting business. We intend to expand the firm, through acquisitions and internal development, into a one-stop investment and estate-planning institution. This means providing all of the money management services we can to as many customers as we can reach."

Don Regan became chairman and CEO in 1970. In 1971, the award-winning commercial, "Merrill Lynch is Bullish on America" swept onto American television screens during a Pirates-Orioles World Series game. Merrill Lynch's aggressive marketing posture spurred investors' expectations and corporations' manipulations. While the oil crisis and recession of the early 1970s tempered stock market machinations, it didn't thwart Merrill Lynch's stampede. According to the company's account: "Don Regan was one of the first to note the changing status of the securities industry, and that of the larger financial services industry of which it was a part. The trend was customer driven. Customers were after integrated planning and management of their financial affairs and receptive to new services and packages of financial instruments that help meet their needs. And they couldn't care less whether the services they wanted were supplied by a banker, a broker, an insurance company—or a merchant."

In 1977, Merrill Lynch introduced its Cash Management Account (CMA), which, according to the company, was "a unique combination of a brokerage margin account, a money market fund into which any cash generated in the account is automatically placed, and check writing and VISA card access to the cash or borrowing power in the account."

The next year Merrill Lynch acquired White, Weld & Co., a prominent securities firm whose strength lay in investment banking. White, Weld's many large accounts enhanced Capital Markets strength and furthered Merrill Lynch's objective of achieving a more upscale retail market mix. At the same time Merrill Lynch began building up its own overall capital-markets strengths by becoming more involved in the financing of mergers and acquisitions, venture capital operations, and increased trading activities.

Despite the fact that the company experienced the economic ups and downs that characterized this era, it also succeeded in giving its customers what they wanted: financial gains. Between 1970 and 1980, revenues increased sixfold to $3 billion, with earnings up fivefold to $218 million. And Merrill Lynch's own shareholders' equity shot from $300 million to $970 million. In the aftermath of the company's first public offering of its own stock in June 1971, Merrill Lynch did for its own investors what it had long been pushing America's corporations to do for theirs.

Redirecting Wall Street (1980–Late 1990s)

American businesses' renewed and intensified passion for mergers and acquisitions began to raise questions among investors as disastrous combinations began to occur. In many instances, executives familiar with certain types of technologies, competitors, markets, and customers could not transfer their skills to managing other types, and before long they began divesting their organizations of units that did not match their abilities. According to Hayes and Abernathy, "Unfortunately, the general American penchant for separating and simplifying has tended to encourage a diversification away from core technologies and markets to a much greater degree than is true in Europe or Japan. U.S. managers appear to have an inordinate faith in the portfolio law of large numbers—that is, by amassing enough product lines, technologies, and businesses, one will be cushioned against the random setbacks that occur in life. This might be true for portfolios of stocks and bonds, where there is considerable evidence that setbacks are random. Businesses, however, are subject not only to random setbacks such as strikes and shortages, but also to carefully orchestrated attacks by competitors, who focus all their resources and energies into one set of activities." In response, they suggested, business must secure more and more creative financing that not only meets their immediate and long-range needs but that encourages investors to adopt longer-term expectations.

In an insightful working paper Lee Tom Perry, a professor in Brigham Young University's Organizational Behavior Program, identified some key financial issues today's executives must consider. First, he insists, investors must overcome their ignorance. Knowing too little about cutting-edge technologies or the strategic risks associated with a particular technology, or the potential of rival, alternative technologies, investors often perceive greater risk than, in fact, exists. Second, investors need adequate monitoring information, but the tried-and-true short-term financial performance criteria used in the past no longer suffice. For ex-

ample, if sizable chunks of funding go to research and development on technologies with promising long-term potentials, but
with no near-term gain, traditional investors may not understand
the potential competitive advantage. According to Perry: "There
is [no] guarantee that the vision will ever be realized; not even
under the best of circumstances is it likely that the break-even
point will be reached, much less surpassed, in the near-term future. For this reason, efforts to develop radical product innovation require both faith and a significant, long-term commitment
of resources." Investors who feel more comfortable with a conservative approach that includes developing existing technologies
and markets and increasing production efficiency will prefer decisions that in the long run can actually undermine the creativity
and innovative ability of the firm.

Perry goes on to note that in the highly innovative firms he has
studied, innovation and creativity require levels of waste, inefficiency, and slack resources that would give any rational manager
pause. And if the manager worries, the investor panics. Healthy,
respectful relationships among managers and investors may forestall the panic, but for how long? Research in this area, and in the
field of mergers and acquisitions, suggests that investors or owners tend to let management run the show as long as things go
well. However, when performance falters, so does the investors'
faith in the managers. Attitudes often change rapidly, and they
typically shift toward more conservative strategies.

To complicate this situation, some managers tend to behave
more conservatively and traditionally than others, often undermining ideological consensus in times of stress. When a crisis
strikes the firm, investors can quickly decide that the more reactionary managers were correct all along, and that the more liberal
heads should roll. In this way a strong culture committed to long-
term gains often falls victim to more conventional wisdom.

In January 1981, when Don Regan resigned his chairmanship
of Merrill Lynch to serve as Ronald Reagan's Secretary of the
Treasury, Roger Birk succeeded him as chairman and CEO. With
regulatory red tape loosening and competition increasing, Merrill
Lynch needed to find a new corporate direction. Although the
company continued building up its capital-markets strengths,
putting capital at risk by financing mergers and acquisitions, venture capital operations, leveraged buyouts, and other creative financing projects, Merrill Lynch chose to move away from a

"product approach" to a more "customer-oriented" or "market-centered" one.

By late 1983 security industry earnings had plunged, with Merrill Lynch reporting a 67 percent drop in third-quarter earnings compared to the previous year. *Business Week* reported that Merrill Lynch was in a "traumatic transition." With the old lines between financial services blurred by deregulation, the firm now found itself competing directly with Sears Roebuck and Citicorp. *Business Week* observed: "In recent years, Merrill has proved itself the equal of anyone in innovating financial products and services. But in the way it delivers them to consumers, in its compensation methods, and in its culture, Merrill Lynch remains quintessentially a brokerage house." The article went on to say that "Merrill's attempt to strike a balance between old Wall Street and the emergence of one-stop financial shopping has trapped it in a truly nasty dilemma."

The dilemma had forced the company to pump a lot of resources and energy into expanding its retail system, but because most of its offerings are funneled through brokers who receive sizable commissions, costs have gotten out of hand. If the firm tampers with the retail sales organization, it risks losing a lot of customers because customers retain more loyalty to their personal brokers than to the company.

Again quoting *Business Week*, "[Merrill Lynch had] extended its lead by building a vast system of retail branches and a huge corps of account executives known for a Marine-like *esprit de corps* and pride in 'Mother Merrill.' The company used its retail-distribution muscle to leverage moves into the institutional brokerage business, trading, and investment banking."

In early 1984, Merrill Lynch's strategic planners concluded that the company needed to take a break from "headlong expansionism." In order to prosper in the deregulated world, Merrill Lynch would have to transform itself from a sales machine to a marketing organization responsive to customers' needs. To gear up for this, Merrill Lynch reorganized and created the two separate units mentioned at the beginning of this chapter—Individual Services Group to serve the retail market and Capital Markets to work the corporate-institutional market.

In 1984, Merrill's president, William Schreyer, told *Fortune* that "after a two-year study, it became clear that the emphasis in the future must be on what the customer needs and demands and not what a financial service company wishes to offer." *Fortune* went on to say that "[Don] Regan first proposed this idea at a contentious 1976 company meeting in Florida. Little has come of it since. The very idea of listening to customers goes against the grain at Merrill Lynch. Since Charles Merrill founded the firm in 1914, it has relied primarily on the legendary ability of those hard-driving account executives to push products out the door."

In 1985, Merrill Lynch opened a "Financial Center" as the base for a new marketing program similar in concept to the "Financial Supermarket" of the seventies but involving much more client counseling. Instead of just offering a wide variety of financial services and letting clients choose what they want, the new approach would, in effect, allow customers to pick from the shelves of financial products those that best suited their needs. For its part, Merrill would provide guidance and advice on what items might best benefit a customer.

With the recent emphasis on marketing, most Wall Street brokers find themselves struggling to balance all of their traditional responsibilities with added marketing activities. *Institutional Investor* reported a new buzzword used to describe brokers' compensation on Wall Street: "asset gathering." Charles Amerkanian of National Recruiting Advisors explained, "The big firms are making a dramatic shift away from transactional volume toward a greater emphasis on managing assets in-house and establishing long-term client relationships."

In an effort to secure greater customer loyalty to the firm, Merrill Lynch altered the compensation system for its brokers by reducing the amount brokers received in commissions on stock and bond transactions but entitling them to a share of the income from Merrill Lynch's other financial services such as Cash Management Accounts and second mortgage loans. As Joseph Grano, Merrill's director of national sales, reported in an *Institutional Investor* interview, "We all grew up chasing gross and transaction volume. Now we are looking for long-term client loyalty. We want a sales force that will concentrate on financial service rather than transaction volume, and our compensation system will support that strategy." Moreover, adds Grano, "The new system is good for the broker, good for the customer, and good for the firm. And for the health of the whole Street, I hope everybody follows suit."

More Enduring Investor Company Relationships

As we begin to weigh the future of capital funding and manager-investor relationships, we would like to acknowledge the groundbreaking research of Jay Barney and William Ouchi of the University of California–Los Angeles Graduate School of Business. Traditionally, resource dependence theory defines the relationships between managers and external sources of capital as adversarial ones. Managers who strive to protect their independence and minimize investor control perceive concentrated outside financial influence as a threat. To deal with that threat they:

- Avoid dependence on a small group of investors.
- Avoid situations where an individual or small group of outside investors own a large percentage of the organization's debt or equity.

However, Barney suggests that when some circumstances require a firm to view concentrated ownership of equity more favorably, it should seek to increase rather than decrease external investors' influence on managerial decision making. Normally, he notes, the interests of management and those of external investors can conflict. For example, managerial decision making can both positively and negatively affect a firm's debt and its equity holders; the most adverse decisions include:

- Decisions to maximize personal political power within the firm or within a division or department in that firm.
- Decisions to maximize chances of organizational survival, not only on an individual or departmental level, but also on an organizational level. With "greenmail," for example, managers often undermine the position of equity holders to ward off hostile takeover attempts. While such a strategy clearly strengthens management's hand, it often runs counter to the best interests of equity holders or of the firm itself, since resultant debt-to-equity ratios can easily become a costly handicap.

- Decisions that squander organizational resources on perks for managerial enjoyment or protection.

External investors have developed monitoring strategies to limit the disparity between managerial interests and their own, but ironically, these strategies, too, can be quite costly. Traditionally, investors have relied on periodically reported financial performance information. In some cases, government disclosure regulations or independent auditors insure accurate and timely monitoring, but in many cases the financials can mislead investors or cause them to assess dangerously limited data. To offset suspicion and hostility, managers often use bonding strategies (stronger interpersonal relationships) with powerful external groups, hoping that friendships might overcome doubts about their trustworthiness and decision-making prowess. In either case, Barney and Ouchi note that, given rapidly changing, highly uncertain, and complex business environments, and the difficulty of monitoring the effectiveness of many complex and ambiguous managerial activities, bonding and monitoring strategies cannot guarantee a greater convergence of external groups and internal managers. This, Barney hypothesizes, becomes reflected in the cost of capital made available to a firm, with some extra cost reserved for an inefficiency or waste factor inherent in conflicting interests. If, working together, investors and managers can develop better bonding and monitoring relationships, costs of capital should decline.

Monitoring activities can mean more than studying financial reports. Requests for additional information or contractual arrangements with management that place limits on managerial discretion may also be called for. For example, banks can demand reduced or eliminated dividends and low-risk corporate investments; and third parties, such as government agencies or external auditors, can play an increased role.

However, in some cases, only close, long-term, continuous relationships between internal and external groups will win the day. Barney concludes: "Finally, under some circumstances, the ability of investors to monitor performance (or, similarly, the ability of firms to demonstrate their performance through various bonding mechanisms) through quarterly reports, audits, or investment contracts may be so limited, perhaps due to the complexity and uncertainty of the business, that these, and similar mechanisms of control, will be inadequate."

Newer forms of management-investor relationships include overlapping boards of directors, overlapping management committees, and common cost accounting, all of which Barney calls "clan arrangements," involving systems of values, beliefs, and management styles shared by both the investors and the managers.

With such noncontractual clan relationships interests of investors and managers are less likely to diverge, for they bind the parties together with interpersonal relationships or "human capital investments" that benefit particular transactions. The resultant close, cooperative ties can transcend formal market transactions and make third-party or government intervention unnecessary. Ultimately, therefore, formal organizational boundaries between the firm and its sources of capital become blurred.

Clan relationships between investors and managers do not come about easily. However, as business strategy and leadership become increasingly complex and ambiguous in highly unstable, rapidly changing business environments, these sorts of relationships clearly offer some advantages. Investors, faced with esoteric future technologies and fluctuating market demand, can never rely solely on conventional capital relationships to assure themselves that management has acted in their best interests. But long-range strategic positioning that evolves from vision and leadership rather than rational analysis and forecasting, and close bonds of trust with managers, can help them overcome much of their uneasiness. Given the difficulty and time it takes to cultivate "clan relationships," they tend to work best with a tight-knit rather than widespread groups of investors, but abuses of such close relationships in the past have led to government suspicion and even legal action. However, Barney and others recommend them for the future, provided all partners arm themselves against certain dangers and potential abuses.

For example, close "clan" relationships between a small, dominant group of investors and managers can easily change and expose the managers to risk. Simply stated, investors, preferring to scrutinize financial statements, have generally been intolerant of qualitative programs and policies that make an organization and its culture distinctive, innovative, and ultimately more competitive. This primarily quantitative focus can easily give investors a false sense of security (or alarm) and lead them to ignore the qualitative side of strategy and culture. Karl Weick, in his book *The Social Psychology of Organizing,* warns: "To get the organization into countable measurable form is to strip it of what made it worth counting in the first place."

In the future we think investors must learn to add qualitative concerns to their calculations of acceptable return, and they must become dynamic, innovative, and synchronous components of the corporate environments in which they invest. Let's see how complexity management can help in this crucial undertaking.

Long-Term Investor/Company Relationships and Complexity Management

Our analysis of corporate financing has convinced us of the need for longer-term, more knowledgeable, and more symbiotic relationships between investors, whether individual or institutional, and the companies they help finance. While American business executives recognize the debilitating effects on their organization of short-term, manipulative maneuvers, Wall Street has clung to its short-term measures of performance. However, recent changes that have taken place seem to indicate a desire by both sides to better align their expectations in longer-term relationships.

At the beginning of this chapter we proposed that executives find better ways of helping investors develop longer-term investment outlooks that will permit executives to formulate and implement longer-term corporate strategies, and we used the experiences of Fred Meyer, Eastern Air Lines, Honda, and Merrill Lynch to illustrate varying levels of success in dealing with the issues that arise in the area of investor-company relationships. Most firms face similar issues today, and successfully resolving them will, in part, determine a company's position among the Future 500. Companies like Fred Meyer must cure the financial manipulation syndrome. Going public, then going private, and, then going public again makes little sense if it does nothing but distort the true picture of corporate performance. Eastern Air

Lines must figure out how to make employee ownership work to the benefit of all concerned. To date, employees' 25 percent ownership of the company has not brought the necessary long-term investor orientation. Can Honda and other Japanese companies use their ownership positions in American firms to imbue in them the advantage of patient capital? If they do so, perhaps American firms can find equally patient equity sources inside their own country.

We believe complexity management can help executives successfully tackle issues related to corporate financing, thus developing the creative capitalists of the future.

Applying Perspective Management

Perspective management will help executives integrate and will bind investor and company purposes in long-term investor/company relationships. Specifically, future executives might:

- Report financial results and major business decisions and actions in the context of their companies' long-term strategic directions (twenty years and beyond) in an effort to attract investors who appreciate the value of such long-term thinking. For example, before Fred Meyer goes public again, it could clearly identify and communicate its long-term strategic direction and express a commitment to reporting and explaining financial performance and major business events within that context.

- Devise a plan to buy back publicly traded stock and reissue it to institutional investors who are willing to forego current earnings in favor of future expansion and strength. For example, Merrill Lynch could offer such a service to corporate clients, institutional investors, and groups of individual investors through special long-term equity brokers.

- Make sure privately held companies match owners' expectations for return with management's expectations for funding. Whether conducted formally or informally, matching expectations should be an ongoing concern. Otherwise, a company will almost surely suffer the adverse consequences of hidden agendas, mixed signals, and power struggles. For example, Eastern Air Lines could take steps to rebuild trust levels with employee owners by initiating a dialogue, deriving from an all-out commitment by management, designed to achieve a match in expectations. Otherwise, it would be met with suspicion and even hostility.

Applying Power Management

Executives and managers should identify those stakeholders who deserve the freedom to bring about desired long-term investor/company relationships. They might:

- Identify an investment banking firm willing to help them find the kind and amount of patient capital they desire. For example, diversified financial firms like Shearson/Lehman Brothers, First Boston, and Merrill Lynch have begun promising to deliver greater value and innovative solutions to corporate clients. Perhaps they deserve the chance to make good on their promises.

- Provide institutional investors and investor groups with freer access to company records and plans in exchange for deepened commitment to long-term strategic priorities. At Honda and in Japan, for example, institutional investors habitually practice patience, but in the United States, patience will come only on the heels of freer access to information. Once public again, Fred Meyer could give committed institutional investors free access to company information.

Applying Pivot Management

Pivot management can help executives uncover ways to improve long-term performance of their corporations to increase the fulfillment of both their investors and their companies. They might:

- Build close relationships with individuals representing institutional investors and investor groups to make sure they intimately understand investors' expectations and needs and vice versa. Such relationships will become increasingly important as a means of improving long-term corporate performance and fulfillment on both sides of the investment equation. For example, Merrill Lynch could facilitate such relationship building through a special services group committed to bringing investors and companies closer together. However, while offering such a service to public companies, Merrill would need to take special precautions about strict observance of SEC regulations regarding insider information and trading.

- Begin building a network of relationships with Japanese and other foreign equity sources who may provide acceptable alternatives to domestic equity markets. For example, Eastern Air Lines might begin looking for a Japanese investor to acquire a major percentage of its stock in order to win the time and money it needs to reestablish itself.

- Communicate constantly with a network of pivotal investors in an effort to make sure relationships remain mutually beneficial. Seek input and feedback, and demonstrate a genuine commitment to investor well-being over the long haul. For example, Honda has convinced investors of its ability to invest time and money in better-built cars, a fact that encouraged investors to remain patient until Honda had time to perform. American firms should learn to do the same with intense communication with key investors.

We think America's corporate future will require the modification of certain SEC laws and many Wall Street practices, and we believe complexity management can help all the participants develop an improved version of creative capitalism. As with the other dimensions of the future, if mutual benefit can override individual gain, the results can be dramatic.

CHAPTER NINE

Ethical Enterprises: Accepting Corporate Social Responsibility

*If we can't do business observing certain
absolute standards, we will simply demur from
doing business. Instead of growing another $30
million in sales we'll grow a little less, but we'll
sleep better for it.*
—W. MICHAEL BLUMENTHAL

The Rise of Business Ethics

Cummins Engine Company, which manufactures and sells a diversified line of in-line and V-type diesel engines, components, and replacement parts to markets throughout the world, has, over the years, set an example in the area of business ethics and social responsibility.

Although Cummins continues to dominate the heavy-duty diesel truck engine market in the U.S. and Canada with more than a 60 percent market share, its earnings have fluctuated in recent years, and sales have not increased dramatically. In a slow-growth market with intensifying competition and a surplus of worldwide diesel truck engine manufacturers, Cummins faces an uphill battle, yet the company's 20,000 employees continue to meet the challenge. The company operates over 30 manufacturing, assembly, and research facilities in nine countries, with 10 divisional and regional offices in North America, 25 international offices,

seven parts distribution centers, 500 distributor and branch locations worldwide, and over 5000 dealers and subdealers in 115
countries. Its customers—who manufacture almost 95 percent of
the heavy-duty trucks in North America—include Ford, Freight-
liner (owned by Daimler-Benz), General Motors, Navistar (formerly International Harvester), Kenworth, Mack (partially owned
by Renault), Peterbilt, and Volvo White. Another 80 customers
around the world put Cummins engines in their trucks and
equipment.

According to a recent Cummins publication, the company is
pursuing a two-pronged strategy: introducing new products, and
improving customer service and internal efficiencies in cost, quality, and delivery. The company intends to maintain its lead in the
U.S. and enlarge its position worldwide by broadening the definition of its present products to include new engines, new components, electronics, service products, and financial services, and
by accelerating its efforts in customer linking, technology, cost,
quality, and delivery performance.

CEO Henry Schacht and his executive team believe that their
long-term viability and success depend as much on high standards
of ethical and socially responsible behavior as they do on high
standards of financial, technological, and production performance. In keeping with this commitment, Cummins has maintained its exemplary position despite financial performance
pressures. Will the company be able to continue this leadership
if maintaining its market leadership becomes even more difficult?

Executives and companies trying to resolve ethical and social
issues in the future must figure out how to help their people and
organizations practice ethics and responsibility without coercing
them. Not every company has been as successful as Cummins
Engine in addressing this problem. Three in particular—Manville
Corporation, Continental Illinois Bank, and E. F. Hutton—have
recently experienced the unpleasant consequences of unethical,
irresponsible decisions. Over forty years ago Johns Manville (as it
was called then) began receiving information that inhaled asbestos could cause a serious lung disease, but Manville's management
suppressed that information from employees working with the
company's asbestos product. Ultimately, a California court held
that Manville had in fact covered up the asbestos danger instead
of looking for safer methods, and a New Jersey court found that

Manville had flagrantly disregarded human rights. Today, Manville has been forced to turn over 80 percent of its equity to a trust for the benefit of those who have sued or plan to sue the company for damages.

Continental Illinois, once the ninth largest bank in the United States, is now the ward of the federal government. The company began its downward spiral when its chairman led an aggressive charge to increase the bank's lending power. Managers became so enthralled with the vision of a much larger and more significant bank that they bought loans from smaller banks with a ruthless disregard for standard control and prudent banking practices. Before long the bank reached its growth goal by building a billion-dollar portfolio of shaky oil loans. When oil prices fell, the loans went from shaky to bad, making it necessary for the federal government to bail out the bank. Despite warning memos from concerned managers, the bank had continued on its blindly aggressive course. Today, approximately 80 percent of Continental Illinois' equity is owned by the Federal Deposit Insurance Corporation.

E. F. Hutton & Company, Number Two among the nation's independent brokers, entered a plea of guilty in 1986 to 2000 counts of mail and wire fraud. In a zealous approach to effective cash management, branch managers had begun drawing against uncollected or nonexistent funds of over 400 banks without paying interest. Without any clear signals from corporate headquarters to the contrary, Hutton's managers assumed that the practice was perfectly legal and even brilliant; they felt, after all, that it merely meant taking full advantage of what bankers and the law permitted. While E. F. Hutton has not suffered consequences as severe as those experienced by Manville and Continental, the company has nonetheless lost much of its good reputation. To date, Hutton has agreed to pay $2 million in fines and $750,000 in government investigation costs, and it has set up an $8 million reserve fund for bank restitution. In addition, many officers have lost their jobs, and some face possible indictments.

In the future managers must build their businesses on the fundamental belief that good ethics equals good business. Before we consider how complexity management can help put that belief into practice, we want to explore the historical evolution of business ethics and social responsibility to gain a better perspective on just what the future might hold.

From Unbounded Power to a Broader Responsibility

Corporations have always compensated their executives and managers for successfully guiding their companies' actions in the marketplace. However, as doing business has become ever more complex in a shrinking world, executives and managers have been forced to shoulder broader responsibilities to individuals and society, and although most still have a long way to go before they perfect their ability to manage their ethical and social obligations, they have also come a long way since the close of the nineteenth century.

Note on chart on page 181 how the eras of ethics and social responsibility parallel the eras of modern management.

Utilitarianism (1910–1940)

The attitudes of business people around the turn of the century reflected the values of social Darwinism. During this so-called Gilded Age, the age of Horatio Alger and New Thought, hardworking individuals could supposedly rise to the top of their organizations and society through the cultivation of virtues prescribed by the Protestant work ethic. Business leaders, having risen according to the law of the survival of the fittest, became the heroes of the time, and they exercised almost absolute authority. Years later Richard Bendix would say in his important book *Work and Authority in Industry,* "They [the employers] interpreted their own success in the struggle as ample justification of their absolute authority in the enterprise, and all those who had not been successful had to submit to that authority without qualifications." In short, economic success came to those who maintained a high standard of personal integrity, while the market supposedly punished their less-virtuous counterparts with economic failure. The losers gave up their rights to manage because they were simply not worthy. The winners enjoyed a "divine right." Naturally, such absolute management authority resulted in exploitation of workers and neglect of their most basic human needs. Before long organized labor attempted to redress abuses of authority by threatening collective economic sanctions, and although many or-

Eras of Ethics and Social Responsibility

| 1890 | 1910 | 1930 | 1950 | 1970 | 1990 | 2010 |

ganizations attacked the labor movement with private police forces and government militias, it steadily gathered momentum during this and subsequent eras.

In those days of unbridled power, business people, claiming allegiance almost solely to the best interests of their stockholders, paid scant attention to the effects of their policies or practices on anyone else. The few exceptions came about when antitrust legislation against Standard Oil, Du Pont, and others prohibited business practices that conflicted with the basic tenets of free enterprise. The government, alert for abuse, passed food and drug legislation and set up the FDA, which would monitor practices and products detrimental to the public's health.

While many wealthy businessmen of this period practiced philanthropy in their later years, they invariably did so as a personal, not a corporate, act. Many of these businessmen may have eventually contributed sizable amounts of their vast fortunes to the public good, but often as a tribute to their own generosity and superiority.

The Cummins Engine Company was incorporated in February 1919 to produce "oil engines." Financed by W. G. Irwin and his family, this new enterprise was run by Clessie L. Cummins in Columbus, Indiana, where for several years the company operated a single factory with fewer than twenty employees. In a company magazine, Frances Schaefer, an executive secretary in 1925, provided this account of working conditions at the time:

> The office and factory were located in the Cerealine Building at Seventh and Jackson, consisting of two small rooms with heat being supplied by a pot-bellied stove. You had to walk across the railroad track to get into the office. Trains ran at regular schedules, and each train passing through supplied us with a fair amount of coal soot, which seeped through the windows. The trains rattled all the windows, calling a halt to conversations whether on the phone or otherwise. In the winter, we were kept cozy by the pot-bellied stove—that is, we were warm on one side and freezing on the other. In the summer, the soot and noise from trains helped to make the heat even more miserable.

During the 1920s Cummins created the first "direct-injection diesel" and "fully-enclosed pressure-lubricated diesel" engines, as well as the first fuel pump that enabled diesel engines to drive variable-speed machinery. Then, building on the research and development of the 1920s, the company developed high-speed automotive diesels in the 1930s. Numerous licensing and quality control problems plagued the company since its founding, and it did not record its first profit until 1936. It survived the utilitarian era because, like many other American companies, it fought tooth and nail to join the ranks of the "fittest." Ethics and social responsibility had not yet entered the picture in a major way.

Constitutional Rights (1940–1960)

Inevitably the abuses of the utilitarian era prompted the extension of constitutional rights into the workplace. Deciding that the collective actions of labor unions, such as general strikes, were too disruptive and that business responses were often too violent, society took matters in hand. Through the Wagner (1935) and Taft-Hartley (1947) Acts, government granted legitimacy to the labor movement and began regulating labor-management conflicts.

The labor movement not only gained strength in response to management's heavy-handed emphasis on the virtues of economic success at any price, but it also appealed to workers who felt oppressed by the new scientific management practices designed to spur productivity, reducing workers and their tasks to precisely analyzed and timed work "units." From labor's perspective, such practices displayed insensitivity to the needs and concerns of workers as people, while from management's perspective labor's rebellion showed too little concern for the requirements of running a successful business. With the two factions at a seeming impasse, government stepped in to minimize destructive conflicts, but succeeded only in institutionalizing them.

Looking back on the situation now, we can see that the government's laudable intentions to guarantee the constitutional rights of workers did little to change the adversarial relationship between management and labor. For example, by the late 1930s Cummins employees had organized the Cummins Employees' Association, but the National Labor Relations Board withheld approval of the union because its proposed officers were too friendly with the company. In another issue of the company's magazine, *Power Team*, K. Stanley Shaw, a longtime Cummins employee and one of the first presidents of the Diesel Workers Union, gave the following account of Cummins' early union experiences:

> When the first union was thrown out, the CIO (United Auto Workers) sent a bunch of organizers in. They were out there every morning, noon, and night. They'd tell us that 85 percent had joined and that the rest of us ought to sign up to make it unanimous. They promised to get us $3.50 an hour (the minimum wage then was 40 cents) and other things like that. That's when we told them that we didn't want any part of it. They went back to Detroit. Then we organized the present Diesel Workers Union.

During World War II military requirements so greatly increased the demand for engines that the Cummins' workforce grew from 600 in 1940 to over 1700 in 1945, with production output more than doubling. After the war, government continued its efforts to protect the constitutional rights of workers, and the labor movement flourished accordingly. In the late 1940s and throughout the 1950s, corporations remained highly structured and rigid environments in which to work, and while government intervention did promote constitutional rights, companies still viewed the individual worker as a unit of production. Even Cummins, a comparatively enlightened company, exhibited this attitude, as this description of its clean-desk regulation clearly illustrates:

> In the days before the open-office concept, our desks were jammed together, row on row . . . At night when we left work, everything—papers, typewriters, mail baskets, dictaphones—had to be removed from the desk tops and stashed out of sight. Not only that, but the telephones had to be placed in the exact top center of the desk so that all phones in an office were aligned.

Such policies were still largely regarded by society as inherently moral and just, and workers could enjoy only those rights that management, the market, or government extended to them.

Justice (1960–1970)

During the 1960s, management's autocratic stance came under increasing attack. Management researchers, for example, began to explore the destructive effects of authoritarian behaviors. In the early sixties, Douglas MacGregor introduced his "Theory X, Theory Y" definitions of management. According to Theory X, traditional management philosophy tended to regard "the average human" as a lazy, unmotivated, and unambitious worker who craves security and avoids responsibility; he must be coerced, controlled, and threatened before he will do his job. In contrast, Theory Y assumes that the "typical human" does not inherently dislike work or avoid responsibility, but rather will aspire to high levels of effort and performance if jobs are satisfying and rewarding. In other words, Theory X applied the stick to the horse's rear end, while Theory Y held out a carrot at the front end. MacGregor's Theory Y offered a clear challenge to the traditional view of labor, and for the first time the virtue and value of worker participation in the management process became apparent. If a company saw its workers as a creative asset, their needs and desires obviously demanded more serious consideration. The old approaches could only exacerbate the very problems they were supposed to solve.

During this era the concept of social justice and equality held sway as movements for civil rights, women's rights, and environmental awareness got underway. Again, government joined the battle by introducing legislation and regulatory agencies aimed at imposing rules regarding civil rights on businesses. When the ecology movement brought the indirect consequences of industry to the public's attention, government passed still more legislation and established regulatory agencies for monitoring business activities and assessing their environmental impact; standards were set for unacceptable levels of environmental damage. The abuses of business in these areas became painfully apparent during this period, and society resorted to legal means for forcing management to define ethical and socially responsible behavior. As a result, management lost many of its previously sacrosanct prerogatives.

At Cummins, the era brought about a new concern for plant site location, product quality, safety, and pollution control. From the beginning Cummins assumed a leadership posture by attempting to eliminate potential consumer and environmental problems before they occurred. Particularly interesting during this period was the relaxation of many of the company's rigid policies and procedures. Prior to the 1960s Cummins had dictated acceptable office garb: white shirts, ties, short hair, and shaven faces for men, and skirts or conservative dresses for women. Slacks were deemed unacceptable for women, as were blue jeans for anyone. If people came to work attired in anything other than the "correct business look," they received immediate reprimands. Now the dress code fell by the wayside as employees adopted the long hair, beards, colored shirts, miniskirts, slacks, pantsuits, and even blue jeans that had become fashionable outside the office.

In an isssue of *Power Team* John Rowell, corporate historian and publications editor, recorded the demise of the company's Saturday morning rule:

> Starting in the 1940s, salaried people were expected to work from 8 to 12 on Saturday morning. Over the years the requirement relaxed to where we needed only to show up during the morning, shuffle papers for a while, and then leave. Eventually, I began to notice that some guys weren't showing up at all and I also broke the Saturday morning habit.

At Cummins and many other companies the rights of individuals to set up their own standards went beyond appearance to ethics, morality, and social responsibility in general. Until now, resolving the larger moral issues had fallen to government, unions, and social pressure, but eventually individual workers began to shoulder some of the burden. In this regard, Cummins again offered something of a model. J. Irwin Miller, grandnephew of W. G. Irwin, the original financier behind Cummins, began working for the company as general manager, and eventually moved on to become executive vice president, president and chairman. Currently chairman of the Executive and Finance Committee of the board, Miller has exerted tremendous influence upon Cummins' ethical standards. A strong believer in the teachings of Jesus Christ, he considered ethical behavior essential because over the long haul, it's the only thing that works. He immersed himself in the civil rights activities of the day, both as chairman and CEO of Cummins and as the first lay president of the National Council of the Churches of Christ. Among his many accomplishments, he instituted the practice of distributing 5 percent of pretax corporate earnings to charity. By the late 1960s the "Cummins Practice on Ethical Standards" guided the whole operation, as the following excerpt demonstrates:

For Cummins, ethics rests on a fundamental belief in people's dignity and decency. Our most basic ethical standard is to show respect for those whose lives we affect and to treat them as we would expect them to treat us if our positions were reversed. This kind of respect implies that we must:

1. Obey the law.
2. Be honest—present the facts fairly and accurately.
3. Be fair—give everyone appropriate consideration.
4. Be concerned—care about how Cummins' actions affect others and try to make those effects as beneficial as possible.
5. Be courageous—treat others with respect even when it means losing business. (It seldom does. Over the long haul, people trust and respect this kind of behavior and wish more of our institutions embodied it.)

By the time J. Irwin Miller stepped down as chairman of the board and CEO in 1969, he had set the tone for Cummins' continued pace-setting leadership as an ethical enterprise.

Role Redefinition (1970–1980)

As the phrase "business ethics" became popular, it ignited discussion and debate in many forums, but it did not lessen confusion over the respective roles of executives, government, and individuals in ethical and socially responsible behavior. Economic issues such as profit maximization, efficiency optimization, cost minimization, and other indicators of economic performance became integrally related to ethical issues. W. Michael Blumenthal, former business executive and Treasury Secretary, described the evolving concern over ethics this way: "People in business have not suddenly become immoral. What has changed are the contexts in which corporate decisions are made, the demands that are being made on business, and the nature of what is considered proper corporate conduct."

During the 1970s, especially after the infamous "payments scandal" revealed that bribery of foreign officials, governments, and businessmen had become almost a business norm, many business leaders concluded that the growing stack of legislation regulating business had done little to resolve the fundamental moral issues. In an attempt to stem the tide of this legislation, improve relations with the public and government, business people out of genuine moral concern began formulating corporate codes of conduct.

The ethical actions of executives and the socially responsible performance of organizations became topics for discussion in the boardrooms and in the annual reports of an increasing number of corporations. In one chapter of the book *Corporations and Their Critics,* Harvey Kapnick quotes Juanita Kreps, former Secretary of Commerce, as saying, "The past fifteen years have seen corporations devote dramatically increased attention to social responsibility." To substantiate this claim, she continues, "In 1977, 456, or 91.2 percent, of the Fortune 500 industrial firms published information about social performance in their annual reports, according to an Ernst & Ernst survey. This is nearly twice the number of firms that did so in 1971."

While the rhetoric of corporate ethics and social responsibility increased during this era, few organizations backed up that rhetoric with clear-cut programs. "We know we should do something, and we *want* to do something," they seemed to be saying, "but what *exactly* should we do?"

Under Henry Schacht, who became Cummins' CEO in 1969, the company continued the course Miller had set earlier. In fact, Schacht further formalized the company's policies after a thorough redefinition of values and responsibilities led to a reorganization of functions to handle those redefined roles. In Cummins' 1972 Annual Report corporate officers outlined the company's ethical and social philosophy and the actions it intended to take to implement that philosophy. A Corporate Action Division was formed to give more formal direction to this area of concern. In the following six propositions (reproduced here in part), the company articulated its commitment:

1. Our success as a corporation will be increasingly influenced by our ability to understand the societies within which we do business.

2. We have a responsibility to use part of our resources to respond to the needs of the society which gives us our charter.

3. We have a responsibility to identify and eliminate potential consumer problems before they occur.

4. We have a responsibility to reexamine constantly the extent to which we promote and affirm humane living.

5. Our responsibility includes working toward achieving population parity in our work force (both vertically and horizontally).

6. We should provide not only resources but a point of view in anticipating and responding to social problems.

In the same annual report Cummins explained that the new Corporate Action Division would function in four major areas: Corporate Philanthropy, Public Affairs and Governmental Relations, Corporate Responsibility, and Corporate and Community Relations. The report concluded with a concise statement of the principle on which Cummins should operate: "While some still argue that business has no social responsibility, we believe that our survival in the very long run is as dependent upon responsible citizenship in our communities and in the society as it is in responsible technological, financial, and production performance."

Human Rights (1980–Late 1980s)

During the next era most organizations experimented with programs for addressing issues of discrimination, sexism, and individual rights. Some interpreted ethics in a broad sense, actively supporting ethical reforms and improvements in everything from education and community economic development to urban renewal and public service. Others lagged behind. As a result, legislation for monitoring and regulating corporate conduct continued. With many constitutional rights having been won during earlier years, attention turned from group to individual human rights, such as employee privacy, confidentiality of personnel files, freedom of speech, conscientious objection, and due process. Employees began demanding certain rights involving desks, files, lockers, and telephone conversations; they objected to the fact that managers could put anything in personnel files, whether the material was relevant and accurate or not; they felt they should be able to publicly criticize a policy or a practice of the organization that they considered immoral or dangerous; they demanded their right to object to an order or request they considered immoral or unethical; and they demanded protection from harassment or termination whenever they voiced honest, concerned criticism of corporate actions.

While some corporations have moved toward protecting these individual human rights, others have not. Unfortunately, those who shrug off the obligation run the risk of the government rushing to fill the gap. As experience has shown, such intervention seldom treats more than the symptoms of a problem.

Throughout this period Cummins has continued its quest for upholding human rights. Addressing the public's right to non-polluted air, the company instituted aggressive measures with emission controls; and it embarked on a concerted effort to protect its employees' rights to privacy. In the first case Cummins advocated a partnership with government that could establish emissions control without a disruptive adversarial confrontation. In the early 1980s Cummins, along with other firms, created a new nonprofit organization, the Health Effects Institute, to study the health effects of emissions from motor vehicles for the Environmental Protection Agency. This "nonadversarial" approach increased the dialogue and collaboration between government and industry. Interestingly, the Institute hired Charles Powers, vice president of Public Policy at Cummins and a past professor of social ethics at Yale University, to direct its efforts.

In the second case, Henry Schacht described the company's approach in an article he and Charles Powers contributed to the book *Corporations and Their Critics*. That article drew important lessons from Schacht's service on an Indiana State commission. Increasingly concerned about the privacy issue, Governor Otis R. Bowen of Indiana had formed a state commission on privacy, on which Schacht served as chairman of the nongovernmental recordkeeping subcommittee, composed of representatives of diverse private sector organizations and individuals who felt they had suffered invasions of their privacy. While the subcommittee found little actual abuse, they found great potential for abuse. Since Cummins was computerizing its employee records at the time, Schacht decided to design a system to thwart that potential. As a result, Cummins' human resources record system became a model for governments and corporations alike. And, most importantly, Cummins' employees *know* that the new system protects their right to privacy.

At almost no additional cost Cummins incorporated a record system it hoped would require little or no modification if and when legislation comes about in this area. Both the subcommittee's report and the principles and methods utilized at Cummins have been picked up by the Privacy Protection Study Commission in Washington and by legislators developing new laws. Quite possibly all of corporate America will benefit from the relative simplicity, effectiveness, and efficiency of a system which evolved from multiple interactions between a corporation and its social-political environment in Indiana.

With this and similar efforts, Cummins entered the ethical leadership era before most other companies. Social activists and business critics have praised Cummins for such leadership and even Ralph Nader's organization had cited Cummins as a "standout" company for its public-spirited orientation, its commitment to consumer advocacy, its role as a corporate philanthropist, and its untiring efforts to assist minority communities.

Ethical Leadership (Late 1980s–Late 1990s)

In contrast to the progressive efforts of companies like Cummins, many, if not most, business enterprises have historically adopted a reactionary stance when confronted by attacks on their moral conduct. In fact, the record shows that business vigorously opposed most of the social legislation currently on the books, including child-labor, antitrust, securities, workman's compensation, social security, minimum wage, medicare, and civil rights legislation. However, if corporate America wishes to avoid potentially stifling government restriction, its executives and managers must begin to lead rather than follow the trend toward ethically and socially responsible behavior. The future of the free enterprise system depends upon it, but it won't be easy because tension will surely continue between the needs of maximizing profits and of maximizing social benefits. This tension reflects yet another paradox the Future 500 must manage: an improved bottom line contributes to the welfare of the corporation, of individuals working for the corporation, and of society at large, but decisions to improve the bottom line can also affect that welfare adversely.

Further complicating the matter, individuals and groups within society and the global community have not, and may never, reach a consensus concerning what's "right" and what's "good." Even when everyone does agree on certain general ethical principles, disagreement invariably erupts when it comes to implementing them. For example, we might all agree that a healthy economy depends on strong family units and that secure families depend on a more comprehensive approach to child care, especially in situations where both parents work, but who should shoulder that responsibility—individuals, corporations, or state and federal governments? If business executives accept the responsibility, encouraging managers to set up comprehensive child-care programs, the managers, expected to produce bottom-line results, might have to cut into those results to establish the required programs, impeding their own advancement. In a corporate system where compensation and promotions depend on financial performance, middle managers and first-line supervisors often feel pressure to compromise ethical standards.

To address this paradox, executives must find ways to establish and manage moral and ethical codes that work toward long-range business and social benefits. Central to the resolution of the paradox will be the corporate code of ethics, written by top management, which enunciates company principles clearly and compellingly. Once the code of ethics has been established, all stakeholders can begin conducting themselves accordingly. As with all corporate behavior, the socialization process begins with the behaviors and role modeling of top management. Research has consistently concluded that the behavior of superiors most strongly influences managers to resort to unethical decisions. Likewise, the ethical behavior of superiors provides the strongest deterrent to unethical behavior by subordinates. A number of academic researchers have remarked that the most ethical and "public-spirited" firms always have strong, moral CEOs who inspire a sense of ethics and social responsibility by example.

Cummins, building on its earlier initiatives, remains a model of ethical leadership. In its continuing effort to integrate more fully both economic and social activities, Henry Schacht and his management team have enunciated four basic premises they feel should drive the corporation's approach to social and political responsibility. The article by Schacht and Powers in *Corporations and Their Critics* sets forth the Cummins code of ethics, key aspects of which are:

1. No corporation has an inherent right to exist. It wins its right by producing needed goods and services within the parameters set by law and acceptable conduct.

2. Within such a view, the corporation is seen as both dependent on and responsible to the full range of people whose lives it affects. A corporation is best pictured, then, as having a full gamut of stakeholders with each of whom a constructive relationship must be established or negotiated.

3. One important aspect of this stakeholder responsibility is the recognition that no product has an inherent right to the marketplace. Customers (the better informed, the better) have much to say about this. But so also has the general public, especially as it expresses its will about the health, safety, and other environmental effects of the product.

4. Each of these points has implications for the way in which corporations reach out to participate in social and political processes, especially the process of public policy formulation.

The ethical leadership era requires an integration of corporate self-interest with the interests of all direct and indirect stakeholders in the corporate ecosystem. Without such an encompassing view, no company can expect to reach, and remain among, the Future 500.

Responsible Leadership

Two events that occurred on the international political arena during 1986 underscore the fact that the worldwide court of public opinion about ethical behavior may be shifting toward consensus. The world community was reluctant to shelter the deposed authoritarian leaders, Ferdinand Marcos and "Baby Doc" Duvalier. The message seems clear: those who disregard their social responsibilities and rob their societies of valuable resources will no longer be able to find a safe place to hide. The same holds true for business leaders, as the cases of the Dalkon Shield and the Bophal disaster so painfully proved.

Admission to the Future 500 will require a belief in and a commitment to the principle that, in the long run, organizational excellence depends on ethical conduct. While those who compromise this principle may win short-term economic advantages, long-term gains will be reserved for those who build their organizations around codes of ethics that enhance the integrity of all who work for them.

The ethical enterprise of the future should seize the opportunity to provide meaning, purpose, and reinforcement to the ethical and moral standards of its workforce, and those standards in turn should promote the well-being of society at large. The new codes can flourish only in an atmosphere of mutual openness and trust among all stakeholders, an atmosphere achievable, at least in part, through proper application of complexity management. Thus those who practice responsible leadership should:

- Commit themselves to environmental protection and apply state-of-the-art technologies to pollution control as well as to research and production.

- Realize that honesty not only enhances the corporation's reputation but also improves its operations.

- Demand examination and discussion of ethical issues with concerned groups, thus keeping the organization not only honest but efficient and effective as well.

- Strive for greater community involvement whereby company employees and officers can help solve local community problems, the resolution of which will result in higher levels of worker satisfaction and fulfillment.

- Protect individual rights of people inside the organization and provide due process, thereby making further government regulation and unionization unnecessary. Critics within the organization, allowed to speak their minds, can serve as early warning systems, providing management with the information needed to deal with problems before they deteriorate into public crises or fiascos.

- Pay equal attention to bottom-line and social performance by inculcating a deep commitment to social responsibility into organizations' strategies and cultures.

- Maintain a long-term commitment to ethical behavior and socially responsible activities regardless of short-term costs.

- Insist that all executives and managers practice what they preach and thus provide examples of ethical and socially responsible behavior.

The complexity managers of the future should not just pay lip service to these principles for appearance's sake, they should make them daily habits that inform all their decisions regarding their own people, their customers, and all other stakeholders.

Responsible Leadership and Complexity Management

We are convinced that ethical and socially responsible behavior will play a steadily increasing role in a world of growing interdependence. Standards of corporate behavior must be established that work constantly toward the benefit of all who live in the world. We believe that the best of the Future 500 will practice responsible leadership and that those who don't will lose their competitive edge as they betray the trust of employees, customers, government agencies, and even competitors. In a world of interdependence, mistrust can kill an enterprise.

At the beginning of this chapter we talked about the importance of executives' encouraging, rather than dictating, ethical and socially responsible behavior in their people and their organizations. Manville Corporation ultimately lost its freedom because it failed to act ethically forty years ago. Today Manville must struggle to regain trust and respect by demonstrating ethical leadership. Continental Illinois faces a similar issue: How does a bank pursue aggressive growth strategies without putting so much pressure on managers and employees that they resort to cutting corners or issuing bad loans? At E. F. Hutton the issue involves establishing an ethical culture in a highly self-oriented industry, while, in contrast, the issue at Cummins involves becoming more profitable without sacrificing a position of ethical leadership. We believe complexity management can help executives resolve issues like these.

Applying Perspective Management

A perspective manager would help find ways to unite employees in a common quest for more ethical and socially responsible behavior by, among other things:

- Publishing company standards of ethical behavior and social responsibility. Any employees unable or unwilling to abide by the standards would be invited to leave the company. For example, Continental Illinois might circulate a strict set of standards for conduct and request that everyone sign an agreement to abide by them. Violators could be warned after the first violation, then helped to find employment elsewhere after a subsequent violation.

- Establishing an ethics council to set company policies and build commitment behind them. For example, E. F. Hutton could establish a companywide council of employees charged with determining the characteristics of an ethical culture. The strongest culture would derive from commitment at the lowest levels rather than from an executive level mandate.

Applying Power Management

A power manager would empower the most ethical employees to influence the actions of all stakeholders by:

- Promoting more ethical and socially responsible managers, giving them more power and freedom in the corporation. For example, Manville could make sure that one of the company's criteria for promotion included demonstrated ethical judgment and performance.

- Allowing employees to question the ethical implications of any corporate practice or policy. Such criticism should never become an obstacle to an employee's progress in the company. For example, Continental Illinois could issue a companywide proclamation that all levels of employees could freely examine the ethical aspects of any and all banking practices and policies, and it could praise and award honest "whistle blowers."

Applying Pivot Management

A pivot manager would take into account the increased performance and fulfillment of individual stakeholders by:

* Conducting one-on-one interviews with any stakeholder inside or outside the company who fails to adopt the company's
  ethical standards. For example, Cummins executives could
  meet with an investor who had criticized Cummins' attention
  to ethical and social leadership as leading to lackluster financial performance, in an effort to determine any validity behind that claim. Perhaps some of the company's social
  responsibility programs are too costly and should be reeval-
  uated. On the other hand, the investor may not be tempera-
  mentally suited to the Cummins environment.

* Producing a quality video program illustrating the benefits of
  ethical and socially responsible behavior. For example, E. F.
  Hutton could produce a thirty-minute film depicting ways to
  curb abuses on Wall Street. Such a film could generate public
  admiration and customer loyalty.

* Inviting each stakeholder to complete an annual ethics and
  social responsibility report card on the company. Executives
  could then address all negative ratings with the goal of improving individual relationships, performance, and fulfillment. For example, Manville could circulate a comprehensive
  questionnaire to customers, shareholders, employees, and in-
  terested citizens as a means of communicating their deep
  commitment to never again disregarding social or individual
  well-being for the sake of profit.

Many executives we have met list Scott Peck's *The Road Less
Traveled,* a rather spiritual work, as one of the books that has
influenced their lives and the way they manage their businesses.
Others cite their religion or their study of philosophy and history
as a source of moral guidance. Whatever the source, a renewed
sense of ethics and social responsibility seems to be on the minds
of many of America's business leaders. For those who want to
place their organizations among the Future 500, we think such
moral foundations should become an even stronger concern.

CHAPTER TEN

Visionary Architects: Designing New Forms of Organization

> *Good architecture is like a piece of beautifully composed music crystallized in space that elevates our spirits beyond the limitation of time.*
> —TAO HO, CHINESE ARCHITECT

Organizational Dynamism

Frito-Lay receives little attention as a corporate performer outside the snack food industry because it operates as a division of PepsiCo. However, we think this dynamic organization deserves a good deal of attention in terms of its bold experiments with organization structure.

Frito-Lay's president, Willard Korn, believed his company can continue to grow in the late 1980s by expanding its snack food markets. As he told *Business Week*, "We'll consider getting into any snack item that lends itself to a store-door delivery system." Leo Kiely III, the company's senior vice president of marketing, enunciated Frito-Lay's market expansion philosophy when he said, "Each new snack increases the total amount of snacking, dormant appetites come into ravening existence." To implement this growth and market expansion strategy, the executives and managers at Frito-Lay have creatively designed an organization that thrives on constant change—in the creation of new products, the exploitation of old ones, or the company's responses to competitive challenges. Frito-Lay embarked on a contingency approach to organization some time ago, yet, paradoxically, as its

past president and the current president of PepsiCo, Wayne Cal-
loway, has said, "The heart of Frito-Lay is consistency."

In addition to product innovations and aggressive competitive
positioning, Frito-Lay has embraced changes made possible by
technology. The company used computer simulation to create its
new, thicker potato chip, O'Grady's. As a result, O'Grady's twice-
as-thick chip can withstand over two times as much pressure as its
conventional rivals before breaking. The chip's off-set ridges (or
waves) create a thicker up-slope for crunchiness and flavor, while
the down-slope provides the needed fragility. Frito-Lay even fine-
tuned the flavor with technology, employing chromatographs to
analyze gaseous flavor compounds of ordinary potato chips in an
effort to achieve ideal ratios of baked-to-fried potato flavor. With
these scientific specifications in hand, the company redesigned
factory machinery to make the new chip.

Frito-Lay's corporate culture fiercely follows a "can do" action-
oriented approach that encourages and demands aggressive,
rapid response to challenges. People take on a lot of responsibility
and strive to perform at the highest possible levels. Some have
called the Frito-Lay culture a pressure cooker that will push you
to the top or boil you alive. By the late 1980s, Frito-Lay had gone
a long way toward securing its position among the Future 500,
but can it extend its success even further?

The blueprints for dynamic new forms of organization will require tremendous design skills because executives will have to
move away from tight structure and control. Most find it psycho-
logically difficult to afford individuals the freedom they need to
produce peak performances. However, business leaders should
take comfort from the fact that although freedom implies less
strict control it does not necessarily imply anarchy. Some organizations must become much more flexible and diverse than their
leaders ever thought possible, but some will also remain fairly
faithful to the old functional, decentralized or matrix forms. Even
those, however, must find creative ways of responding to the increasing dynamism of other organizational structures.

Several problems and opportunities will attend the rise of more
dynamic forms of organization. As new forms arise throughout
the organizational landscape, executives and managers must answer a crucial question: how can new forms foster flexibility, diversity, and change while allowing for necessary control and
direction? Consider how three companies have been trying to

answer this question. Du Pont recently set up a distributor marketing network composed of thirty-five distributor marketing managers whose responsibilities include discussion of common problems, market trends, and requirements for change. Ideally, the steering committee should streamline and enhance collective learning from companywide experiences and perspectives. Meetings of the committee include discussions led by market researchers, consultants, and distributor marketing managers from other noncompetitive companies. This kind of networking and organizing of distributors illustrates flexibility and adaptability that will characterize dynamic networks of the future.

Galoob Toys Inc. also uses futuristic organizational forms. The company's action figures and other fashionable toys produce a sales volume of over $60 million, despite the fact that Galoob only employs 115 people. Most of the company's products come from independent inventors, most of its design work is performed by outside engineering specialists, and its manufacturing and packaging are contracted out to a handful of Hong Kong enterprises. Independent manufacturers' representatives distribute the toys and Commercial Credit Corp., another independent company, collects its receivables. The company structure involves a network of relationships among independent entities with Galoob at the center of communications, which it effects with telephones, facsimile machines, and telexes. Although the company has been struggling lately to meet sales projections, it has successfully experimented with a radical new form of organization.

The Gaines Food Plant located in Topeka, Kansas, once owned by General Foods, is now operated by Anderson Clayton, and may soon be sold to Quaker Oats. All the apparent interest and disinterest in this food plant has come about partly as a result of its surprising organization form. From the beginning the Gaines plant replaced traditional management hierarchies with work groups that the company's corporate parents have had trouble managing traditionally. The plant has attained high performance marks over the years as its work groups have organized themselves, hired new employees, monitored quality control, run maintenance programs, set strategies, and, in general, determined their own destiny. Given this freewheeling environment, the work groups resist control from above.

Before we discuss how complexity management can help fuel the proliferation of organizational forms in the future, let's re-

view the development of organizational forms during the past
hundred years.

Evolution of the Modern Organization

Good architects nurture the psychological, mental, and spiritual
needs of the people who will inhabit their structures. As Arthur
Erickson, a leading Canadian architect, once said, "Life is rich,
always changing, always challenging, and we architects have the
task of transmitting into wood, concrete, glass, and steel, of transforming human aspirations into habitable and meaningful space."
In a similar fashion, the designers of tomorrow's forms of organization should concern themselves not just with lines of responsibility, channels of internal communication, and organizational
charts, but the psychological and spiritual needs of individuals,
and they should always consider the relationship of each structure
to its environment, from a crosstown competitor to a supplier of
raw material on the other side of the globe.

The forms of organization have evolved from the rather
straightforward and small structures of the early 1900s to the
exceedingly complicated and large structures of today. Consider
how these organizational eras correspond to the management
eras presented in Chapter 2.

Functional Organizations (1890–1925)

At this point in history technological advances, from streamlined manufacturing processes to the completion of nationwide
transportation and communication systems, permitted manufacturers to create goods in high volume, and distributors to quickly
market the high volumes over broad geographical areas. Seizing
the opportunities inherent in these developments, organizations
grew rapidly by coordinating and integrating the processes
of mass production and mass distribution, until the old single-
product, single-function, single-location approach no longer suf-
ficed. Inevitably multiple-function organizations evolved, either
through vertical integration or horizontal combination. In the
former instance, single-function enterprises linked multiple eco-

Organizational Forms

| 1890 | 1910 | 1930 | 1950 | 1970 | 1990 | 2010 |

Functional Organizations

Decentralized Organizations

Matrix Organizations

Neo-Contingency Organizations

Dynamic Networks in a Constantly Changing Environment

Structure

Productivity

Systems

Strategy

Culture

Innovation

Leadership

Complexity Management

Management Eras

nomic functions vertically (for example, adding shoe distribution to shoe production), while in the latter instance, they linked them horizontally (for example, adding shoelaces to footwear distribution).

Mass producers, foreseeing the advantages of creating their own marketing and distribution networks, favored vertical integration. With technological advances having made it possible for them to expand their output, they could best maintain the new high volumes by building their own marketing networks, coordinating the flow between production and marketplace. Furthermore, many producers required specialized distribution and marketing services beyond the capabilities of existing general marketers.

Other firms chose the horizontal path, which usually involved mergers or acquisitions. Most early mergers and acquisitions, like those today, came about when firms within a given industry achieved a certain organizational "critical mass." However, early mergers differed from contemporary ones in that they often began as trade associations managing cartels within a single industry and ended up with the federations legally consolidating into a single firm, usually a trust or holding company. After the consolidation, these new firms would continue to grow through further mergers and acquisitions or through vertical integration.

In order to serve their markets effectively, these new large organizations needed to maintain a steady flow of products to their consumers, which required close coordination among the various economic functions. Since a company typically organized each functional activity as a separate department with its own bureaucratic structure and its own autonomous head (usually a vice president), coordination depended on the vice presidents forming an executive committee, possibly located in a central office, that could control overall operations.

The potato chip industry nicely illustrates this first organizational era. According to accepted lore, the potato chip was invented in 1853 by George Crum, an Indian/Mulatto chef at the Carey Moon Lake House in Saratoga Springs, New York. A much admired cook, Crum could afford a few eccentricities, such as not accepting reservations and keeping all patrons, even such luminaries as President Grover Cleveland or Jay Gould, waiting in line. He never responded gracefully to criticism. If a dissatisfied diner sent food back to the kitchen, Crum would often "improve" the offending dish by burning it beyond recognition or mixing it with something quite unpalatable. One day, the story goes, Cornelius Vanderbilt complained that his french-fried potatoes were not sliced thinly enough and tasted like cardboard. Crum promptly replaced the original dish with a "new and improved" version: *extremely* thinly sliced potatoes fried in a large quantity of hot oil and liberally doused with salt. To Crum's amazement, Vanderbilt adored the new "potato chips," and Moon's Lake House Restaurant added another dish to its menu.

As the potato chip captured the imagination of gourmet restaurateurs around the country, some enterprising folks saw it as a logical product for mass production and distribution. In 1895, a visitor to Cleveland would have marveled at William C. Tappenden's horse-drawn wagon delivering one of the country's first non-restaurant-manufactured potato chip products to local eateries. As the market for the so-called "Saratoga Chips" expanded, Tappenden converted a barn behind his home into a potato chip factory, and by the early 1900s he was distributing potato chips in an electric car. Before long, similar operations had sprung up all over the country, with such companies as Num Num Foods in Cleveland and Barrett Foods in Atlanta building their own local and regional production facilities and distribution networks. Num Num Foods produced pretzels and other snacks besides potato chips, distributing them to taverns, grocery stores, confectionary stores, school lunch programs, and other institutional buyers. The visionary behind Num Num was Harvey Noss, an exceptionally persuasive and organization-minded man. Potato chip industry historians credit him with establishing Cleveland as the "Vatican City of the potato chip industry." In keeping with organizational developments of the day, Noss vertically combined production and distribution, horizontally added crackers, nuts, and popcorn to the product line, and carved out new distribution territories. Eventually, he helped form the Potato Chip Institute International for which he served as executive secretary for many years. In 1959, Num Num Foods merged with the Frito Company.

Barrett Foods, headquartered in Atlanta, became one of the country's earliest "major" snack food companies. Barrett employed a distribution system of route salesmen who both sold and delivered snack products. The company's three plants, situated in Atlanta, Memphis, and Jacksonville, Florida, fed the company's growing distribution network. The Barrett organization would later employ Herman Lay as a route salesman's helper, and later, when he bought the firm from the founder's widow, the company's name was changed to H. W. Lay & Company.

Decentralized Organizations (1925–1960)

By 1925, corporations in many sectors of the economy had grown so large via integration of mass production and mass distribution processes, that their functional components could only achieve further growth through product diversification. This meant developing dissimilar products, through acquisition or internal expansion, that could take advantage of similar technological, production, or distribution processes. However, as organizations ballooned to include new products and businesses, traditional departments organized by economic function could no longer handle the load.

To regain lost efficiency, executives broke their unwieldy functional organizations into product divisions, each responsible for a different product or group of products, and each with its own set of functional departments, such as marketing, sales, finance, and purchasing. The collection of product divisions was in turn controlled by a central office from which emanated the policy framework within which division executives made all their decisions. General Motors pioneered this movement by installing one of the first decentralized multidivisional organizational structures. Other companies, especially those like Standard Oil, that grew through acquisitions or mergers, used the holding company to accomplish decentralization, while still others adopted some combination of the two forms, a hybrid approach the potato chip/snack food industry illustrates beautifully.

C. E. Doolin, founder of the Frito Company, and Herman W. Lay, the head of H. W. Lay & Company, shared some striking similarities. Both started out in 1932, both aimed their sights on the fledgling snack food market, and both borrowed $100 for the initial capitalization of their businesses. While Doolin bought the recipe for a new Mexican product made from corn masa or dough, Lay purchased a distributorship from Barrett Foods.

In the late 1930s, Lay rescued Barrett Foods, which had been floundering in the wake of a stockholder dispute and defection, by buying the company's two plants in Atlanta and Memphis for

$60,000 ($5,000 from his own distribution company, $30,000 borrowed from the bank, and the issuance of preferred stock to the Barrett family). A year later Lay bought the Florida plant, which continued to produce and distribute products in Florida under a franchise arrangement; then over the next few years he acquired The Richmond (Virginia) Potato Chip Company, Tas-Tee Pretzel and Potato Chip Company (West Virginia), Halter's Pretzels, Inc. (Ohio), Brooks Potato Chip Company (Missouri), Red Dot (Wisconsin), and Frito Company capital assets in Bethesda, Maryland. In addition, he built plants in Mississippi, Kentucky, North Carolina, Georgia, and Washington, D.C. To manage this sprawling conglomeration of snack food companies, Lay imposed a decentralized organizational structure that was half holding company and half product divisions. In some cases acquired companies continued to operate independently, while in others the operations of two companies joined forces. In some areas of the country, production plants and distribution operations remained separate independent divisions, while in others the production and distribution came together in a regional or local division.

When C. E. Doolin founded the Frito Company in San Antonio, he became the trademarked producer of corn chips. In 1946, H. W. Lay & Company acquired the franchise to produce "frito chips" around the country, thus forming an alliance between the two companies long before they actually merged with one another. Frito came to dominate snack food markets in the southwest, while Lay controlled the southeast. Throughout this period Frito itself acquired companies such as Num Num Foods in Cleveland. Doolin, like Lay, built a decentralized organization to accommodate his company's increasing size, complexity, and broader geographical product distribution.

Matrix Organizations (1960–1980)

Throughout this period many organizations attempted to take full advantage of all that had transpired during the preceding eras. Since both the centralized characteristics of the functional organization and the decentralized features of the holding company offered advantages and disadvantages, the matrix organization seemed to promise the best of both worlds. Ideally, a matrix form balances the need for centralized, functional management with the need for decentralized, product or business division management. The most complex and sophisticated matrices, such as the ones at ITT and Digital Equipment Corporation, often gave managers two bosses, one centrally and functionally oriented, the other decentrally and product-, business division- or geography-based. Although a synthesis of the earlier forms, the matrix style represented a major step toward complexity. Managers operating under the functional form combined line and staff responsibilities, while those working under the decentralized form separated those responsibilities. In the latter case, division managers retained authority over divisional functions, thereby reducing the need for staff managers, who theretofore tended to serve as the CEO's staff. Under the matrix form, the power of staff executives often increased to the point that confusion sprang up over the distinctions between line and staff responsibilities.

Not all organizations employed model matrices during this era; some simply moved to balance centralized functional management with decentralized divisional management. The product management practices of companies such as Procter & Gamble and General Foods provide good examples of this blend. At these companies, product groups operated fairly independently as quasi-divisions but still relied on some centrally managed functions such as production and sales. For example, a production supervisor at General Foods would report to both his production boss and the Kool-Aid product manager. This dual reporting system provided the benefit of both product and production perspectives.

During the 1960s conglomerates mushroomed as companies acquired existing enterprises, quite often in unrelated fields. Instead of growing internally like the large, integrated, and diversified food companies, most conglomerates grew externally. Such conglomerates seldom made sense in the capital-intensive, mass production, mass distribution industries, where large integrated enterprises had entrenched themselves, but they frequently arose in industries where smaller enterprises had remained competitive. These conglomerates also struggled to balance centralized functions and decentralized operations. ITT, for example, adopted a decentralized form but gave substantial line management authority to executives responsible for central functions such as finance.

In 1961, The Frito Company and H. W. Lay & Company merged to create Frito-Lay. When C. E. Doolin died, just before the merger, Herman Lay became the new company's first CEO. Four years later, Frito-Lay itself merged with the Pepsi-Cola Company, resulting in PepsiCo, Inc. Within the PepsiCo organization, Frito-Lay operated as a separate division, but, true to the purpose of the matrix form, obtained the benefits of some centralized functions such as planning and control systems.

When the Frito and H. W. Lay companies merged, they kept their respective operations highly decentralized and operated as distinctly regional enterprises. The only centralized direction from the parent corporation came from the creation of zones (regional groupings) that operated with financial autonomy. However, in the late 1960s and early 1970s, PepsiCo and Frito-Lay brought a good deal of central direction and structure to bear, balancing central functional with decentralized geographical control. Quite naturally, a type of matrix organization began to emerge at Frito-Lay as strong functional departments at the Dallas headquarters set policies for the geographically dispersed sales and manufacturing zones around the country. This new organizational approach brought functional centralization along with decentralized operations to an industry that had never experienced it before. Adding the centralization to the decentralization in a modified matrix form made it possible for Frito-Lay to take advantage of the increasing importance of national advertising and marketing through television and the increasing standardization around national brands of supermarket chains. The results were breathtaking. Frito-Lay quickly became the first snack food company to produce national brands and soon dominated the industry with as much as a 75 percent share of some markets.

Neocontingency Organizations (1980–Late 1990s)

As the brontosaurus proved several million years ago, sheer size can become a hazard. Business executives, with ever larger and more complex organizations under their command, began to worry about the compatibility or "fit" among organizational forms and their companies' various strategies and cultures. As a result, *relationships* among the many components of the corporate environment began to matter as much as the structures of the components themselves, and executives started developing organizational structures contingent upon all the success variables. Consistent with the "culture" management era, the neocontingency organization era focused executive attention on strategy implementation and corporate culture, leading to a marked increase in flexibility when it came to structure. New human resources management concepts, new leadership styles, increased complexity, and greater competitiveness conspired to make the careful handling of organizational issues top priority for most firms. Contingency theories of organization had been around for a long time by the 1980s, but had never produced the kind of flexible organizational structuring to accommodate the increasing number of variables seen in this era.

As this era continues to unfold, we think we will see more and more flexibility and experimentation with structural forms. Standard Oil's unique arrangement with Analog Devices to fund new and emerging ventures provides just one example of the inventiveness we foresee. Given the preoccupations that characterize the "innovation" management era, we expect executives to search high and low for creative ways to organize and structure their businesses.

During this period, Frito-Lay has been experiencing what one of its managers called "a state of constant reorganization." What accounts for it? "Fit." Intent on making organizational structures contingent upon changing processes, strategies, systems, and priorities, Frito-Lay has freely tinkered with its organizational forms. In the early 1980s the company distinguished between salesmen and merchandisers working within Frito-Lay's famous store-door delivery system. Merchandisers became those 2,000 salesmen who called on and delivered to major outlets. They used the larger goose-necked trucks and trailers to transport the snacks. The other 8,000 salesmen continued to be called salesmen, and they sold and delivered to smaller outlets and convenience stores, using the more familiar Frito-Lay vans. The separation was *contingent* upon the need to tailor service to the different needs of different outlets. Later, another organizational experiment sent marketing people out into the field to work side by side with salespeople. Traditionally, the marketers had stuck close to headquarters, but Frito-Lay made a change *contingent* upon the need to improve communication between marketers and salespeople, thus obtaining more accurate feedback, more highly tailored marketing approaches to unique regional differences, and greater integration of marketing and sales efforts. Other organizational changes included the separation of manufacturing and sales management within the zones or regions, the combination of engineering and research and development, and a general move toward "business unit" organization. This contingency approach to organizational structure has helped Frito-Lay attain faster growth than the industry as a whole, greater profits than most competitors, and a continuation of sixteen years of record sales and profits, all of which add up to dominance of an industry.

Dynamic Networks in a Constantly Changing Environment

We think neocontingency organizations will lead to a rich assortment of forms in the future. Paralleling the "leadership" era in management, the neocontingency era will foster more experimentation and flexibility and make possible an unprecedented variety of innovative forms. Most such forms, flexibly designed to respond to rapid change, will be contingent upon circumstances. They will span the continuum of possibilities: functional organizations, decentralized organizations, matrix organizations, neocontingent organizations, brand-new forms, and combinations of all conceivable forms. Despite the range of forms, however, we think they will all contain elements of what we call the "dynamic network," by which we mean an organizational architecture that accommodates constant and accelerating change while at the same time stimulating components of the corporate environment to build deep and lasting relationships. As a child grows up, it may experience traumatic changes, but the parent's love remains constant whether the child wins a Nobel Prize or runs afoul of the law. Similarly, stakeholders in the corporate environment may take surprising turns, but the relationships among them should survive both stupendous successes and dismal setbacks. The flexibility of the dynamic network will allow for maximum diversity of organizational forms thriving side by side within the corporate ecosystem.

The true dynamic network:

- Maximizes flexibility.

- Allows for diversity among functions and divisions.

- Contains dependent, independent, and interdependent parts.

- Displays the attributes of the pivot organization (see Chapter 3).

- Is both simple and complex.

- Is both fragmented and unified.

- Remains always contingent upon needs/circumstances/stakeholders.

- Permits and even encourages constant internal change, renewing itself smoothly and naturally.

- Anticipates and even creates relevant external changes.

- Allows for both formality and informality.

- Continues to invent new organizational forms.

Not all Future 500 companies will assume the dynamic network form, but all will come under its influence one way or another. A small company may assume a functional form itself, then enter into a dynamic network relationship with other small companies. A large global corporation may keep the traditional decentralized structures that provide stability for some of its divisions, while at the same time creating dynamic networks for other divisions that require greater flexibility.

By observing the principles of complexity management, executives can orchestrate a wide range of organizational forms as they encourage individuals and groups inside and outside their corporations to shoulder more responsibility for structuring their own working environment. Despite the great diversity of future forms, we suggest that the dynamic network will help maintain dynamic equilibrium among them all.

Dynamic Networks and Complexity Management

Numerous types of organizational structures have arisen to cope with the increasingly complex nature of the business world. In the beginning of this century executives preferred simple and straightforward forms, but they quickly designed more complex and flexible ones in a growing climate of uncertainty and change. The direction seems clear: our organizations will become more and more dynamic as they afford people the ability to structure their working arrangements to meet the challenges of the future.

As we proposed earlier in this chapter, future executives must learn to develop dynamic networks that foster flexibility, diversity, and change while providing needed control, direction, and consistency. How can a company like Du Pont use extra-organizational or super-structure techniques, such as the national distributor marketing network, to facilitate needed communication and coordination? At Galoob Toys, what kind of organizational forms lie beyond the loosely tied network the company currently favors? Can the network continue to work as the company grows? Can the Gaines Plant find a parent company enlightened enough to accept and profit from its organizational uniqueness? How can Frito-Lay help people use an environment of constant change to their own and the company's benefit?

We think complexity management holds some of the keys to answering these questions. In fact, without it, we fear executives will cling to the old organizational forms in order to maintain a false sense of security in a world of constantly accelerating change.

Applying Perspective Management

By assuming the attitude of perspective management, executives can open their minds to diverse organizational arrangements while fostering unity and oneness of purpose. With it, they can:

• Open the doors to innovative organizational arrangements by encouraging managers and workers to initiate new arrangements as long as they "fit" with corporate principles. For example, Frito-Lay could diffuse any frustration with constant change by asking individual workers and managers to find better ways to organize themselves in accordance with corporate guidelines. In this way people would come to see organizational change as positive opportunity for achieving both individual and corporate goals.

- Prepare internal reports on the successes of organizational innovations for distribution throughout the company, thus providing others with insights into how they might achieve similar successes. For example, Du Pont could prepare an internal report on the success of the distributor marketing network and suggest that others look for opportunities to develop innovations in their organizational arrangements to better meet their specific objectives as well as the firm's common objectives.

- Conduct a management development and training course on structuring futuristic organizations during which managers learn how to configure diverse organizational arrangements while promoting greater unity of purpose throughout the corporate environment. For example, Quaker Oats could conduct such a course using its potentially new Gaines Plant as an example of an alternative approach to organization at the manufacturing plant level.

Applying Power Management

By assuming the posture of power management, executives can properly bestow freedom to act on those individuals capable of using it to further organizational innovation. With it, they can:

- Give committed and proven managers the freedom to experiment with alternative organizational forms that can improve the company's operations and results. For example, Galoob Toys might give key managers license to enter into new and different organizational arrangements that could become vital to Galoob's future. An organization with such a history of flexibility needs to give people the freedom and power to act even more flexibly in the future. Otherwise, they could naturally gravitate toward reduced flexibility as the organization grows.

- Avoid demanding that every department and function follow the same approach to organizational structure, regardless of the requirements of the corporate compensation system or traditional personnel practices. For example, Quaker Oats should not force Gaines or another organizational unit to conform to corporate personnel or to compensation systems that do not fit its unique style. Rather, the parent should act as a true power manager, allowing Gaines managers the freedom to structure and control their own environment as long as they continue embracing and accomplishing Quaker Oat's common purposes with acceptable results.

Applying Pivot Management

By assuming the outlook of pivot management, executives can carefully consider the individual's role in the organization. With it they can:

- Give every individual in the corporation the mandate to suggest improvements in organizational structure that might improve individual performance and fulfillment. Corporate managers may find it difficult to deal with a barrage of suggestions, but doing so can pay off handsomely, particularly if managers sort the good suggestions from the bad. For example, Frito-Lay could initiate an internal advertising campaign asking every employee to offer organizational recommendations to their bosses. In this way employees can become the agents rather than the victims of change.

- Analyze the impact of any organizational form on each individual and identify opportunities for organizational change that could increase performance and/or fulfillment. For example, Du Pont could incorporate an organizational component in its annual review process. Review sessions might take more time, but they would help ensure the constant refining of mutually beneficial new forms.

- Adopt a policy that every committed employee must accept responsibility for making the organization work, even if that means reconfiguring a structure to suit the unique needs of individuals in a given department or modifying it to meet the needs of just one person. For example, Frito-Lay could adopt a corporate policy of organizational adaptability that gives even the newest employee guidelines for organizational change at different corporate levels. Of course, the newest employee's sphere of influence would be small, but the policy would set people on the right path from their first day on the job.

We believe that with the coming proliferation of organizational forms, complexity management can be used to build unity in the midst of diversity and to empower people to attain peak performance and individual fulfillment. The ability to manage such diversity will, in part, determine a company's ranking among the Future 500.

CHAPTER ELEVEN

Corporate Orchestras: Integrating Subcultures

> *It is one thing to make an individual conform,*
> *and another altogether to make him keep his*
> *identity within a group of equals while he is*
> *trying to find the common ground with them.*
> —WALTER GROPIUS

Integrity and Interdependence Among Subcultures

Dayton Hudson topped *Fortune* magazine's 1987 list of most admired corporations for retailing companies. In addition to the company's overall effectiveness, it deserved that honor for one clear reason: its ability to maintain both integrity and interdependence among its many businesses and their respective subcultures. Its many diverse subcultures work together harmoniously, but when the parent organization determines that one of its units might benefit from a better fit elsewhere, it doesn't hesitate to move, as the selling of its B. Dalton Bookseller chain to Barnes & Noble illustrates.

We expect to see competitive battles among retailers intensify during the late 1980s and early 1990s, with those who try to be "all things to all customers," as Dayton Hudson and its rivals did in their early years, losing market niches to competitors who master more careful market segmentation. As the survivors take a hard look at their internal operations and expenses in an effort to lower overhead costs, they will surely pay a lot of attention to both the independence and the interdependence among their various units and their respective subcultures.

Dayton Hudson has apparently found a successful formula for balancing operating autonomy and standardization in its four main businesses: Target, Mervyn's, the Dayton Hudson Department Store Company, and the Specialty Merchandisers. The company's participative management process is well defined and encompasses strategic, financial, and human-resources planning. By involving management in the planning process, Dayton Hudson effectively ensures management commitment and support throughout its organization.

Dayton Hudson doesn't really care whether its product line is low margin or high margin, books or shoes, as long as it's profitable. Maintaining these profitable businesses and holding down expenses in its maintenance businesses will remain a top priority for Dayton executives in the coming years. The merger between May Department Stores Company, one of Dayton's archrivals, and Associated Dry Goods Corporation will dislodge Dayton Hudson from its fourth-largest retailer position, knocking it down to number five. More importantly, continuing consolidation in the industry will place tremendous pressure on Dayton Hudson to manage expenses.

For executives trying to create, maintain, and integrate subcultures, the main concern will be increasing unity while at the same time fostering greater diversity. Many issues will spring from this apparent paradox, and many companies besides Dayton Hudson will struggle with them. For example, EMI Ltd., an entertainment and electronics company based in the United Kingdom, achieved a remarkable technological breakthrough over a decade ago when it created the first CAT Scanner, a device doctors could use to analyze a patient's total health status. In fact, the company's distinguished scientist, Godfrey Hounsfield, won the Nobel Prize for the accomplishment. Unfortunately, EMI failed to maintain its initial market lead because the company's management insisted on centralizing decision making in London even though the principal market for new scanners lay in the United States. The gap between market needs and corporate direction widened, EMI began losing money, and it eventually succumbed to a takeover bid from Thorn Electric Industries. The company assumed it could function as one global entity without regard for market differences and strategies that demanded separate corporate subcultures, and in doing so, the company chose a self-destructive road.

By contrast, Shouldice Hospital may be the most profitable hospital in the world, according to John Heskett of the Harvard Business School. How do they do it? The hospital segments the market on the basis of medical conditions, then targets the segments it wants to go after. What follows is simple but brilliant. The targeting of very specific market segments allows the hospital to create a focused facility, precisely trained staff, and dedicated subcultures that can provide the best service and value for the price. Competitors find it almost impossible to compete. When Shouldice attacked inguinal hernias, the second most frequently performed operation in the world, as a target market, it attracted patients from around the world to its hernia facility. By relating this and its other subcultures under the umbrella of unified strategic and cultural philosophy, Shouldice produces unity in purpose and philosophy and diversity in application.

In another industry, Eastman Kodak Company recently underwent a major reorganization that may hold very significant consequences for its future. Under the new organizational plan, Kodak hopes to become more customer oriented, with important decisions residing at the lowest possible levels. As a result, the revitalized company encourages risk taking and rewards innovation as never before, seeing employees at all levels as potential leaders who will move the company forward. The goal of all this reorganization has been to create an environment in which subcultures can more easily come into being and align themselves with other groups and the umbrella organization. For example, Kodak has divided the new Photographic and Information Management Division into eighteen separate business units, each of which it has grouped with other business units that share common technology, products, or markets. The plan allows for both unity and diversity. If Eastman Kodak can continue this direction, it will surely win a strong position among the Future 500.

Complexity management offers a natural solution to all these contemporary issues surrounding the management of corporate cultures and subcultures. Before we explore the ways in which it can do so, we want to look at the history of subcultures in organizations to gain greater insight into the future.

From Stifling Sameness to Standout Uniqueness

By subcultures we mean any work group, department, function, division, subsidiary, strategic business unit, or affiliate company that maintains a separate identity within a larger organizational framework. Throughout this century executives have gone from robbing subcultures of their identities to protecting their unique attributes.

Notice in the chart on page 220 how the history of subcultures parallels the history of management.

Systematic Attack on Subcultures (1910–1935)

Around the turn of the century production largely depended on the traditional master-servant relationship between "inside" contractors and their crews of workers. Contractors retained the power to hire and fire workers, while skilled craftsmen retained the right to determine how and at what rate required work would be performed. Entrepreneurs, relying on the expertise of the contractors and craftsmen to keep production flowing smoothly, felt no need to interfere with this process. Thus, workers, especially the skilled craftsmen, developed strong subcultures based on centuries-old guild traditions.

Eventually, however, these strong subcultures caused problems for business people. First, as entrepreneurs watched the inside contractors reap substantial profits, they sought ways to retain those profits for themselves. Second, as skilled craftsmen grew increasingly powerful with newly organized work unions, they demanded better compensation, working conditions, and other benefits. As a result of these pressures, business leaders launched an "Open Shop" campaign in the early 1900s. The resultant attack on the principles and character of the labor movement and its organizers enjoyed only limited success.

In the midst of worker-owner conflict, the writings of Frederick Taylor began to attract attention. Whereas the Open Shop campaign had attacked the laziness and sloth of workers and promoted the hard-earned absolute authority of the employer, Taylor called for a "great revolution" in the attitude of workers

History of Subcultures

| 1890 | 1910 | 1930 | 1950 | 1970 | 1990 | 2010 |

Above timeline (History of Subcultures):
- Systematic Attack on Subcultures
- Struggling for Understanding
- Recognition of Subcultures
- Exploration of Subcultures
- Legitimizing Corporate Cultures
- Celebrating Subcultures
- Interrelated Subcultures

Below timeline (Management Eras):
- Structure
- Productivity
- Systems
- Strategy
- Culture
- Innovation
- Leadership
- Complexity Management

Management Eras

and managers alike. According to Taylor, "scientific management" could avert attention from the fair division of the "surplus"
or profits and turn it more productively toward increasing the
size of the surplus, which would benefit both employer and
worker through higher profits and increased wages. To accomplish this goal, Taylor advocated the scientific determination of
"the one best way" to perform any task, which eventually resulted
in time and motion studies, production planning, cost analysis,
task specialization, and the assembly line philosophy.

Various forms of scientific management appealed to managers,
who saw them as a way to strip workers of their control over the
production process. In the end, various versions of Taylor's system concentrated control in the hands of management, eroding
the power of the unions.

Not surprisingly, Taylor attacked worker subcultures and their
tendency to promote "natural soldiering" as unnecessary and
even downright dishonest. In *The Principles of Scientific Management*, Taylor painted a portrait of workers as inherently lazy victims of natural soldiering, always seeking to thwart an employer's
desire to make them work harder. Unfortunately, Taylor's scientific management theories evolved into the scientific planning,
analysis, and control techniques that ignored the mutual benefit
that Taylor himself had proposed as the philosophical basis of
this ideology. Eventually even Taylor decried the increasing use
of scientific management techniques that merely exploited workers.

As management searched for methods to force employees to
produce more for less pay, and as they sought means of crushing
"dysfunctional" social relationships and subcultures, they soon hit
upon industrial psychology as a most promising tool. Psychological testing techniques that the military had refined during World
War I drew considerable attention during the 1920s because they
held forth the possibility of selecting the right person for every
job. Presumably, with appropriate psychological selection techniques, business could ensure worker satisfaction with jobs—a
heightened satisfaction that could, in turn, forestall dysfunctional
social relationships. In other words, by focusing on the individual,
managers might be able to avoid dealing with groups and subcultures. This sort of approach reached its zenith in the mid 1920s,
then gradually receded as it became clear that industrial psychology could not deliver on its early promises.

In its continuing quest to blunt perceptions of exploitation and to undermine the labor movement and worker subcultures by duplicating some of their perceived benefits, management moved toward paternalistic personnel programs during the 1920s. Loren Baritz, in his important work *The Servants of Power*, observed that management during this period took care of workers in the hope that they would reciprocate with appreciation, loyalty, and harder and more efficient work. Welfare plans covered virtually every aspect of the worker's life, from the moment he or she was hired by a centralized and "scientific" employment department to his retirement with subsequent pension benefits. Attempts to secure the support and cooperation of the workforce became increasingly popular and culminated in the human relations movement of the mid and late 1930s.

The Dayton Company aptly illustrates the paternalistic attitude assumed by many companies during these years. However, unlike many more cynical organizations, The Dayton Company's approach sprang from a genuine concern and feeling for its employees and thus smoothed the way for a graceful transition to the conscious management of subcultures.

George Dayton started out as a banker in the late 1800s, eventually investing in a dry goods store he later bought from his two partners. By 1910 Dayton and his two sons, Draper and Nelson, all of whom expressed a genuine concern for the company's employees, were running The Dayton Company. Through his own example George taught his sons the value of frequently communicating with employees through short messages, praise, and notes of good cheer included with employees' paychecks. An editor of the local paper once wrote: "Dayton employees are the highest paid in the city—part in cash, part in fatherly advice." A biographer of George Dayton wrote: "From the beginning he had enjoyed the sense of being patriarch to his growing family of employees." In fact, people often used the term "Daytonia" to describe the Dayton community of workers.

By 1917 The Dayton Company workforce had grown to 600, and by 1935 it numbered well over 1000. The company prospered and grew during this era at least partly because employees, gladly becoming members of the company's patriarchal corporate culture, worked together in harmony. The problems of destructive subculture did not afflict Dayton because the firm operated only one store, and because George Dayton and his sons drew all individuals and groups within the company into one well-functioning family.

Struggling for Understanding (1935–1955)

This era began with the translation of Max Weber's theories on bureaucratic organizations, the rise of the human relations movement, and the modern managerial theory promoted by such works as Chester Barnard's *The Functions of the Executive*. All of these developments strongly affected management's views of subcultures.

Max Weber sought to prove that bureaucracy, an inevitable result of industrial growth and an extension of the Western trend toward the "rationalization of social life," could provide the ideal organizational state. According to Weber, the "passionless organization" should surpass all other forms in terms of efficiency. The perfect bureaucracy, he insisted, would "dehumanize" organizations, eliminating irrational and unproductive personal emotions and feelings.

Bureaucratic management expanded and refined the mechanisms of managerial control introduced earlier under the auspices of scientific management. By coupling impersonal standards, rules, and procedures with careful specialization and division of labor, bureaucracies attempted to limit individual worker authority, personal discretion, and opportunism by concentrating power in the hands of top executives. Such a bureaucracy could supposedly "transcend" social groups and subcultures within the organization. Although bureaucracies did remedy many of the managerial evils and abuses of authority that were becoming common in business and government, they never achieved Weber's "passionless" ideal.

Then the pendulum swung again as the human relations movement got underway. This reaction against scientific management tried to reemphasize the effects of human sentiment and behavior on productivity and efficiency, and it found in the Hawthorne Experiments (described in Chapter 2), a strong argument for doing so. The Hawthorne Experiments concluded, among other things, that informal social relationships—organizational subcultures—controlled and regulated production. Why shouldn't businesses find a way to make these informal group relationships congruent with the goals of management?

In his book Chester Barnard recommended that management accept the obligation to "rationally" define and set the goals of the organization independent of the input of "non-logical" and, by implication, irrational individuals or representative groups. For their part, workers should accept the obligation to cooperate in the attainment of those goals. Whenever leadership fails, workers must also accept a certain amount of blame because real power and authority reside not with those who give the orders but with those who choose whether or not to carry them out. Further, once business has met "the level of the bare physiological necessities," workers should, according to Barnard, find sufficient motivation and satisfaction through nonmaterial incentives. This sort of thinking strongly influenced the early human relations movement.

One major aspect of the movement involved industrial counseling; company counselors would listen to worker frustrations and problems, allowing people to vent their feelings to provide catharsis and give the counselors a chance to reassure the frustrated worker that everything was all right. The company and its counselors offered a sympathetic ear without feeling compelled to make changes to eliminate the cause of frustration. In effect, companies hoped that their counseling programs would displace worker subcultures and the need for labor unions.

Barnard's logic also led to the commencement of motivation studies that tried to identify social and other noneconomic incentives that might improve worker performance. After analyzing the results of a number of "attitude studies," human relations experts began emphasizing "fair treatment" as the most effective antidote to industrial workers' frustration. Not surprisingly, their studies focused on social, not economic needs. At this point even unions fell into a social, rather than an economic category. If companies fulfilled their workers' social needs, unionization should become unnecessary.

Despite the new emphasis on social needs, this era witnessed continued managerial antagonism toward subcultures. However, Barnard had sown some seeds that would sprout and flourish through the next era, when management learned the hard way that they could no longer combat subcultures by avoiding and denying them.

When George Dayton died in 1938, his son Nelson became president of The Dayton Company. Continuing his father's tradition, he strove to keep his employees content by offering job security, encouraging managers to hone their human relations skills, and adopting his father's paternal posture.

The company experienced great growth and development during this period. Not wanting to exit either the high-price or the low-price market segments, Nelson pushed the company into horizontal expansion, whereby Dayton could sell more merchandise to all customer segments by offering more and more variety. The plan included selling more sports clothes by offering better sports clothes and attracting more customers by opening a bridal boutique and an interior decoration department. As the company grew larger and more complex, Nelson Dayton and other members of the Dayton family (both Nelson's and Draper's sons had joined the business) struggled with ways for the firm to become more efficient and effective. In keeping with the wisdom of the day, management adhered to the concepts of scientific and bureaucratic management, with emphasis placed on the theory and technique of merchandising. The resultant "by the book" approach accounted for every item of merchandise and every activity of every department. However, in the midst of all this scientific, bureaucratic, and control-oriented management, Dayton held onto some of the basic principles of "people management" that had so concerned its founder, allowing Dayton to begin understanding how to manage subcultures. One biographer made an insightful observation about Nelson Dayton: "Nelson's ability to make his sons feel a comfortable identification with the store and also to make each of the five feel an identification with each of the others in a cooperative enterprise, may well account for the phenomenon of a family-owned institution in which there is partnership without rivalry, departmentalization that makes good use of diversified talents, and an overall harmony that has been the marvel of the trade." This family subculture thrived in an era when scientific and bureaucratic management theory argued that subcultures and subgroups should be expunged from organizations.

Later in this same era Dayton inaugurated employee selection and training processes, developed sophisticated employee evaluation and career planning tools, adopted innovative retirement and insurance programs, and expanded aggressively into the suburbs of Minneapolis. Nelson Dayton died in 1950, but his influence would continue into later eras.

Recognition of Subcultures (1955–1970)

Eventually the limitations of bureaucracies became painfully apparent. The "passionless organization" fell into disrepute because no amount of managerial control could ever eliminate the impact of individual emotions and social relationships on the management of an enterprise. Thus the impact of subcultures on organizations, especially on public bureaucracies, came under intense scrutiny, particularly by the Institutional School of Research, championed by Philip Selznick. In his famous *TVA and the Grass Roots*, Selznick explored how competing subcultures can subvert even noble and moral organizational goals and turn them into instruments of private gain. When the principles of equal opportunity and individual rights get swept aside by the conflicting demands and economic pressures that characterize American enterprise, something has to give. Since ultimate goals, ideals, and principles frequently remain vague or unspecified, the opportunist can usurp them to his or her own advantage. Selznick warned executives never to underestimate the potential corruption of opportunism. Vested interests will inevitably arise, and they will concentrate on maintaining personal power and influence.

However, in *Leadership in Administration*, Selznick concluded that with appropriate leadership managers could obtain positive results from subcultures. If managers exercised what Selznick called "institutional leadership" they could wring from social groups tremendous benefits for both the organization and its employees. Selznick's brilliant analysis shaped one of the cornerstones of the corporate culture movement, which began consciously to tap the potential of subcultures.

Perhaps the strongest contribution of the human relations movement was in managerial training and development—managers obtained and sharpened the process and persuasion skills they needed to minimize conflict and justify their authority and control. Many writers continued to define human nature as fundamentally irrational and illogical, regarding workers as "social creatures" who want little more from life than to look good in the eyes of others. The managerial elite could supposedly exploit this fact of life by controlling their own sentiments and emotions, and by developing their logical thinking.

Organizational development (OD) specialists put one of the first modern tools, sensitivity training, into the hands of the paternalistic managerial elite. In the fifties the National Training Laboratories began preaching the value of sensitivity training, claiming that it would help managers improve their interpersonal styles through T-group feedback. Many tried it, but many failed to change their ingrained sentiments and interpersonal styles. When the researchers gave up on altering individuals, they tackled work groups and other organizational subcultures instead. Team building and a variety of related OD interventions focused on teaching the communication skills that can resolve group conflicts and facilitate cooperation. This was a noteworthy turning point: attention now turned toward the problems and needs of *groups*, rather than individuals, but this brand of OD also failed to deliver on its promises of dramatic change.

Then, in the early 1960s, Douglas MacGregor ignited an ideological revolution with his "Theory X, Theory Y" definitions of management, already mentioned in Chapter 9. Theory X represented the old school of thought, Theory Y a radically new school. In a bold, new way management was told that workers are an organization's most valuable asset, one which the old-fashioned paternalistic and authoritarian management behaviors can never fully exploit.

The revolution in thinking took time, however, because management initially used Theory Y to justify its authority and control. Despite the philosophical differences between the two, Theory Y argued less against high levels of managerial control than against certain forms of control MacGregor thought destructive. As MacGregor himself said, managers can use Theory Y "to provide an improved basis for the prediction and control of human behavior in industry." Many executives understandably fell in love with MacGregor's ideas and, ironically, opened themselves to a perspective that would finally lead them to incorporate employee subgroups into their management strategies.

The Dayton Company continued to grow during this era as the family-owned independent chain of stores strove to compete with the national chains. Having pioneered the idea of specialty units within department stores, Dayton set its first expansion sights on setting up a national chain of specialty shops, and the company's specialty and discount operations, such as Target, began dotting the retail landscape. The strategy effectively drew upon the company's recognition of the importance of subgroups inside the company and its knowledge about integrating them into the whole. In the mid 1960s, Stuart Wells, the first non-family Dayton Company president, gave employees a great deal of freedom to experiment with new ideas and to participate in decision making at all levels. Throughout this era, Wells's attitude helped instill a spirit and style that made Dayton a model for the effective management of subcultures.

In 1969, Dayton merged with J. L. Hudson's, a Detroit company founded in 1881 by a young Englishman. Together, Dayton's and Hudson's generated an annual volume of $800 million, with profits of $24 million and a combined staff of 22,000 full-time people. The merger brought with it two major benefits: Hudson's added a strong position in real estate and retailing to Dayton's discount and specialty operations; and the increased size after the merger offered employees more development and promotional opportunities. Additional acquisitions after the merger remained under autonomous management and kept their own names. Kenneth Dayton, an executive vice president, remarked in a local newspaper that, "each of our operations has its own character, its own flavor, its own trade territory."

By the end of this era Dayton Hudson had proven its ability to unify employees while allowing for the integrity of subgroups, whether departments, specialty units, stores, chains, or autonomous acquisitions. Even when it operated under non-family presidents like Stuart Wells, the philosophies and orientations of founder George Dayton still permeated the company.

Exploration of Subcultures (1970–1980)

By the beginning of the 1970s concern turned toward the work environment and how it might be improved. Some attempts to redesign the workplace, such as job enlargement or enrichment, returned partial responsibility and control over the work process to the workers themselves. In setting up autonomous work teams, managers were recognizing the value and desirability of subcultures. Other job redesigning efforts addressed the physical layout of working environments; many companies restructured work areas to reinforce social relationships and subcultures to attain higher degrees of motivation and productivity.

Labor participation in management and the quality of life movement also represented a logical extension of Theory Y. If executives accepted employees as knowledgeable, creative, and full of potential, shouldn't they include workers in the decision making process? Increasingly, both formal and informal employee groups became respected sources of information, creativity, and innovation, and managers who ignored those capacities did so at their own peril.

Executives began to worry about business sectors, market segment economic niches, and value chains. Devising strategic business units, product groupings, and organizational entities capable of responding more effectively to growing competitive challenges, they tacitly admitted that well-managed groups within groups could strengthen strategic planning.

During this era Dayton Hudson's store-within-a-store concept proved the value of healthy subcultures. One of Dayton Hudson's senior vice presidents for store operations enunciated the company's philosophy in *Merchandising Magazine:* "We use the store-within-a-store idea when it's appropriate, such as for hi-fi. As a concept, the store-within-a-store works throughout Dayton's, even when the category is not as sharply defined physically as the sound rooms are. We encourage customers to think of Dayton's as specialists in all the areas the traditional department store has encompassed."

However, as can easily happen to a company operating in the vanguard of new ideas, Dayton Hudson began drifting toward philosophies that hampered its ability to manage and integrate increasingly diverse business entities and subcultures. The executive who replaced Joe Hudson at Hudson's, Edwin Roberts, encouraged his staff to develop a "killer instinct." One Hudson executive said of Roberts, "He'll ask you very nicely and quietly what you do and how you run your business, and you'll think 'What a great guy.' Then the next day, he'll fire you." *Business Week* reported in 1972 that Dayton Hudson's CEO, Ken Dayton, liked to see lots of competition among his various companies and divisions. A few years later, *Forbes* reported that "Target store managers are like automatons." According to the *Forbes* report, Target managers had lost responsibility for pricing and merchandising decisions because they followed a lock-step "plannogram," a comprehensive blueprint that strictly identified the location of every item, shelf, and department. In 1980 *Business Week* observed that "since 1974 Dayton Hudson has been centralizing operations and building in rigid financial controls that outsiders now see as its strong suit." Before long such regimentation caused alarming management turnover problems.

After a number of people left to join the rival May Company, Dayton Hudson decided to offer highly competitive compensation packages, but according to *Business Week,* "Although well-compensated, company managers operate under a performance standard believed to be the industry's most stringent; slavish devotion to return on investment . . . brooks no excuse for failure." Would such hard-nosed performance standards, internal competition, and stringent management blueprints compromise the ability of Dayton Hudson's executives to function as individuals and manage subgroups? Or, could Bill Andres, Ken Dayton's successor, find a way to bring complementarity, rather than conflict, to the dual forces of freewheeling autonomy and centralized control? While the business press waited for answers to these questions, a new era began to unfold.

Legitimizing Corporate Cultures (1980–1985)

By the early 1980s, management began to tap the potential benefits of subcultures. Many companies toyed with adaptations of Japanese techniques. Productivity teams, quality circles, and similar groups designed to obtain worker feedback that could help improve quality and productivity became popular, and since they practiced some degree of self-regulation, they reinforced the importance of independent worker social systems. William Ouchi's *Theory Z* served as the bible for much of this activity.

Increasingly throughout the eighties, corporate leaders placed strong emphasis on worker involvement and the related issues of innovation, productivity, and employee satisfaction. In the face of stepped-up foreign competition and stepped-down worker productivity, such issues became crucial to the profitability of many firms. Tom Peters and Robert Waterman led an almost patriotic chorus when their *In Search of Excellence* proclaimed that "there is an art of American management, and it works!" Capitalizing on the research of James MacGregor Burns, Philip Selznick, and others, Peters and Waterman tried to show how American business could realize the sort of "ideal" organization proposed many years before by Chester Barnard. Management responsibility, they argued, revolves around identifying the values that lead to corporate excellence. These, gleaned from scrutiny of America's "best" companies, could be condensed into eight attributes, which Peters and Waterman promoted as a recipe for success. Like Barnard, Peters and Waterman implied that "excellent" organizations are inherently moral, and that they build on traditions of moral and transforming leadership, "that builds on man's need for meaning, leadership that creates institutional purpose."

According to the "excellence" model, a charismatic leader carves out a purpose, identity and mission—usually early in the history of an organization—that employees, then subsequent leaders can inculcate through dogged persistence and consistency. Managers must become leaders, whose roles go far beyond the bounds of rational management. Such leaders fashion a sense of identity and purpose for employees, securing in return high levels of motivation, commitment, and performance. The leader becomes a new sort of patriarch.

Such a formula may have worked historically for some of America's best-run companies, but could it work for existing groups and organizations desiring change? The corporate culture movement tried to answer that question by studying systems of shared beliefs and values. Unfortunately, when the entire organization becomes the unit of analysis, effectively creating, managing, or changing corporate culture takes on gigantic, even impossible, proportions. While executives recognized the power and potential of strong corporate cultures, they soon found that dealing with them on an organizational scale, especially when they wanted to make changes, could be an ambiguous, complex, and frustrating task.

Under Bill Andres' leadership, Dayton Hudson went a long way toward resolving the apparent conflict between operational (subgroup) autonomy and corporate control. In an important speech on the subject, Andres shed light on the reasons for his company's success in this area: "At Dayton Hudson, we believe the best way to attract the best talent, to keep and motivate that talent, is by granting a high degree of autonomy to our operating companies . . . by creating a spirit of teamwork and participation throughout our organization. We have carefully thought through which functions should be centralized, and which should be decentralized. And where we come out is this: We think it's critical to keep the operating and merchandising decisions out in the field, close to the customer—where the action is. We place the responsibility for operations right where it belongs—squarely on the shoulders of our operating company CEOs. We expect them to look out to their environments and to their customers, and not back to the corporation for guidance in making their operating and merchandising decisions. But we balance this autonomy with corporate accountability when it comes to ensuring that we have the strategic plans, the people and the capital to grow."

In an interview with *Stores Magazine*, Andres further clarified the company's formula for success when he described the Dayton Hudson culture as simultaneously people-oriented and strategy-oriented. Strategies may originate at headquarters, but employee feedback, discussion, and listening programs try to involve all the company's people. Further, each Dayton Hudson employee works out an individualized development plan with a supervisor. Kenneth Macke, Andres' successor as CEO, summarized his own philosophy in the company's 1984 annual report: "The most important thing I can do as CEO is to get our people to think about how they can do things better. My job is to create an environment that helps them to think." This commitment to individual and group innovation combined with common purpose helped create a healthy corporate culture at Dayton Hudson. Chain presidents, granted freedom to operate as they deem necessary, encourage standardized approaches to many aspects of their businesses, while allowing individual store managers to use discretion where it really counts. In this way Dayton Hudson operating units, with their distinct subcultures, can embrace the larger values of the corporate culture without sacrificing autonomy, creativity, and experimentation.

This dynamic interaction may in part explain why Dayton Hudson won accolades from the University of Southern California School of Business Administration in 1984 as the best-managed company in America. When USC presented the Vanguard Corporation Award to the company, the school cited its "unusual dynamism and entrepreneurial zeal" and "uncompromising ethical standards." Only the company itself found flaws in its management when it scolded itself for not "finding more ways to create satisfying career paths for part-time employees."

Celebrating Subcultures (1985–Late 1990s)

Quite naturally management researchers began trying to turn the lessons learned from the corporate culture movement into practical principles any company could apply. Many focused on the ways a leader can establish and reinforce central values, foster creativity and innovation, and provide a sense of direction, vision and purpose. At the same time, culture researchers began to tackle more accessible units of analysis, focusing on subunits, subcultures and their interactions. As business came to understand the nature and functions of both the "institutional" and the "cultural" leader, and as research deduced principles that work for small groups, the corporate culture movement has gradually evolved a useful set of tools for management.

Alan Wilkins, a well known corporate culture observer, notes that unified corporate cultures, wherein the entire organization shares certain beliefs and values, do not come easily. To understand the "culture" of an entire organization, one must begin by examining the values of subunits including functions, divisions, departments, work teams, and managerial groupings. Further, researchers from Selznick on down have repeatedly argued that one must adopt a developmental approach by looking into corporate history. The years ahead will culminate in transformation only if executives successfully implement such advice.

In 1985, *Fortune* magazine reported that a shakeout among department stores was under way due to an excess of selling space and fewer shoppers. However, *Fortune* said that "overstoring does not much bother what industry observers like to call power retailers—those confident merchandisers such as R. H. Macy & Co., Dayton Hudson Corp., and The Limited, Inc., that have such financial strength, marketing skill, and reasonably priced quality merchandise that they can bull their way into any market, however saturated, and make a profit." In addition to the strength derived from sheer size and profitability, Dayton Hudson early on began celebrating subcultures and linking them together into an integrated whole. One key to its success has been its ability to manage change. The company has always prided itself on adjusting to the fast-changing trends of merchandising, but it has tried not to do so at the expense of culture.

But don't strong corporate cultures thrive on consistency? Yes, they do, but if their values run deeply enough, cultures can adapt quite easily to changing circumstances. Having learned to pay attention to subcultures early in its history, Dayton Hudson can maintain deep-seated values despite a rapidly changing industry. Today Dayton Hudson is a growth-oriented retailer composed of over 1200 stores in 48 states dedicated to providing value in assortment, quality fashion, competitive prices, and convenience through multiple retail formats and autonomous operations. The company's Target Stores, with revenues of $4 billion, operate in 22 states with 226 low-margin stores. Its Mervyn's unit currently produces revenues of $2.5 billion with 148 value-oriented department stores in nine states. And the Dayton Hudson Department Store Company operates 37 stores in 7 states and currently produces $1.5 billion in revenues. The company's specialty merchandisers include Lechmere with 10 stores in New England and revenues of almost $1 billion. The company as a whole currently employs 128,000 employees, enjoys revenues of almost $9 billion and earnings of close to $300 million, and it has so far managed to balance the autonomy of subcultures and the common commitment to Dayton Hudson principles.

Much of Dayton Hudson's future success will depend on its continued ability to spot and capitalize on consumer trends. Recognizing market niches and devoting the appropriate amount and type of customer service to each should continue to be a major preoccupation. In some cases, technology will replace human workers, as with a system called Touchcom that presently lets customers shop for furniture via computer. Finding ways to meet customer needs while keeping staffing levels at a minimum will also preoccupy Dayton Hudson's leader. Because Dayton Hudson offers so many types of products, from high-margin to low-margin goods, it must always worry about adapting appropriate selling techniques to each product group.

Managing Interrelated Subcultures

Executives planning for the future must discover how to orchestrate corporate environments that nurture and harmonize subcultures and substrategies, and we think this can be done by applying the principles of complexity management.

Until now, many managers and management researchers have thought of culture in rather vague, general terms. Culture is "who we are," a sort of collective character, and if management doesn't like that character, it can change it with an appropriate redirection of corporate strategy, policy, and leadership styles. Unfortunately, corporate character resists such a simplistic approach to change because it is based on a complex set of organizational assumptions and habits rather than on a new collection of traits. The simplistic approach lends itself to a black-or-white mentality, while a look at assumptions and habits takes into account the gray areas that characterize so much of corporate culture. No culture is perfect: an excellent one today may wither without constant caring attention, and yesterday's weak one may grow stronger with patient nurturing. In either case, change does not occur overnight but gradually over years and even decades.

Further complicating the picture, actions to maintain or improve culture in one area can inadvertently undermine efforts in other areas, because the actions that foster technical, manufacturing, and marketing innovation may not only differ, they may conflict. Research suggests that as a company becomes competent in fostering a certain type of innovation such as in marketing, it systematically loses its capacity to innovate effectively in other areas, such as manufacturing and engineering. Ironically, the solutions to today's problem may turn into the causes of tomorrow's crisis.

How do managers deal with such ironies? The answer comes, once again, from an understanding of paradox management. The leaders of the Future 500 will have to learn how to blend the old and the new as circumstances force them to shift strategic emphasis from one area to another.

Many managers make the common mistake of allowing groups and individuals to abandon guiding principles when embarking on specific new programs, policies, and practices. In such instances freedom can deteriorate into anarchy. While principles without applications are the assassins of success, the converse also holds true: actions that abandon guiding principles are the murderers of unified cultures.

Translating principles into practices poses one of the great challenges of the future because any attempt at rigid standardization of practices, policies, structures, systems, and reporting procedures, although it may reinforce efficiency in some areas, will undermine it in others. Again, executives must maintain a process perspective wherein practices and subcultures change over time but principles that form the basis of the corporate culture remain more consistent and unchanging.

Strong, unified corporate cultures offer concurrent advantages and risks. Any culture that encourages its members to define themselves, their goals, and their integrity according to a central value system generates high levels of productive commitment, but such commitment can easily turn unproductive when circumstances change. As early as 1957, Selznick noted that institutionalization creates a situation wherein cultural values may improperly override organizational tasks or functions and vice versa. A strong marketing culture can dampen product innovation, and overemphasis on product development can short-circuit the need to get new products to market.

Can executives really expect the different subcultures under their direction to retain highly autonomous, independent institutionalized values and norms when such norms contradict those of other subcultures?

Sheri Bushnell beautifully described how this can be done in her working paper "Borderguard." As Bushnell sees it, the borderguard recognizes the natural boundaries subgroups draw around themselves and knows how to translate the terminology, concepts, and thinking used by one subgroup into language and ideas another subgroup can understand. For example, suppose a company has designed a new product, the specifications of which must be communicated from the design department to manufacturing for cost and production analysis. Since the designers and producers work within fairly strict boundaries and use their own special languages, a borderguard research and development manager might need to serve as a translator between the two groups.

By using multiple organizational contacts, borderguards defuse potentially explosive intolerance of differences between individuals or groups. They also function as buffers, making deals and trades between subcultures. Careful and timely representation can avoid a lot of unnecessary conflict without damaging the integrity of each subculture. Trades and deals also include negotiating with other groups for necessary resources. For example, an innovative team within an organization may be able to exist only insofar as its members can barter and trade for the resources they need to accomplish a specific assignment.

Think of borderguards as agents of change who can minimize the negative effects of change. Sometimes they encourage minor modifications in tasks and objectives, while at other times they foster dramatic changes, even to the point of creating a brand new subculture. Regardless of the degree of change involved, however, borderguards must always account for both the internal state of the organization (the strivings, inhibitions, and competencies that exist within each subculture) and the external demands for survival of the organization as a whole. With this perspective, the complexity manager, acting as a borderguard, can adapt the guiding principles of the organization to changing conditions without serious violation of those principles.

Another key to the successful management of change involves the selection of a "social base," the business or organizational environment in which the subculture can most comfortably operate. To select the right social base the complexity manager assesses a subculture's ability to live within the guidelines imposed by coalitions of powerful organizational, professional, and even governmental restrictions.

Just as organizations can rely on a variety of mechanisms to buffer themselves against the demands and inconsistencies of their external environments, so can subcultures employ a variety of tactics to ameliorate the negative effects sometimes created by the demands of the umbrella organization. In most cases organizations and their subgroups resolve such inconsistencies by decoupling alignments between imposed structures and their own activities. Specifically, they try to replace regimented evaluation by outsiders with more informal internal measures. The successful management of informal measures depends a great deal on trust, confidence, and good faith on both sides. Otherwise, informality will create suspicion and bring back the undesired formal structure and controls. For example, Dayton Hudson's Target Stores have been blazing a trail in new and innovative retailing formats since 1962, and the chain has been able to maintain its autonomy, set its own course, and measure its own results because its umbrella believes in supporting subcultures. However, if Target Stores had not been so successful, the umbrella might have folded and introduced a set of corporate controls and measures.

In their early stages, subcultures are like seedlings, susceptible to many threats from their environment. Until they have sufficiently matured to withstand sudden changes in the environment, these seedlings thrive best in relatively protected isolation. However, once they have matured, they can survive quite strong pressures from the outside, even from the umbrella organization itself.

Given a number of healthy, thriving subcultures, a certain amount of organizational rivalry becomes inevitable. However, this rivalry need not be destructive because, when properly controlled, it can assure the organization of a diverse range of creative styles. No one style can ever provide all the solutions to all the problems an organization encounters, and borrowed or traded traits can help each subculture refine its own unique style. As we saw earlier in this book, independence and interdependence, like freedom and responsibility, form two inseparable parts of the same equation, and balancing the equation results in the sort of dynamic equilibrium that Future 500 companies need to thrive.

Interrelated Subcultures and Complexity Management

Historically, subcultures have steadily evolved from sameness to uniqueness, a direction that clearly mandates executives to weigh more thoroughly than ever the ways they manage them within their corporate ecosystems. Not only must executives continue creating distinctive subcultures, but they must also strive to integrate and interrelate all their subcultures with one another.

How can executives create, maintain, and integrate subcultures so that they simultaneously foster both unity and diversity? This question has obviously been on the minds of managers at companies like EMI, Shouldice Hospital, Eastman Kodak, and Dayton Hudson.

At EMI, now owned by Thorn Industries, executives must figure out how to manage subcultures in the first place. At Shouldice they must decide how to perpetuate and expand upon previously successful subculture management practices, while at Eastman

Kodak they must resolve the issue of making the new emphasis on innovation and subculture autonomy really work without succumbing to the traditional traps of the past. And at Dayton Hudson they must continue grappling with the balance between subculture diversity and centralized standardization and control. In each case, making subcultures independently effective but at the same time congruent with one another and with the overall corporation will spell the difference between success and failure. How can complexity management help guarantee success?

Applying Perspective Management

Since perspective management respects diversity, executives can use it to maintain the integrity of subcultures, while simultaneously marshaling all subcultures behind a common purpose. Perspective managers can:

- Insist that division, department, function, and area managers relate their organizational unit's purpose and activities to all those with which it interacts, including the corporation as a whole. If the corporation has established clear and concise principles, responsibility for integration can reside at the lowest levels of organization. For example, Thorn Industries could place the responsibility for determining areas of independence and interdependence directly on EMI's management. Such a tactic could shore up EMI's own awareness of subculture management.

- Include a culture and subculture analysis in the strategic planning process, thus helping business units tie their strategies to their culture and subculture development plans. This added attention should cause managers to address in an ongoing way the balance between independence and interdependence. For example, Dayton Hudson could include a culture and subculture review section in the strategic planning guidelines distributed to divisions and subsidiaries.

Applying Power Management

Since power management provides freedom for subcultures to act, executives can use it to strengthen diversity and unification behind a common purpose. Power managers can:

- Give managers the freedom to become strong leaders who mold their own subcultures within their respective spheres of influence and authority. Then managers could properly take into account the unique characteristics of their people, their tasks, and all relevant aspects of their respective environments. For example, Shouldice Hospital could convince business unit heads that different organizational units focusing on different medical procedures and market segments can and should operate very differently from one another.

- Encourage managers to avoid placing their subcultures at odds with the rest of the corporation. Vigilance should be maintained against harmful "we-they" attitudes. For example, if a division manager at Eastman Kodak were to use the newly granted power and freedom of the company's reorganization to rebel against Kodak's common purposes and the company's mutually benefitting principles, the company should help that manager change his or her attitude. If the person cannot change, termination or reassignment would become necessary.

- Give employees the freedom to join subcultures without the usual obstacles to corporate transfer. Employees should be encouraged to seek out subcultures within the corporate ecosystem that fit them best. For example, Dayton Hudson could encourage more active transferring among its divisions and subsidiaries to give employees the freedom to select their own work environments. Such an orientation could greatly increase the commitment of people to the common purposes of the company.

Applying Pivot Management

Since pivot management enhances individual performance, executives can use it to promote both subculture and corporate culture values. Pivot managers can:

- Allow individuals within subcultures to develop work groups and form the relationships they need to perform their jobs. In order to maximize performance and fulfillment, the corporation should extend the same flexibility that fosters subculture development to every individual employee. For example, Eastman Kodak could encourage managers to make changes in their own spheres of influence and authority similar to those that the corporation made in its overall corporate environment. This would mean cascading the principles behind the reorganization down to every individual, making all individuals shapers of their own experiences and encouraging them to take risks and to innovate.

• Encourage all subculture managers to develop relationship networks with other subculture managers in order to share experiences and ideas more effectively. For example, Dayton Hudson could teach managers to develop relationships with managers throughout the corporation for the purpose of sharing perspectives and innovations. Such a heightened emphasis on networking could greatly accelerate the development of strong, cohesive subcultures throughout the company.

In the end, the accomplishment of individual and collective purposes in the most fulfilling ways possible will create winning organizations. Companies, processes, systems, strategies, and cultures are the means to fulfillment, never ends unto themselves. When the means allow for both individual and collective well-being, integrity and interdependence among subcultures become a reality.

CHAPTER TWELVE

Individual Fulfillment: Tuning Every Employee into the New Millennium

Man is more interesting than men. It's him, *not* them *whom God made in His image. Each is more precious than all.*

—ANDRÉ GIDE

The Sanctity of the Individual

AT&T was the largest private business organization in the world prior to the divestiture of the Bell Operating Companies at the end of 1983. Although much smaller after divestiture, AT&T remained a vast enterprise operating in high technology and the long-distance telephone markets. Each of the Bell Operating Companies, in turn, itself became a large enterprise.

More than anything else the breakup has forced AT&T and the operating companies to face new dimensions of competition that have placed great pressures on all employees to develop new skills, capabilities, and strengths. This development will preoccupy AT&T for some time, but unless the company brings these new capabilities to bear on its customers, the customers will turn to its competitors for service; if it doesn't respect its competitors, its competition will do it in; and unless it honors its own individual workers, the best ones will leave for greener pastures.

To its credit, AT&T has begun to infuse a marketing aggressiveness and innovativeness in its people. When competitors started to enter AT&T's overseas market, AT&T cut prices, and when GTE, Sprint, and MCI became aggressive at home, the company worked to win regulatory approval to reduce its long-distance rates for small businesses. Randall Tobias, chairman of AT&T Communications, Inc., told *Business Week*, "The innovation is coming from us now." Good marketing sense? Yes, but a sense of individual worth as well.

AT&T must also decide which new businesses it should enter. Under the divestiture agreement, it can freely attack the computer and data processing markets, but some Wall Street computer experts have argued that computers may not be a worthwhile venture because AT&T lacks the refined salesmanship that has made IBM such a powerhouse. Perhaps AT&T's future profits will depend more on its old phone business than ever.

In fact, AT&T has shown little interest in confronting IBM in its bread-and-butter mainframe computer line. Instead, AT&T has set its sights on the faster-growing automated office equipment market. Since most information processing in the future will take place at scattered locations with terminals and networked desktop personal computers, perhaps AT&T can exploit its communications expertise by linking offices together better than anyone else.

Still, no matter which strategies AT&T pursues, it must overcome ongoing public relations problems. Since the general public associated AT&T with more than just long-distance service prior to the divestiture, AT&T waged an enormous marketing campaign in 1985 and 1986 to change that perception, but many consumers still express confusion. Given a longstanding skepticism toward Ma Bell, consumers will continue to keep a watchful eye on changes in cost and service.

Can AT&T reach out to both its old and new customers in a way that its formerly regulated environment never required? Apparently, it can. Already company operators have begun to solicit subscribers, and their pitch has clearly won over many confused or undecided consumers.

The success of AT&T's marketing program for its long-distance service partly offset 1985's poor showing on the company's equipment side. This prompted Jack B. Grubman, a Paine Webber Inc., analyst, to say in a *Business Week* interview, "Before the breakup, when people got excited about AT&T, they got excited about their technology, the promise of computers and high-growth markets. Ironically, the most innovative and best-managed piece of AT&T has turned out to be the long-distance unit."

None of AT&T's new product lines or consumer marketing programs can succeed without the continued dedication of the company's employees. Just as its business has begun evolving into a new form after the divestiture, the AT&T culture has begun changing, too, because not even the best new product in the world can score unless an astute salesperson can sell it, so AT&T must now launch a major sales training effort.

In addition to retraining, the company has also undertaken major changes in the way it treats employees on the job. *Fortune* magazine describes the current situation this way: "The huge staff divisions at corporate headquarters—Ma Bell's 'general departments'—used to issue tomes of detailed instructions on how every task should be performed. 'You weren't measured by your success but how little trouble you caused,' says one former executive. The general departments don't exist anymore, and nowadays employees are held accountable for what they accomplish."

Another important concern for AT&T will be its relationship with the communications unions. After the divestiture, AT&T and the CWA (Communications Workers of America) enjoyed a fairly cooperative relationship compared to the adversarial one that afflicted the Bell Operating Companies. On June 1, 1986, 155,000 union workers struck after rejecting a proposed 8 percent pay increase over three years. Then on June 26, 1986, the strike ended when the union knuckled under to the 8 percent increase.

In spite of some clear progress, AT&T managers and employees are still struggling for clear direction. Change has shocked the 100-year-old culture. Can the company fashion a new one for the future? *Fortune* magazine succinctly summed up the situation: "Ironically, the old culture AT&T is trying to shed had much in it that enlightened American companies are trying to achieve today. AT&T was famous for guaranteeing lifelong employment, for the loyalty it inspired among employees, for promoting from within, for its consensual decision making style, and for the high quality of its services and products—many of the characteristics that books on managerial excellence tell us are behind the Japanese success. The problem was that these values had grown up in a sort of cocoon of guaranteed profits, not in response to market needs or competitive pressures."

To thrive in the future AT&T and other organizations must create mutual benefit for all stakeholders. By mutual we mean the fulfillment of each individual as well as the organization. Can leaders really satisfy the desires and needs of individual stakeholders in the corporate environment while meeting the performance demands and expectations of the corporate entity? We think they can but we also recognize that establishing and maintaining a balance between individual and collective well-being will be hard.

Take the Ford Motor Company, for example. Formerly antagonistic UAW officials now meet with Ford's Board of Directors to provide input and join in discussions in a whole new spirit of cooperation and partnership. As a result, Ford and the UAW have agreed in the last few years to such things as profit sharing, wage restraints, plant closing limitations, and job security programs. In addition, the company has instituted new approaches to training, retraining, and problem solving. Today management and union individuals share a new perspective on establishing an environment of mutual benefit.

When Chevron and Gulf Oil merged, human resources manager Frank Dickson and strategic planner Joe Synan opted for early retirement. Now these two men help other companies design outplacement programs that help organizations and individual employees deal gracefully with layoffs and terminations. Dickson and Synan, having experienced outplacement firsthand, now help executives and companies recognize properly handled layoffs or firings as potentially positive for both the company and individuals. Sensitive outplacement programs can help people find jobs as good as, if not better than, the ones they have lost. Joe Synan recently told Perry Pascarella in an *Industry Week* interview, "If managers were aware of the good things we have seen happen to people who go through outplacement workshops, they wouldn't be so afraid of firing people." Even in the aftermath of difficult downsizing or cost cutting decisions, individuals as well as organizations can win.

Any discussion of mutual benefit would not be complete without mentioning IBM, where respect for the individual has benefitted all concerned. Well-trained executives at this highly successful company recognize the individual as the key to dealing with change and the future. IBM adheres to a full employment practice whereby no employee loses his or her job involuntarily. When change may require downsizing, cost cutting, or staff reduction in a division, employees (and customers, investors, and other stakeholders, for that matter) know exactly how the change will affect them. The company's approach to cutting the workforce involves not firing people but stresses, instead, opportunities for transfer, relocation, retraining, or otherwise redirecting careers. Effective communication helps immensely and weekly and monthly publications, meetings, retreats, hot-lines, and open-door policies implement IBM's philosophy of mutual benefit.

Before considering how complexity management can help fulfill individuals, let's review the historical roles and paths of individuals in American corporations.

The Maturing Management of Individuals

During this century management of individuals has become a greater concern as workers have steadily demanded higher levels of meaning and fulfillment in their organizational lives.

The diagram on the following page compares the growth of management of the individual eras with the management eras we presented in Chapter 2.

Controlling the Individual (1910–1960)

Unlike other elements of the corporate environment, human beings actually shape their landscapes, but they can also be shaped by them.

At the turn of the century, organizations reflected the personalities of the entrepreneurs who founded them. Such founders felt they had won an absolute right to control their companies' and their employees' affairs according to the principles of the Protestant work ethic. Their organizations, they believed, had come into being as a result of their superiority and existed primarily for their own benefit. The thought of others reaping substantial benefits from their organizations seemed not only

Management of Individuals

1890	1910	1930	1950	1970	1990	2010

Controlling the Individual

Recognizing the Individual

Honoring the Individual

Individual Fulfillment

Structure

Productivity

Systems

Strategy

Culture

Innovation

Leadership

Complexity Management

Management Eras

repugnant but "unholy." Employees, lacking the industry and "virtue" of the founders, did not deserve such benefits.

These attitudes faced two challenges: the growing muscle of organized labor and the increasing power of managers. As we discussed earlier, a master-servant relationship between "inside" contractors and their crews of workers governed the work process in the pre-modern management age, and owner/entrepreneurs felt little need to control the process, depending instead on the expertise of the contractor foremen to keep production flowing.

Eventually, however, workers, especially the skilled craftsmen, found wages and working conditions inadequate and, in some cases, subhuman. Their control of the production process and a centuries-old guild tradition gave them a potentially powerful tool with which they could win concessions from their employers. If employers felt entitled to ignore basic human needs and desires, the craftsmen, in turn, felt entitled to secure them by force. Eventually labor unions derived their justification from this conflict. As owners/entrepreneurs searched for ways to combat organized craftsmen, their growing army of managers searched for an ideology that would legitimize and expand their own individual power. The owners/entrepreneurs and their professional managers eventually accepted a form of scientific management because it helped strip workers and inside contractors of their control over the production process. The moral justification was clear: By remaining in operation over time a business gained the right to control its employees. Of course employees could quit their jobs, but if they stayed they must submit to the "divine right" of a morally justified hierarchy.

Industrial psychology also traces its roots to this era. As indicated in Chapter 11, psychological testing techniques refined in the military during World War I drew considerable attention during the 1920s, with the new industrial psychologists hoping to achieve the same sophistication in understanding workers that managers had developed in understanding the production process. If engineers, using scientific methods of observation, experimentation, and analysis could plan out the production process to the smallest detail, and design machinery to perform to their minutest specifications, why couldn't industrial psychologists, through similar methods, help organizations select and train workers and put into management's hands the "psychological levers" they needed to get employees to perform according to tight specifications? Attempts to answer that question carried an implicit definition of individuals as little more than living cogs in a machine designed to benefit owners and managers.

Later in this era came the translation of Weber's theories on bureaucratic organizations, and the development of the human relations movement, both of which attempted to control individuals in organizations, though neither went beyond the old "unit of production" definition of the individual.

Through impersonal standards, rules, and procedures, coupled with careful specialization and division of labor, Weber-style bureaucracies sought to control the amount of authority, personal discretion, and opportunism available to individual workers. In effect, bureaucracies tried to supplant individual needs and desires with organizational ones derived from supposedly more objective, universal, and, of course, morally justified criteria. Many of the best leaders during this era assumed what they thought of as a morally noble patriarchal responsibility for their employees, taking care of the organization's subjects in a paternalistic way, exercising their right and their inherent responsibility to determine what is best for both the organization and its workers.

Returning again to the Hawthorne Studies and the subsequent works of Mayo, Rothlesberger, and Dickson. This early research concluded that workers banding together to regulate production through informal social relationships, rather than the efforts of management, primarily controlled production. Mayo considered social groups that restricted production as primarily irrational in nature. Consequently early efforts in human relations focused on undermining them and replacing them with more formal organizational ones. Mayo and other researchers seemed to ignore the fact that workers gravitated toward informal control mostly as a defense against layoffs, poor working conditions, and lower piece rates, all of which were resulting from increased production and volatile economic conditions. Although the Hawthorne Experiments might have eventually revealed this fact, those studies ended prematurely when extensive layoffs changed the composition of the experimental groups so much that researchers could not rely on the data.

Throughout the early human relations movement individual needs fell into a social, rather than economic category, a classification that, in part, produced the sort of industrial counseling where company counselors would listen to worker frustrations and problems as a means of catharsis rather than change. In the long run the counselors failed to subvert social alliances such as unions because they never believed in the economic purpose of those alliances.

As noted earlier, the human relations movement initiated the whole field of managerial training and development, which tried to give managers process and persuasion skills to minimize conflict and justify their authority and control. However, the human relations movement widened the chasm between labor and management. On the one side stood the workers—base, irrational individuals who defined themselves according to informal social relationships and conspired against their employers from motives of selfishness, greed, and laziness. On the other side stood the managers—scientifically selected, morally justified, and trained in business schools, who have transcended their irrational natures and offer other individuals a chance to do likewise. Of course, no amount of sensitivity training or counseling could close the gap between such adversaries.

So researchers turned their attention to groups and organizational development. With its team-building techniques and a variety of related interventions designed to give managers better communication skills for resolving conflicts and obtaining cooperation from work groups, this marked a turning point in the history of the management of individuals. If managers couldn't control individuals, maybe they could control groups. But organizational development also failed to deliver dramatic improvement.

American Telephone and Telegraph Company (AT&T) began operations in 1885. Alexander Graham Bell had invented the telephone, but Theodore Vail invented the Bell System after Gardiner Hubbard, Bell's father-in-law and an original backer of Bell Telephone, hired Vail as general manager of Bell Telephone in 1898. In 1911 Vail proceeded to organize AT&T's subsidiaries into operating companies.

AT&T's philosophy, culture, structure, and employee relations policies came under Vail's strong influence as he assumed moral and physical leadership of the company. During his tenure, AT&T thoroughly standardized all operating procedures and anything else that wasn't already tied down. Adopting an Army-like organizational structure, the company became an epitome of bureaucracy. Internal competition substituted for external competition, and a comprehensive rating system quantified and compared workers' output across departments and divisions.

For fifty years standardization guided every job, every piece of furniture, even the company's product, "POTS" (Plain Old Telephone Service). By routinizing the "production" process, management strove to maintain tight control over all workers and their roles. Although this paternalistic approach treated workers as production units, it also created a good deal of job mobility because a Bell employee could leave a job in one city and pick up the same role the next day somewhere else. According to Alvin Toffler in his revealing book *The Adaptive Corporation,* based on a four-year study of AT&T, "AT&T became identified with the supposedly scientific attempt to reduce each individual job to a standardized sequence of 'most efficient' routines!" You could deduce a person's job role and level of responsibility by simply noting his or her immediate environment: a Level 1 manager sat in an open area with no partitions and used phones with no additional lines; group supervisors occupied semiprivate offices; and district heads inhabited private offices with carpeting and other amenities.

According to another chronicler, Sonny Kleinfield, in his book *The Biggest Company on Earth,* "On the one hand, AT&T zealously guards the privacy of its employees; on the other, it inevitably intrudes into their personal lives, encouraging, if not exactly enforcing, what some AT&T people speak of as a numbing uniformity of attitude, appearance, and action." Not surprisingly, Vail's six-word mission statement for the company, which became the driving force throughout this era, proclaimed, "One System, One Policy, Universal Service."

When Walter Gifford became president of AT&T in 1927, he continued strengthening Vail's paternalistic philosophy. While Vail had laid the foundation and structure for the faith, Gifford completed the work by enshrining the AT&T culture based on the "One System" bible. Even though the company conducted many programs and studies to improve employee satisfaction and productivity, these efforts merely reflected a desire to prevent deviation from the uniformity of AT&T's strict policies. The famous Hawthorne Studies at Western Electric, the maker of Bell telephones that AT&T acquired in its early days, resulted in counseling programs designed to let employees air personal or job-related problems. However, these programs only augmented management's control over the productivity and conformity of individuals. Eventually, the company abandoned the counseling program when it became clear that mere talk would not satisfy discontented people.

Nevertheless, employees during this era felt a sense of loyalty to an organization that tended to their needs with lifetime benefits and a "family" atmosphere. Submitting to the company's uniform practices and policies, they seldom rebelled against the parental control of management. To be sure, employees distrusted the company's elaborate and dehumanizing measurement systems, but they also accepted management's explanation: "If it doesn't get measured, it doesn't get done." Believing they worked for a "good" company, employees saw little reason not to obey and conform, and corporate personnel people would instinctively bristle at the sight of a nonconformist—somebody who might not function as a "systems person" in AT&T's "One System, One Policy" culture. Kleinfield quoted one personnel manager's attitude about nonconformity, "Sometimes I can spy someone who won't work out just by the look in his eye."

Recognizing the Individual (1960–1980)

As we have noted before, Douglas MacGregor introduced an ideological revolution in the early sixties with his "Theory X/Theory Y" ideas.

For the first time management heard reasons why it should recognize the valuable potential of individuals. A subsequent re-evaluation of authoritarian management behaviors led many forward-thinking executives to realize that dictatorial control tended to exacerbate the very problems it attempted to solve. Could they create healthier organizational environments if they paid more respect to individuals and individual differences? However, executives still clung to many of their manipulative paternalistic attitudes and simply added a new dimension to the same old style. Nevertheless the notion of responsible leadership lost some of its self-righteousness as managers paid more attention to individuals.

In the 1960s and throughout the 1970s the focus shifted toward improvement of the work environment. Soon attempts got underway to redesign the work environment in ways that might make jobs more meaningful, rewarding, and satisfying for workers. Job enrichment efforts experimented with providing workers with more interesting tasks. For example, instead of just turning a couple of screws or performing a couple of welds, a worker might assemble an entire component or rotate through a series of tasks to cut down on assembly line monotony. Some job enrichment efforts returned some responsibility and control over the work process back to the workers. For example, some workers became responsible for inventory and quality assurance tasks as well as production. Although still paternal in origin, these experiments did prove management's willingness to address the needs and desires of individuals.

Logically extending Theory Y, some business thinkers and practitioners began looking at ways labor might participate in management. If employees are knowledgeable, creative, and full of potential, why not include them in decision-making processes once restricted to their paternal leaders? Increasingly, organizations set up both formal and informal employee groups they hoped would grow into sources of information, creativity, and innovation. Even executives who followed this approach, however, often operated like unwise parents who might let their children voice their preferences but would themselves ultimately decide the issue. The full extension of responsible leadership to individuals, allowing each to achieve maximum fulfillment and actualization, would still take years to arrive.

Other job redesigning efforts, focusing on the physical layout of businesses, tried to restructure work areas to reinforce rather than undermine social relationships. Many of these made workers more motivated and productive.

During this era AT&T made breathtaking technological advances that enhanced business but began suffocating workers. When employee morale declined perceptibly, the company launched a series of studies to determine the level of discontent, and after each study the company embarked on a new solution to the problem—a human relations-oriented work group, an employee counseling center, or some other manipulative technique. As a result, a new "AT&T employee" began to emerge. People no longer accepted everything their managers said or did but rather asked questions and demanded recognition, not just as achievers of productivity gains, but as flesh-and-blood human beings.

One phone worker, Lou O'Leary, reflected on the "new" Bell employee in a conversation with Kleinfield: "You see, there is this new employee. Much less amenable to external discipline. He has the Protestant Work Ethic, but he wants to be talked to. If you send him across town, he wants to know why. I never had to be told why. I was told to move and so I packed my belongings and moved. The new worker wants explanations. We've got to involve the worker in the work. You don't do this by the 'How's the wife and kids?' routine. It's asking workers what they need. What do they need to do their jobs?"

Beginning to respect the desires of individual customers, it introduced color telephones for the first time, and with an eye on the needs of individual workers, it used technological innovations to replace very long production runs with very short ones, a move that brought a general decline in the number of repetitive tasks in all functional areas. In the early 1960s, Western Electric initiated an "Operational Communications" program designed to elicit employee participation in the very definition of the organization. Despite these efforts, in 1970 the Equal Employment Opportunity Commission, citing the company as the largest oppressor of women workers in the United States, filed suit against the Bell System's discriminatory employment practices. The complaint charged that women and minority employees were losing nearly a billion dollars a year due to employment policies that confined them to low-paying positions. After Bell itself conducted a survey of the attitudes of managers in five Bell companies, it concluded that many respondents felt the company didn't really care about employees as people, that results were more important than service, and that the direction of the company was not clear. In response to these problems, AT&T selected a structural solution. In September 1970, Chairman H. I. Romnes said, "Earlier this year, AT&T undertook a restructuring of its top management that explicitly recognizes the importance of the human element to the success of our business. In the course of this restructuring, we appointed an Executive Vice President— Human Affairs whose special responsibility it will be to see that human considerations are given full weight in the highest councils of management." Unfortunately, this structural change failed, largely because a decades-old attitude didn't change with it. Within a few years, the human affairs organization fell by the wayside in the wake of more pressing public policy issues. Before it did, though, it set the stage for the "professionalization" of the personnel function and the enhancement of the company's overall benefits program. In 1972, AT&T changed the name of its Personnel Department to the Human Resources Development Department, but instead of more actively involving itself with the typical Bell employee, as the new name suggested, the department worked mostly on executive incentive compensation programs.

This same year John deButts became chairman of AT&T and began orchestrating the first major change in business strategy since Theodore Vail's administration. This change came about primarily as a response to accelerating changes in technologies and markets. In brief, deButt's strategy involved:

- Total corporate reorganization (titles, responsibilities, and assignments would change for a third of the AT&T workforce).

- A new marketing orientation (new products would compete with computer offerings).

- A plan for handling the complex regulatory environment by accepting the possibility of competition if the government did not drop its campaign to break AT&T into separate parts.

- A reorientation of AT&T employees toward competition. As described by *Business Week*, "to tackle this job, AT&T is mounting its most ambitious training program ever in an effort to make its employees think in terms of selling and not of taking orders, of dealing with competitors and not regulators, and of making profits as well as providing services."

In 1973, Archie McGill, a former marketing VP from IBM, joined AT&T as the firm's first marketing manager. McGill's recruitment as the first top executive hired from outside AT&T marked the beginning of an aggressive program to bring people in from strong marketing-driven organizations and his responsibilities included enlightening the AT&T management team about marketing strategy.

In 1977, AT&T made its first move to restructure along market segment lines rather than functional departments. When it had enjoyed a virtual monopoly over the telephone business, the company had not needed to consider individual consumer's needs, but the new competitive environment demanded a strong emphasis on customer service. Of course this new emphasis required a major change in how AT&T's individual employees did their jobs.

Recognizing the need to rely on the individual worker to bring about necessary changes, AT&T inaugurated an extensive retraining drive, putting its top 1,800 managers through a corporate policy seminar on how to manage and market in Bell's changing environment. And it has given 15,000 lower-level managers and supervisors at least some marketing training.

Honoring the Individual (1980–Late 1990s)

By the early 1980s, management slowly began to honor the fullness of individuals—customers, workers, and competitors. Productivity teams, quality circles, and similar groups cropped up throughout American enterprise as executives began welcoming worker feedback and participation. At last they gave up trying to eradicate workers' social systems and began using them to improve quality and productivity. At the same time Japanese management methods, with their emphasis on worker involvement, reached American shores.

Gradually "leadership" began to replace "management." By definition, leaders should do more than merely manage their enterprises—they should somehow, possibly by example, exert the sort of influence on the organization that would motivate individuals to the highest levels of performance. But doesn't this all sound suspiciously like the paternalism that dominated the first two thirds of the century? In the hands of some executives, leadership did in fact degenerate into the old master/servant model, but in the hands of many others, who based their leadership on a profound respect for the rights, abilities, desires, and needs of individuals, it went from manipulating people to motivating them.

Even when the new-style leaders genuinely fulfill individuals' social and esteem needs, continued high levels of performance require the utmost diligence because shared beliefs and values can easily produce a harmful uniformity among the workforce, which can stifle innovation and adaptation to change. If individuals value their culture over vital organizational tasks or functions, they may resist and even vigorously oppose necessary strategic changes. For this reason, some strategists suggest that good managers should avoid overemphasis on their organization's short-term objectives. Rapidly changing business conditions demand continual revision of corporate strategy, and the more emphasis on short-term strategy, the more difficult it becomes to persuade the organization to turn to different goals when needs and conditions shift. When establishing systems of values, perspectives, and principles that will meet individuals' needs for identity, purpose, and meaning, the wise leader makes sure they are specific enough to serve the short term but general enough to survive the long term as well. The right principles can survive most crises. Uniformity becomes especially costly whenever it stymies individual innovation and creativity. Unless a leader systematically champions and reinforces a variety of perspectives and subcultures, the organization can lose a vitality that comes from a liberal plurality of viewpoints. Innovation and creativity cannot survive confinement to familiar channels.

On January 8, 1982, AT&T and the Justice Department announced the Modification of Final Judgement Consent Agreement whereby the company would divest itself of certain units by January 1, 1984. On that date, Ma Bell split herself into seven operating companies—Ameritech, Bell Atlantic, Bell South, NYNEX, Pacific Telesis, Southwestern Bell, and US West—and the so-called "Baby Bells" found themselves needing to almost completely reverse the ways they treated employees, customers, and competitors. Instead of rewarding standardization, homogeneity, and internal competition, the new units began rewarding internal entrepreneurial behavior, striving to please customers and respecting external competition. Training sessions were held to teach the newly desired managerial behavior (risk taking, innovativeness, and initiative) and all employees, despite their discomfort over the divestiture, dove in head first to help management unbundle AT&T. Leadership communicated the changes and divestiture plans clearly to the Bell employees, but not surprisingly, many felt extremely confused about their new roles in the divested organization.

In 1983, AT&T introduced the Total Life Concept, an innovative plan for treating some of the tensions surrounding divestiture. The program, which included exercise, nutrition, and stress-control classes, reflected management's awareness that successful divestiture depended on strong, healthy individuals, the sort of people who can make independent and responsive decisions without waiting for headquarters to tell them what to do.

In *The Adaptive Corporation*, Alvin Toffler described the traits

AT&T employees would need in order to thrive in their newly deregulated and competitive industry: "The ad-hocracies of tomorrow will require a totally different set of human characteristics. They will require men and women capable of rapid learning (in order to comprehend novel circumstances and problems) and imagination (in order to invent new solutions). In short, to cope with first-time or one-time problems, the corporate men of tomorrow will not function 'by the book.' Instead, they must be capable of exercising judgments and making complex value decisions rather than mechanically executing orders sent down from above."

To its credit AT&T has charted a course in this direction, but it and all other companies intent on making the Future 500 will run up against many obstacles on the road to their ultimate destination, and one of the largest of these will be the ingrained tendency to view individuals from a paternalistic point of view.

Individual Fulfillment and Organizational Excellence

Each individual brings to his or her employment a set of skills and talents that can lead to excellence in some area of endeavor. Peak performances do not derive from some sort of "natural endowment" restricted by birth and fate to a select few, but lie within the power of every human being. They come about when individuals discover who they really are and strive to realize their personal destinies. Unfortunately, in a society that idealizes certain professions and lifestyles while denigrating others, people can be easily seduced by a profession that does not develop their individual talents and natural gifts or promote their personal destinies.

When an individual chooses (or is forced to choose) a wrong job, or adopts an incompatible work style, the consequences not only affect his or her fulfillment, they also wreak havoc on organizational performance. If an individual cannot commit himself to his personal integrity and excellence, he will never commit himself to others. Since commitment to others lies at the heart of a strong corporate culture, the whole culture will suffer.

David Norton coined the phrase "moral nobility," an attitude toward oneself and one's relationship with others that goes beyond self-actualization to the actualization of all. The history of management in this century has been the saga of moral nobility in the sense that moral responsibility has steadily cascaded from one managerial level to another until reaching the most important level: the individual human being.

In the future, organizations must institutionalize principles of moral nobility and act to preserve and maintain conditions that lead to the self-actualization of all stakeholders—employees, investors, customers, and competitors. Otherwise they will never achieve the equilibrium that occurs when unique individuals work toward the common good without setting aside their own special desires and needs. On the other hand, uniformity and conformity, derived from the dictates of the autocrat or the rules of the organization, can strip individuals and subcultures of the opportunity for self-actualization and plunge the whole culture into frustration and confusion.

To strike the right balance, the complexity manager should champion individuality and collective culture at the same time. We think this will be one of the most pervasive paradoxes of the twenty-first century, and that it will require a vigilant and consistent application of perspective, pivot, and power management. As constant agents of change, complexity managers must place moral nobility (responsible leadership) where it belongs, with each individual employee.

As with so many other dimensions of the future, management of the individual depends more on a new mind-set than on a specific set of skills or tools. While the early entrepreneurs looked down from on high at their organizations and their people, and the professional managers assumed a similar perspective, and while the culture builders of recent years have climbed a long way off the throne to work with their people as colleagues, complexity managers should actually look *up* at their people. This does not mean that they will fear the power of individuals and their group relationships, nor does it mean they will abandon their leadership roles, but it does mean that they will treat people with the deepest respect, trust, and integrity. This goes far beyond "executive ethics" or "corporate responsibility," because it is a basic principle from which ethics and moral responsibility derive.

More importantly, complexity managers should not confine this responsibility to the offices of the corporation but should let it govern their treatment of competitors, thus helping resolve the paradox of competition versus collaboration; and they should direct it toward a true concern for the satisfaction of customer needs and social well-being thus helping achieve equilibrium between what's good for the company and what's good for the society and the world. Cynicism, fear, distrust, and frustration could vanish if this outlook became a central, daily habit. The novelist Frederick Forsyth summed up this phenomenon nicely: "My ideal qualities . . . strength without brutality, honesty without priggishness, courage without recklessness, humor without frivolity, humanity without sentimentality, intelligence without deviousness, skepticism without cynicism."

Individual Fulfillment and Complexity Management

During the past 100 years the individual in the organization has progressed from an interchangeable unit of production to the focal point of organizational performance, and we imagine that this trend will continue in the future. If so, executives and managers must work harder than ever to understand and appreciate each individual who comes into their spheres of influence.

Earlier in this chapter we identified one major issue that executives will encounter: How can leaders truly satisfy the desires and needs of individual stakeholders without sacrificing the performance demands and expectations of the corporate entity? Companies like Ford, Chevron, IBM, and AT&T have all been wrestling with this issue.

Ford Motor Company has struggled with melding the viewpoints of management and labor for the benefit of each individual and the well-being of the corporation. Chevron has dealt with lessening the trauma of the layoff experience. And IBM has tried to maintain its highly regarded focus on the individual while at the same time increasing its lackluster profit picture. For its part, AT&T may face the most difficult challenge of all because its environment has changed more than anyone else's. In each case, however, we believe complexity management can help these and other companies tap the full potential of individuals.

Applying Perspective Management

The perspective manager grasps the big picture of the corporation while zeroing in on each individual member of it. With perspective management, an executive can:

- Make sure each individual in the organization works harmoniously toward the corporation's common purposes through its mutually benefitting principles. If an individual fails to do so, the perspective manager exhausts efforts to help him or her change before deciding to help him or her find suitable employment in a more compatible environment. For example, IBM has been a recognized leader in this regard and could even strengthen its leadership by instituting an annual or semiannual "Congruence Review" in which every individual stakeholder would have an opportunity to confirm or deny his or her compatibility with corporate purposes. By the same token, this sort of review would afford individuals the chance to help modify corporate purposes for greater individual and organizational fulfillment.

- Review corporate principles to make sure they mutually benefit all individual stakeholders and that each principle allows ample opportunity for individual fulfillment throughout the corporate environment. For example, Ford could establish a principles review committee composed of people from all areas of the company to examine each of the firm's mutually benefitting principles and consider ways in which they could be improved to achieve even greater fulfillment.

Applying Power Management

The power manager empowers individuals to reach for higher levels of fulfillment. With power management an executive can:

- Bestow on committed and responsible managers the freedom and power to devise arrangements, programs, and approaches for increasing the fulfillment of all individuals under his or her charge. For example, Chevron could allow selected managers to create personal development programs, flex-hour policies, four-day work schedules, educational assistance arrangements, work group realignments, rotational work assignments, new challenging product or process development projects, entrepreneurial business opportunities, and so forth in an effort to increase the fulfillment of each person working in a particular division, department, or functional area.

- Award each employee the freedom to create his or her own work objectives and priorities, subject to corporate principles and management review and approval. While many companies attempt to do this, they rarely allow individuals to set actual priorities and objectives. For example, AT&T could make individual planning part of its annual strategic planning process. Individual plans could then affect each business unit's overall strategic direction.

- Allow individual customers to specify their preferences for service. Again, an annual customer planning component could be incorporated into the larger strategic planning process. For example, IBM could initiate such a planning process that would go even further toward giving the customer options and choices for service and attention.

Applying Pivot Management

The pivot manager tunes in to the performance and fulfillment of every individual. With pivot management, an executive can:

- Prepare individual fulfillment plans for the sole purpose of attending to and planning for the increased fulfillment of each stakeholder. This would apply not only to employees, but to customers, investors, and competitors as well. For example, AT&T could include such fulfillment assessments as part of an annual performance appraisal process.

- Offer career fulfillment counseling along with help at broadening an individual's options for enhancing the quality of professional and personal life. For example, Ford could offer such counseling to union employees, giving them the opportunity to go anywhere and do anything within the company.

- Work to make the organization an accredited corporate university capable of bestowing bachelors and masters degrees upon deserving employees, thus providing sophisticated continuing education to employees, customers, and other stakeholders. AT&T could hire high school graduates and put them through an individually tailored corporate curriculum. Graduates could then combine their schooling with applied experiences thereby enhancing career opportunities and fulfillment.

- Closely monitor individual fulfillment among all stakeholders. Every corporation should develop some means of accomplishing this essential task. For example, Chevron could set aside one month a year as "fulfillment month" in which every stakeholder is encouraged to function as a pivot manager in assessing the fulfillment level of all other stakeholders with whom they interact.

We have concluded our tour of several critical dimensions of the future with a consideration of individual fulfillment because we think the fate of every Future 500 company will begin and end there. Whether a company is high tech or low tech, operating in an age-old industry or one of the newer service or knowledge ones; whether it employs a thousand or a hundred thousand people; and whether it serves one market niche or vast worldwide markets, its success will depend, more than anything else, on the satisfaction of the needs and desires of each unique stakeholder in its environment.

As we proposed at the beginning of this book, achieving that satisfaction will require not just a refining of existing management techniques but a genuine and fundamental new way of thinking about management. That sort of thinking begins, of course, in the mind of the individual.

SELECTED BIBLIOGRAPHY

Auletta, Ken. *Greed and Glory on Wall Street*. New York: Random House, 1986.

Bass, Bernard M. (ed.). *Stogdill's Handbook of Leadership*. New York: Macmillan Publishing Co., Inc. (The Free Press), 1981.

Bellah, Robert N.; Madsen, Richard; Sullivan, William M.; Swidler, Ann; and Tipton, Steve M. *Habits of the Heart*. Berkeley: University of California Press, 1985.

Bennis, Warren, and Nanus, Burt. *Leaders: The Strategies for Taking Charge*. New York: Harper & Row, 1985.

Botkin, James; Dimancescu, Dan; and Stata, Ray. *The Innovators: Rediscovering America's Creative Energy*. Harper & Row, Publishers, Inc., 1984.

Bower, Joseph L. *The Two Faces of Management: An American Approach to Leadership in Business and Politics*. Boston: Houghton Mifflin Company, 1983.

Bower, Marvin. *The Will to Manage*. New York: McGraw-Hill Book Co., 1966.

Culbert, Samuel A., and McDonough, John J. *Radical Management: Power Politics and the Pursuit of Trust*. Macmillan Publishing Co., Inc. (The Free Press), 1985.

Chandler, Alfred D., Jr. *The Visible Hand: The Managerial Revolution in American Business*. Cambridge, Massachusetts: Harvard University Press (The Belknap Press), 1977.

Chandler Alfred D., Jr., and Daems, Herman. *Managerial Hierarchies: Comparative Perspectives on the Rise of the Modern Industrial Enterprise*. Cambridge, Massachusetts: Harvard University Press, 1980.

Clifford, Donald K., and Cavanaugh, Richard E. *The Winning Performance: How America's High-Growth Midsize Companies Succeed*. New York: Bantam Books, 1985.

De Bono, Edward. *Six Thinking Hats*. Boston: Little, Brown and Company, 1985.

Drucker, Peter F. *Innovation and Entrepreneurship: Practice and Principles.* New York: Harper & Row, Publishers, Inc., 1985.

Durant, Will, and Durant, Ariel. *The Lessons of History.* New York: Simon and Schuster, 1968.

Fombrun, Charles; Tichy, Noel M.; and DeVanna, Mary Anne. *Strategic Human Resource Management.* New York: John Wiley & Sons, 1984.

Foster, Richard. *Innovation: The Attacker's Advantage.* New York: Summit Press, 1986.

Gifford, Pinchot, III. *Intrapreneuring: Why You Don't Have to Leave the Corporation to Become an Entrepreneur.* New York: Harper & Row, Publishers, Inc., 1985.

Heskett, James L. *Managing in the Service Economy.* Boston: Harvard Business School Press, 1986.

Kelley, Robert E. *The Gold Collar Worker: Harnessing the Brainpower of the New Workforce.* Reading, Massachusetts: Addison-Wesley Publishing Company, Inc., 1985.

Kotler, Philip; Fahey, Liam; and Jatusripitak, Somkid. *The New Competition: What Theory Z Didn't Tell You About—Marketing.* Englewood Cliffs, New Jersey: Prentice-Hall, Inc., 1985.

Kotter, John P. *Power and Influence: Beyond Formal Authority.* New York: Macmillan Publishing Co., Inc. (The Free Press), 1985.

Levinson, Harry, and Rosenthal, Stuart. *CEO: Corporate Leadership in Action.* New York: Basic Books, Inc., Publishers, 1984.

McCormack, Mark H. *What They Don't Teach You at Harvard Business School.* New York: Bantam Books, 1984.

McKenna, Regis. *The Regis Touch.* Reading, Massachusetts: Addison-Wesley Publishing Company, Inc., 1985.

Mills, D. Quinn. *The New Competitors: A Report on American Managers from D. Quinn Mills of the Harvard Business School.* New York: John Wiley & Sons, Inc., 1985.

Mills, D. Quinn, and McCormick, Janice. *Industrial Relations in Transition: Cases and Text.* New York: John Wiley & Sons, Inc., 1985.

Ohmae, Kenichi. *Triad Power: The Coming Shape of Global Competition.* New York: Macmillan Publishing Co., Inc., 1985.

O'Toole, James. *Vanguard Management: Redesigning the Corporate Future.* Garden City, New York: Doubleday & Co., Inc., 1985.

Porter, Michael E. *Competitive Advantage: Creating and Sustaining Superior Performance.* New York: Macmillan Publishing Co., Inc. (Free Press), 1985.

Rodgers, F.G. "Buck." *The IBM Way.* New York: Harper & Row, Publishers, Inc., 1986.

Schein, Edgar H. *Organizational Culture and Leadership.* San Francisco: Jossey-Bass Inc., Publishers, 1985.

Schlesinger, Arthur M., Jr. *The Cycles of American History.* Boston: Houghton Mifflin Co., 1986.

Scott, Bruce R., and Lodge, George C. (eds.). *U.S. Competitiveness in the World Economy.* Boston: Harvard Business School Press, 1985.

Sloan, Alfred P., Jr.; McDonald, John; and Stevens, Catharine (eds.). *My Years with General Motors.* Garden City, New York: Doubleday & Co., Inc. (Anchor Books), 1972.

Susman, Warren I. *Culture As History: The Transformation of American Society in the Twentieth Century.* New York: Random House, Inc. (Pantheon Books), 1973.

Thurow, Lester C. (ed.). *The Management Challenge: Japanese Views.* Cambridge, Massachusetts: The MIT Press, 1985.

Thurow, Lester C. *The Zero-Sum Solution: Building a World-Class American Economy.* New York: Simon & Schuster, Inc., 1985.

Toffler, Alvin, *The Adaptive Corporation.* New York: McGraw-Hill Book Co., 1985.

Walton, Richard E., and Lawrence, Paul R. (eds.). *HRM Trends and Challenges.* Boston: Harvard Business School Press, 1985.

Wriston, Walter B. *Risk & Other Four-Letter Words.* New York: Harper & Row, Publishers, Inc., 1986.

For further information on implementing the concepts in THE FUTURE 500 contact:

Senn-Delaney Leadership Programs
5150 E. Pacific Coast Highway
Long Beach, California 90804
(213) 494-3398

INDEX

Printed in the United States
by Baker & Taylor Publisher Services